The Keys and the Kingdom

The Keys and the Kingdom

The British and the Papacy from John Paul II to Francis

Catherine Pepinster

Bloomsbury T&T Clark
An imprint of Bloomsbury Publishing Plc

B L O O M S B U R Y
LONDON · OXFORD · NEW YORK · NEW DELHI · SYDNEY

Bloomsbury T&T Clark

An imprint of Bloomsbury Publishing Plc

Imprint previously known as T&T Clark

50 Bedford Square	1385 Broadway
London	New York
WC1B 3DP	NY 10018
UK	USA

www.bloomsbury.com

BLOOMSBURY, T&T CLARK and the Diana logo are trademarks of Bloomsbury Publishing Plc

First published 2017

© Catherine Pepinster, 2017

Catherine Pepinster has asserted her right under the Copyright, Designs and Patents Act, 1988, to be identified as Author of this work.

British Library Cataloguing-in-Publication Data

A catalogue record for this book is available from the British Library.

ISBN:	HB:	978-0-5676-6630-7
	PB:	978-0-5676-6631-4
	ePDF:	978-0-5676-6632-1
	ePUB:	978-0-5676-6633-8

Library of Congress Cataloging-in-Publication Data

A catalog record for this book is available from the Library of Congress

Typeset by RefineCatch Limited, Bungay, Suffolk

Printed and bound in Great Britain

To the memory of my late Catholic relations:
Henriette Michotte
Germaine Pepinster
Julian Pepinster
Michel Pepinster

And my Anglican ones:
Joan Bowen
Winifred Pepinster

Requiescant in pace

Set we forward: let
A Roman and a British ensign wave
Friendly together
WILLIAM SHAKESPEARE, CYMBELINE

CONTENTS

11 What makes for the 'x' factor? The pope as modern
leader

12 The grit in the oyster: Church, state and domestic
politics

PLATES

ACKNOWLEDGEMENTS AND LIST OF INTERVIEWEES

The following kindly agreed to be interviewed at length for this book:

- Nigel Baker, October 2015.
- Lord Camoys, January 2016.
- Francis Campbell, October 2014.
- Archbishop Leo Cushley, March 2016.
- Fr Jock Dalrymple, March 2016.
- Sean Donlon, January 2016.
- Eamon Duffy, December 2015.
- Tim Fischer, October 2015.
- Archbishop Michael Fitzgerald, January 2015.
- Dame Helen Ghosh, July 2015.
- Professor Lord (Peter) Hennessy, October 2014.
- Mgr Mark Langham, October 2014.
- Clifford Longley, October 2014.
- Denis MacShane, March 2015.
- Andrew Mitchell, February 2015.
- Archbishop Sir David Moxon, October 2015.
- Cardinal Cormac Murphy-O'Connor, February 2015.
- Cardinal Vincent Nichols, March 2015.
- Lord (Chris) Patten, January 2015.
- Sir Ivor Roberts, October 2014.
- Edward Stourton, January 2015.
- Mgr Philip Whitmore, January 2015.
- Lord (Rowan) Williams, July 2015.
- Baroness (Shirley) Williams, July 2015.
- Charles Wookey, October 2015.

I am also grateful to diplomatic officials of the Holy See who prefer to remain anonymous.

This book is also informed by conversations with many people over the years. They include John Wilkins, John Cornwell, Michael Walsh, Nicholas Lash, Austen Ivereigh, Jack Valero, Colette Bowe, Tina Beattie, Julian Filochowski, Chris Bain, Cherie Blair, Carla Powell, Fr James Leachman OSB, Fr Daniel McCarthy OSB, Fr Christopher Jamison OSB, Diana Klein, Robert Mickens, David Willey, Fr Keith Pecklers SJ, Philippa Hitchens, Fr Norman Tanner SJ, Andrew Brown, Linda Woodhead, Stephen Bates, Richard Collyer-Hamlin, Archbishop Justin Welby, Alana Harris, Margaret Archer, Sally Read, Fr Gerald O'Collins SJ, Peter Stanford, Fr Timothy Radcliffe OP, Fr Richard Finn OP, Fr Liam Walsh OP, Fr Alban McCoy OFM, Grace Davie, Fr James Hanvey SJ, Mgr Roderick Strange, Fr Michael Holman SJ, Archbishop Bernard Longley, Bishop Mark O'Toole, Sr Bernardette Hunston SCSJA, Sr Jane Livesey CJ, Sr Gemma Simmonds CJ, Marco Politi, Michael Phelan, Paul Vallely, Jimmy Burns, Ruth Gledhill, Cathy Galvin, Mary McAleese, Bishop Paul Tighe, Mgr Tony Currer, Tim Livesey, Conor Gearty, Cole Moreton, Nicholas Pyke, Michael McCarthy and Raymond Whitaker.

The staff of *The Tablet* over the years were always a dedicated, stimulating and supportive team and I had numerous conversations with them during my editorship of the journal that have proved so important for this book. My thanks to Elena Curti, James Roberts, Christopher Lamb, Liz Dodd, Sean Smith, Rose Gamble, Megan Cornwell, Abigail Frymann, David Harding, Iain Millar, John Shirley, Michael Holland, Isabel de Bertodano, Michael Hirst, Christopher Herdon, James Macintyre, Thomas Norton, Philip Crispin, Brendan Walsh, Brendan McCarthy and Joanna Moorhead. My PA, Isabel Gribben, was always on hand to dig out that vital story I couldn't find.

The origins of this book lie in a sabbatical from *The Tablet*, spent as a Visiting Scholar at St Benet's Hall, Oxford. I am grateful to St Benet's Master, Professor Werner Jeanrond, his wife Betty, and the staff and students for making me so welcome and my time there so productive. Unfortunately that time was marred by serious ill health and I am indebted to the staff of Charing Cross Hospital, particularly Professor Justin Stebbing, for their care.

A different, but equally meticulous care, was given to this book by my editor, Dominic Mattos, who showed unstinting enthusiasm for the project and provided invaluable advice. My copy editor, Lisa Carden, brought her marvellous eye for detail to the task. Any errors that remain are my responsibility.

Finally, my friends and family looked after me and nurtured me through this project, especially during my ill health. Thanks go to Sophie Treszka, Veronica Lachkovic, Pauline Gilbertson, Ann and Dave Ryan, and Liz and Brian Croft, as well as my relatives in Louisiana, Wales and North Yorkshire, especially Jean and John Gabriel, Caroline Ashley and Nicole Pepinster Greene. Above all my thanks go to Kevin who sustained me, as he always does, with love.

Introduction

Stonor Park is a quintessentially English estate, tucked in the folds of the Chiltern Hills, close by a curve of the Thames, with deer wandering among the trees. The same family has lived there for over 850 years, tracing their origins back to one of the leaders of the English at Agincourt. Yet this is English history with a twist: one of the most patriotic of ancient families also remained loyal to Rome despite the English Reformation. The Stonors of Oxfordshire were not persuaded to cut their ties with the Catholic Church; indeed they sheltered priests who came to celebrate Mass, including Edmund Campion, honoured as one of the great English martyrs. Stonor is a puzzle to many of its visitors; it is a part of English history they don't know about. To them, Catholicism is something a bit different, rather foreign, even rather exotic.

As a child, raised as a Catholic, the religion did seem rather different to what else was around me. My Belgian father and I were the only Catholics in our road in west London in the early 1960s. Fellow pupils at my Catholic primary school and the convent school I later attended had parents who were Irish, Italian, Polish, Hungarian, Ukranian, Czech and Keralan. Catholic schools in the 1960s and 1970s were ethnically diverse long before it became the norm for the rest of education in Britain. My mother, a nominal Anglican, declined to convert to Catholicism on her marriage, but she took very seriously the promise she made to bring up any child of the marriage as a Catholic. Some of that commitment was easy to fulfil: I was sent to Catholic schools where I was prepared for life in the faith; my mother made me broderie anglaise dresses for my First Holy Communion and Confirmation. But what else to do? She hit upon a simple solution: every Christmas and Easter she sat me down in front of the television to watch the pope give his *Urbi et Orbi* blessing, to the Church and the world. It also imparted a particular message to me, and no doubt to all those watching, that Catholics were part of a huge community of people that stretched way beyond our everyday lives and the countries in which we lived. The man on the balcony in Bernini's stunning setting was in some way strongly connected to any Catholic. I might be British but I was also rooted in this global Church, this huge family that could be found in all continents.

Today that family of the worldwide Catholic Church totals over a billion people. It is used to being the dominant faith in countries across the world, to exercising influence with a self-assurance that befits an organization that bestrides the globe. In Europe, though, that influence is waning; once devout Catholic countries such as France and Spain, and even Italy, have high rates of cohabitation, divorce, abortion and small families are now the norm. People no longer feel duty-bound to attend Mass every Sunday. Meanwhile the Church is growing in parts of the developing world: baptisms and Mass attendance are rising in African countries.

The demographics mean that the Church needs to rethink its relationship with these countries and figure out what the consequences are of being a religion with considerable, yet limited power in the West, while imagining a new axis of influence elsewhere. In such circumstances, Britain, where Catholics make up a significant minority in an increasingly secular society that is also ethnically, culturally and religiously diverse, becomes no longer an oddity for Rome, but a source of useful experience for dealing with the new normality. For in many ways Britain has been seen as an oddity, regarded for centuries as a nation with a curious relationship with the papacy. Once a Catholic stronghold, it severed its ties in the most dramatic and bloody way. The papacy was despised and rejected by Englishmen; loyalty to it was a mark of disloyalty to the country. Rome mourned the loss of England after the break with the Church, caused by Henry VIII's frustrated demands for the pope to annul his marriage to his first wife, Katherine of Aragon. The journey back to first, limited mutual tolerance, later tentative communication and now mutual regard – albeit with occasional clashes – has been long and difficult.

Catholics today form a sizeable minority in Britain. Its one million communicant members mean that it is overtaking the Church of England as the biggest denomination of practising Christians in Britain. The country attracts people from the very countries where Catholicism is thriving, thus making it of huge interest to the papacy. The way in which the Church works in secular British society, choosing at times to be pragmatic and find accommodation with that society, and at others to challenge that secular status quo, has made the Church in Britain a vital testing ground for reassessing the Church's place in Europe as its traditional power is challenged by secularism.

During the past thirty years there have been three popes: John Paul II, Benedict XVI and Francis. This book covers their pontificates, an era when the relationship between the British and the papacy has evolved far beyond the antagonism of the previous 450 years and the mutual ignorance of the pre-Vatican II twentieth century. During my thirteen years as editor of the Catholic weekly, *The Tablet*, and since, I have watched that evolution take place. Post-war social and cultural changes, and particularly the reforms of the Second Vatican Council, have to a great degree brought down the walls of the fortress church. Catholics were once distinctive in this country because of the demands of their faith that so shaped the pattern of their lives, from their weekly Mass-going to what they ate on Fridays and their frequently large families. Those tribal codes and customs have largely faded, although the bishops have tried to revive fish on Fridays. Even they, though, make decisions that lessen Catholic distinctiveness, ruling that some of the great feasts of the Church are no longer holy days of obligation and are instead celebrated on the nearest convenient Sunday.

Whilst there are still hints here and there of a latent suspicion towards Catholics in Britain, perhaps typified by the fact that in the UK still people are described, whether in information kept in their hospital notes about their religion or about their preferences for their children's education, as *Roman* Catholics. As the sociologist Grace Davie notes: 'The British are, of course, the only people to employ the adjective Roman, thus accentuating the foreignness of Catholicism.'[1]

Nevertheless, Catholicism has in many ways been normalized in Britain and it is Islam that has replaced Roman Catholicism as chief religious bogeyman in Britain today. The recusants remain, as do the poor migrants who nowadays are more likely to be Polish or Colombian rather than Irish, but arguably the most significant aspect of English Catholics is that they form a substantial subsection of the middle class and many of them have made their mark in the public arena. Their role has lessened suspicion of the institution to which they belong and today a Catholic child is just as likely as any other to rise to the top of his or her chosen path, a path which usually began at their local Catholic school. From the people in the pew to the priests and bishops, Catholic schools matter deeply and education remains one of the frequent battlegrounds between the Catholic Church and the state, as well as with secularist pressure groups such as the National Secular Society and the British Humanist Association.

This crucial background to how Catholics are present in public life today is the basis from which this book examines the changing relationship between the papacy in Britain in the modern era. In this first part of the book I chart the background to the restoration of Catholicism in England and the beginnings of diplomatic relations between the UK government and the Holy See. I show how this relationship has developed from initial frostiness into a mutually beneficial relationship in which the British influence in Rome is both significant and at times surprising.

I examine the relationship between the Catholic Church and the British government and how it is shaped by the bishops and politicians of this country, but also formed by the Foreign Office and the unique organization of the Holy See's diplomatic service. The Catholic Church has a role, a power and an influence in the world unlike that of any other Christian denomination, and I show how it has found at times the United Kingdom to be both an ally and a combatant. I also explain how the UK matters to Rome because of its significance on the world stage, through its status at the United Nations, in NATO, and in the EU (although it remains to be seen how this may change following the results of the June 2016 referendum). Rome, meanwhile, with its global network of diplomats, its contacts with other religions and Christian denominations, has proved to be a source of useful intelligence for the UK.

The era covered in this book includes the latter half of the reign to date of Elizabeth II. She holds the title bestowed on her predecessor, Henry VIII, of Defender of the Faith, and her role in building relationships with Rome has been highly significant yet so far barely recognized publicly, although Rome is clearly a deep admirer of her as a Christian leader.

Photographs of the queen with the popes of the twentieth and twenty-first centuries fill tables in the British embassy to the Holy See in Rome. Also on display are pictures of popes together with the prime ministers of the past sixty years: from Macmillan and Heath to Wilson, Callaghan, Blair, Brown and Cameron. It is clear that the encounters have become more frequent, although as shown in these pages, the relationship can often be testy. Here in the UK, other than in places like Lewes on Bonfire Night, the pope today is usually not regarded as a foreign tyrant who threatens the Crown and even Englishness itself. Now he is a global celebrity, attracting as many headlines as a movie star, appearing with increasing frequency in people's lives via their Twitter feeds, Facebook pages and the pope app. He is also increasingly an actor in global diplomacy: witness the involvement of Pope Francis in rapprochement between Cuba and the US, and in focusing attention on the plight of refugees. It was a wider engagement with the world that was central to the papacy of John Paul II as well, although the two pontiffs are very different characters and different in their approach, evidenced by John Paul's intractable opposition to Communism.

In examining this changing attitude towards the papacy (and towards Catholicism more generally), it becomes clear that a strident secularism has overtaken Protestantism as Catholicism's staunchest opponent in the UK. Christians of many denominations watched the TV coverage of Benedict XVI's visit to Britain in 2010, examined in detail in this book, and were enthused by a Christian leader speaking so clearly about the role of faith in society. The once pronounced religious divides in society no longer seemed to matter, as Christians from all backgrounds listened to an articulate exposition of the role of faith in a society that has become so secular, even though religion plays such a great a role on the world stage.

The Catholic Church today is both insider and outsider in Britain. It is this paradoxical position, and the ways in which this position enables the Church to play a powerful, often subtle, often remarkable role in the life of the UK, that forms the crux of this volume. From the Church's engagement in Northern Ireland during the Troubles, to rethinks on public policy on poverty, on inner cities, on climate change, on human trafficking, the Church in British public life continues to surprise and to wield real power.

Britain, meanwhile, plays its role in Rome. It had a significant part in ensuring the election of Pope Francis. In other words, the United Kingdom has influenced the most significant reform of the Catholic Church for half a century. This book explains how it came about, and examines the unexpected contemporary relationship between the papacy and the nation that once turned its back on Rome.

An example of how significantly things have changed is in the relationship with the institution that attempted to replace Catholicism, the Church of England. Today the two churches are friends, not foes. In November 2015, Westminster Abbey – the cathedral that could arguably be described as the nation's parish church – played host to Raniero Cantalamessa, preacher to the papal household, the man who instructs the pope himself in the faith. But on this occasion, Fr Cantalamessa was instructing others, namely the highest echelons of the Church of England, on the occasion of the opening of the tenth five-year term of its General Synod. Among those listening was the Primate of All England, the Archbishop of Canterbury, Justin Welby, and the head of the Church of England, Elizabeth II. Cantalamessa did not steer away from the obvious – that he came among them as a Catholic at a time when attention is turning to commemoration of the quincentenary of the Protestant Reformation. 'It is vital for the whole Church,' he said, 'that this opportunity is not wasted by people remaining prisoners of the past, trying to establish each other's rights and wrongs'.[2]

'Prisoners of the past.' The relationship between the British and the papacy is complex, shot through with hints of the past and yet it is also being constantly reinvented. The historian Eamon Duffy, whose research into the English Reformation led to a rethinking of the people's response to Henry VIII's violent schism with Rome, has perceived how different the English experience of Catholicism is from that of its near neighbour, Ireland, where he lived until he was thirteen years old.

'For the English, loyalty to the papacy has to co-exist with loyalty to the UK, the Queen and the flag. For the modern Irish, their Catholicism is part of their identity and that makes a huge difference. There's that Seamus Heaney poem that sums up the feeling: "Be advised my passport's green/ No glass of ours was ever raised to the Queen",' said Duffy.

'If you think of the Irish republic, there was an attempt to create a nation whose laws conformed with Catholicism. But English Catholics had to keep those things separate.'[3]

English Catholics – and indeed British Catholics – have found a way to reconcile these distinct aspects of their identity in a society that is today both more tolerant and more intolerant of difference than it has been in the past. This book explains how they have done so, and forms part of a bigger account of a fascinating and evolving relationship between a nation and a global religion.

Notes

1   Davie, Grace (1994), *Religion in Britain Since 1945: Believing without Belonging*, Oxford: Blackwell.

2   'Rebuild my house: sermon to the General Synod of the Church of England', by Fr Raniero Cantalamessa, 24 November 2015. Available online: http://www.anglicannews.org/news/2015/11/rebuild-my-house-sermon-to-the-general-synod-of-the-church-of-england-by-father-raniero-cantalamessa.aspx

3   Interview of Eamon Duffy by Catherine Pepinster, December 2015.

PART ONE

1

The entirely trusted stealth minority:

How Catholics became part of Britain today

If ever a British city could be said to be a Catholic city, then it would be Liverpool. Its Catholic glory days are behind it now – churches have closed as poor Catholics have grown affluent and moved out – but its Catholic identity emerged in a city that was once deeply divided. The *Liverpool Mail* in July 1851, for example, claimed of Irish migrants that: 'Popery has so completely polluted their mental faculties and debased the physical and moral habits of the Irish peasant that it is impossible to ameliorate his condition as a social animal.'[1]

Contrast that with the enthusiasm, in recent times, for 'popery'. Two popes, John Paul II and Benedict XVI, have visited Britain, with a night-time prayer vigil in Hyde Park led by Benedict in 2010 leading to a huge newspaper headline the following day: 'Glastonbury with God.'[2] And when a picture of Pope Francis hugging a disfigured man appeared on the *Daily Mail* website it attracted millions of hits, more than some images of the Duchess of Cambridge or stars like David Beckham.[3] Meanwhile the Catholics of Britain – some of them the descendants of those Irish migrants so vilified by the *Liverpool Mail* – have reached some of the highest offices in the land in recent years, including Cabinet Secretary, Director-General of the BBC, Vice-Chancellor and Chancellor of Oxford University and Director-General of the National Trust. They not only play their part in British society but in doing so have helped to dissolve some of the traditional prejudices against Catholicism in general and the papacy in particular.

To understand how great an achievement this is and to comprehend the unique relationship that exists today between the papacy and Britain, particularly with its establishment, it is necessary to chart how it has developed in the past 480 years since Henry VIII and his heirs, Edward VI and Elizabeth I, tore up the bonds that secured England's relationship with the pope.

Mass forbidden

England's fidelity to Rome was broken in 1532 when Henry VIII, previously awarded the title of Defender of the Faith for his support for the Church in the face of growing Protestantism, and his chief minister, Thomas Cromwell, removed papal power in England. Pope Clement VII's refusal to allow the annulment of Henry's marriage to Katherine of Aragon enraged the king. A year later the break was further confirmed, with Katherine's marriage being declared invalid and Henry marrying Anne Boleyn. The split with Rome took many forms: the monasteries were dissolved and their lands requisitioned; statues of saints removed from churches and pictures disappeared beneath whitewash; priests, monks and bishops were imprisoned, and some executed; the Latin Mass forbidden.

After the break with Rome instituted by Henry, and the excommunication of his daughter, Elizabeth I, by Pope Pius V in his 1570 bull *Regnans in Excelsis*, popes did not recognize the legitimacy of English (later British) monarchs and in turn, Catholics in England and Scotland were prevented from voting, becoming MPs and joining learned professions.

Until the Catholic Relief Act of 1791, even to attend Mass was illegal. It was forbidden to build Catholic places of worship and Catholics were persecuted for their faith. The act of 1791 did permit the construction of churches so long as there were no bells and steeples (a ban kept in force until 1926), and the numbers of Catholics rose dramatically. Yet Englishmen – and women – who looked to Rome were still considered disloyal to crown and country. It was deemed a foreign, alien faith.

While the 1791 act permitted Catholics to practise law and run schools, Catholics were still excluded from both Houses of Parliament. The iniquity of the situation was highlighted by the landslide by-election in 1828 of Daniel O'Connell, an Irish Catholic, who despite his electoral victory was not legally entitled to sit in the Commons.

Wellington, the Catholics' champion

It was the man perceived to be the most English of heroes, the Duke of Wellington, who began to turn the tide. Wellington, himself in fact Anglo-Irish, the man who saved Europe from Napoleon, served as Tory Prime Minister after his successes on the battlefields, and became convinced that only repeal of discriminatory laws could save England and Ireland from war. This conviction left him and his Home Secretary, Robert Peel, ranged against the king, George IV, who regarded giving way as a threat to the Church of England. Something of the flavour of these times can be seen in the collection of political cartoons kept at Wellington's London home, Apsley House. One of them depicts Wellington's famous duel in 1829 with the Earl of Winchilsea. The Duke is dressed in a monk's habit and holding a rosary as he fights the earl, one of Catholicism's most trenchant enemies. Even after the king was persuaded to capitulate – not least by Wellington's threatened resignation – and agree to the emancipation of Catholics with the Catholic Relief Act of 1829, which allowed them the right to vote and hold public office, prejudice continued. One year later, though, came an intriguing insight into how British opinion might be changing: the Waterloo Chamber was built at Windsor Castle and dedicated to the defeat of Napoleon at Waterloo. It featured a series of portraits commissioned by George IV from Sir Thomas Lawrence of all the allies who joined together to defeat Bonaparte and the secularist French, whose 1789 revolution had so unsettled the English royals. Among those allies – and his portrait still hangs today in the chamber – was Pope Pius VII, who no longer seemed as threatening to the English as 'alien' French. It was a pragmatic case for the English of an enemy's enemy being a friend.

In 1851, thirty-one years after emancipation, came the restoration of the Catholic hierarchy in England and Wales by Pope Pius IX. The bishops frequently prioritized school-building over church construction, with land and buildings paid for by money from the collection plate. The establishment of the Catholic Poor School Committee in 1847, just four years prior to the restoration of the hierarchy, was a deal between church and state that suited both – it helped increase school places and gave the government some influence over the education of Catholics, whose numbers were being swelled by potentially troublesome migrants.

Catholic restoration

The word 'restoration' is telling. The bishops were allowed back to Britain after a break of 300 years but in describing it as a restoration the papacy reminded the established Church of England that this was no Johnny-come-lately but the real thing: Anglicans were the usurpers in the eyes of Victorian Catholics. Nicholas Wiseman, the first Archbishop of Westminster, stoked controversy when he issued a letter to faithful Catholics, entitled 'Out the Flaminian Gate' (referring to one of the original gates in Rome), in which he declared:

> The great work, then, is completed; what you have long desired and prayed for is granted. Your beloved country has received a place among the fair Churches which, normally constituted, form the splendid

aggregate of Catholic Communion. England has been restored to its orbit in the ecclesiastical firmament, from which its light had long vanished, and begins anew its course of regularly adjusted action round the centre of unity, the source of jurisdiction, of light, and of vigour.

He then spoke of his new domain: 'Till such time as the Holy See shall think fit otherwise to provide, we govern, and shall continue to govern, the counties of Middlesex, Hertford and Essex as ordinary therefore . . .'[4]

The government and the Church of England were outraged, and Parliament quickly passed the Ecclesiastical Titles Act, prohibiting among other things the naming of new Catholic dioceses after medieval (now Anglican) ones, while *The Times* published an excoriating leader titled 'Papal aggression'.

Wiseman went further to explain why he chose 'Westminster' as his title, which although not an ancient name used by the Church of England, had long been considered a centre of Anglicanism. In a moving pamphlet, 'Appeal to the Reason and Good Feeling of the English People', he went on to explain what his Westminster consisted of:

Close under the Abbey of Westminster there lie concealed labyrinths of lanes and courts, and alleys and slums, nests of ignorance, vice, depravity, and crime as well as of squalor, wretchedness and disease, whose atmosphere is typhus, whose ventilation is cholera, in which swarms a huge and almost countless population, in great measure, nominally at least, Catholic; haunts of filth, which no sewage committee can reach — dark corners which no lighting-board can brighten. This is the part of Westminster which alone I covet . . .'[5]

A church of the poor

In many ways, Wiseman set the template for Catholicism in this country: a Church of immense global wealth would focus in Britain on the people at the bottom of the economic heap. No wonder then that ever since the restoration of the hierarchy, the bishops and archbishops of English Catholicism have set so much store by education and the building of schools – perhaps even more than they did by the building of churches.

Other distinctive strands have shaped English Catholicism since the nineteenth century: as well as being a Church of the urban poor – a group at one time dominated by Irish workers – it has consisted of recusant gentry descended from those who stayed loyal to Rome through the dark years of persecution, mostly European migrants, and converts. Prominent English figures have frequently 'crossed the Tiber', as the British quaintly put it, with a reference that ensures Catholicism's foreignness is alluded to. Their number includes in particular notable writers, from John Henry Newman and

Ronald Knox to Graham Greene, Evelyn Waugh, Muriel Spark and Beryl Bainbridge. Former Anglicans would have found in the middle of the twentieth century a quite different, Catholic culture, with its own schools and colleges, publications and history, and a distinct Irish influence. Among the more prosperous English Catholics, according to the Dominican Fergus Kerr, there was a history of 'a conscious sense of superiority mixed with a much less conscious sense of social inferiority'.[6]

Today, British Catholics are a much broader group than they were even fifty years ago. There are not only recusants and those with Irish roots but also Poles, Croatians, Colombians and Bolivians. In the mid 1960s, a study of British Catholics described it as a world of 'unbourgeois extremes, of an upper class and abundant mass'.[7]

Middle-class religion

Today, however, substantial numbers of Catholics are notably middle-class. They include second- and third-generation migrants, among them people of great achievement who have reached the top in politics, business, the law, the arts and the media. This in turn has reinforced the view that the Catholic Church and its leadership is not something alien, but rather an institution with which the United Kingdom can do business, both domestically and on the world stage, via diplomacy.

Cardinal Cormac Murphy-O'Connor, the emeritus Archbishop of Westminster, believes that Catholicism – and therefore the papacy – have become more accepted in Britain over the last thirty years. The Second Vatican Council, which made Catholicism a more 'accessible', ecumenical religion, and the papal visits of 1982 and 2010 helped change opinion, he believes, but above all, the improved education of Catholics due to the 1944 Education Act has had the greatest impact. After the Act, when the Church of England agreed to hand over its schools to the state, Catholic bishops fought to retain control of theirs, striking a deal whereby Catholic schools became voluntary aided, with half of their funding coming from the state and half from the Church. Alongside them, major private schools such as Ampleforth and Stonyhurst became rivals to the Anglican public schools of Eton and Harrow. 'It gave more Catholics entry into the middle class,' said the cardinal.[8]

The historian Peter Hennessy, himself a product of postwar Catholic schools, agrees that the integration of Catholics in British society is down to education:

The key thing that changed everything was the 1944 Education Act. Catholics became a stealth minority, as author Denis Sewell memorably put it. By the time someone such as Gus O'Donnell [the former Cabinet Secretary] reached Whitehall, faith wasn't an issue.

In postwar Britain, people's multiple identities emerged. Because of the rise of the middle class, Catholics came to the fore and they played a particularly prominent role in public service. Whitehall civil servants like Sir Michael Palliser, Sir Michael Quinlan and Sir David Goodall – all involved in policy over the nuclear bomb – emerged from Catholic education and were all entirely trusted. There was no suspicion there.

And yet Hennessy indicates that there is a certain clubbishness, a particular code that Catholics understand, indicating their abiding sense of being outsiders while also now being on the inside:

> You can spot the fellow believers instantly. It is a shared patois, so when someone has been moaning, you say, 'offer it up'; you get the same linguistic signals. There are those other linguistic signals, the very posh ones, where the letter A is the great giveaway where people talk about going to 'Maaaaass'. Catholics, and there were an abundance of them from Catholic grammar schools, were social amphibians.[9]

Hennessy puts his finger on it when he talks of 'social amphibians' – the way in which Catholics have adapted and become in many ways an essential part of the British make-up. But the Church is not entirely as 'inside' as Hennessy perhaps suggests.

For although Catholic schools have made huge achievements and helped create a successful Catholic laity, one that is accepted and even part of the Establishment, and thereby have confirmed that the Church to which they belong can be trusted, both in Britain and on the world stage, the Church's *hierarchy* is a different matter. At times it seems still outside the Establishment, not quite clubbable, not quite accepted, and can still sometimes have an awkward relationship with government, particularly over education.

Michael Hornsby-Smith noted this aspect of English Catholicism in his 1987 study when he wrote: 'Historically there appears to be evidence that English Catholics in particular have wished to maintain a low profile politically in a predominantly Protestant and sometimes hostile society . . . [they have] only emerged as a political force in defence of what they have regarded as their vital community interests, notably the continuation of a viable separate Catholic schools system.'[10]

There was a moment, though, when Catholicism seemed to leave behind its traditional reticence in Britain. When a new Archbishop of Westminster was chosen in 1976 to succeed Cardinal John Heenan, senior Catholics were in prime position to influence who would be the next most senior cleric of their Church in England and Wales. Not least among these senior figures was the then Sir John Hunt, the Cabinet Secretary of the time (and the first Catholic to hold the position since its creation in 1916). His second wife, Madeleine, was the sister of the abbot of Ampleforth, Basil Hume, a man many Catholics of a similar sensibility to Hunt – educated, liberal, devout and also steeped in British values – thought would be ideal. Discreet lobbying of Rome by notable liberal Catholics over the vacant archbishopric succeeded in getting Hume chosen by Pope Paul VI for England's foremost see.

For a Church that had long been shaped by Irish migration, tempered with recusant memories, Hume was entirely different. Not that he was English through and through – his Catholicism derived from his French mother – but he was English enough to seem to the British Establishment 'one of us', to use a phrase coined at that time by the Thatcher fraternity. He also had a confidence and self-assurance derived from his education and his middle-class family's standing that was not always possessed by Catholic hierarchs in England and Wales.[11]

Cardinal Hume transformed the Catholic Church in England and Wales during his time as Archbishop of Westminster from 1976 to 1999, to the extent that Paul Vallely, in his annual Newman Lecture of 2008, described it as the 'Hume Dispensation', indicating a Catholic national Church at ease with itself and sure of its position. Hume became a regular broadcaster, popular author and leading religious figure of quiet authority. He stood up for Catholics but he was confident in dealing with Rome too, refusing to be cowed by officials of the Roman Curia.[12]

The Catholic Church of England and Wales seemed comfortable in its own skin during the Hume era, and at ease with the ruling class. Its relationship with the royal family, for example, symbolized this. By 1994, the Duchess of Kent converted to Catholicism, and a year later the Queen attended vespers at Westminster Cathedral, the first English monarch to attend such a Catholic service since the Reformation. She developed a bond of mutual respect and admiration with the cardinal. At the time, says historian Peter Hennessy, 'Number 10 [of John Major] wanted Basil to be in the Lords'.[13]

Hume was unsure and the plan fizzled out, although it was revived when Gordon Brown wanted Hume's successor, Cormac Murphy-O'Connor, to become a life peer. Rome was not convinced of a peerage's merits, and effectively blocked it because of its lack of enthusiasm. But these invitations did highlight how far Catholics had come in public life in Britain.[14]

One leading public figure who exemplifies the remarkable changes in the fortunes of Catholic postwar boys and girls is Chris Patten. The child of second-generation Irish migrants, Patten grew up in the very ordinary London suburb of Greenford, where he attended the local Catholic primary school. After passing the 11-plus he secured a scholarship place, funded by the local council, to the Benedictine public school of St Benedict's, Ealing. This schooling set him on the path to Balliol, Oxford, a career in politics that included Cabinet office and becoming the last governor of Hong Kong before being appointed a life peer, European Commissioner, chancellor of Oxford University, and chairman of the BBC Trust.

'Before Vatican II we Catholics were seen as a bit odd but more open than the Freemasons,' recalled Patten. 'People thought our services were mumbo jumbo, that we were foreigners, either Italian or Irish, some of us strange snobs. That has been transformed in my lifetime. It is no longer the case that being Catholic is an odd thing to be.'

Lord Patten gives credit for the change to Basil Hume's character and to that of his successor at Westminster, Cormac Murphy-O'Connor, but also, like Peter Hennessy, to Catholic education:

> Catholic schools really made the difference to the fortunes of Catholics in Britain. Today the best state schools in London for boys are Catholic schools. They have a very mixed ethnic base. When Benedict XVI visited this country the Catholics who came out for that visit showed a range of ethnicities and ages, and that was very attractive. I look around at the congregation at my local church and that of my daughter's in West London and I see a very normal slice of middle class England with people of every colour and shape.[15]

To understand what a seismic difference Hume made, one needs to recall how, even a few years before his appointment, there was still suspicion of Catholics in public life. The religious commentator Clifford Longley, himself a Catholic convert, recalls that in 1969, the appointment of Sir Charles Curran as director-general of the BBC led to Home Office memos about his suitability. 'They did not need to spell out this – there was inherent suspicion of a Catholic,' recalled Longley.[16]

It was Hume's character and his approach to public life in Britain that was so different to that of other Catholic clerics. This made a significant difference his standing and that of the Church, Longley said: 'Basil Hume was an exceptional aberration. He stepped right outside the usual culture of Catholic priests.' This may seem curious to non-Catholics, for the cardinal, the son of a devout French Catholic, had been educated at a Catholic school. But the usual route for English Catholic priests at this time would have been possibly a junior seminary, followed by a seminary, rather than Hume's route of monastery and university. This difference became apparent to Longley when he helped to write the 'Common Good' document in 1996, which the Catholic Bishops' Conference of England and Wales, with Hume as its president, commissioned as electoral guidance ahead of the forthcoming general election: 'I was surprised by the tension between Archbishop's House [HQ of the Archbishop of Westminster] and Eccleston Square [HQ of the Bishops' Conference]. Hume was from a different class; he knew the Tory establishment.'[17]

By the end of the twentieth century and the early years of the twenty-first, matters were very different. Hume had been succeeded by Cormac Murphy-O'Connor, another man who was at ease with the great and the good, who preached at Sandringham and entertained the Queen and Prince Philip to lunch at Archbishop's House when he retired (Murphy-O'Connor had the canny idea of placing next to Her Majesty an Irish nun from his household who knew nearly as much about horse racing as the monarch; the conversation never faltered, said one witness). And yet for all his humour and avuncular style, Murphy-O'Connor was different to Hume: there was his strong Irish background, and a more tribal approach to Catholicism; the guests at receptions at Archbishop's House were always Catholic, rather than ecumenical. The same went for the next archbishop, Vincent Nichols, whose Liverpudlian Catholicism has also given his tenure a more tribal feel. Both Murphy-O'Connor and Nichols had been educated at the English College in Rome, a seminary more prone to encouraging obedience than imagination in its students. Hume, on the other hand, had attended the University of Fribourg, which gave him a sense of independence from the Vatican, while Murphy-O'Connor and Nichols seemed to derive their Catholicism from Rome. There was a *romanità* about it. Longley agreed that the Catholic Church's bishops have reverted to type since Hume's day.

Tribalism

'Catholic bishops tend to be from grammar schools and possibly redbrick universities so they are very different from the Anglicans, who often tend to have been at public school and Oxbridge. The Catholic bishops' attitude to Rome suggests an adolescent relationship. Going to the English College is an isolating experience. They are inside a bubble,' said Longley.[18]

This was something that Peter Hennessy also recognized: 'Bishops signed up and went off so early to seminary they carry within them a loyalty and obedience the rest of us Catholics don't have.'[19]

The historian Eamon Duffy went further, arguing that Rome's influence can lead to only the most obedient of priests being considered for high office – something that was particularly apparent during the pontificate of John Paul II. He warned: 'Even when there is a new pontificate the problems remain for the individual. The pope might change but Rome doesn't.'[20]

While Rome remains in this way consistent, the world most certainly does not, and the relationship of the papacy and the Catholic Church to society changes accordingly. Rome has continued through the ages to wield its influence in political and world affairs, but that role has at times been under the radar in the United Kingdom. Then 9/11 changed everything. The destruction of the twin towers in New York confirmed that not only was there a threat from highly militant Islamists to Western culture, but it was a reminder that religion was once more part of the global political map. As the title of Adrian Wooldridge and John Micklethwait's account of religion puts it, *God Is Back*.[21] In these circumstances an institution such as the Catholic Church could prove useful to the British Foreign Office, not only for its own role, but also for the expertise and experience it could draw on in dealing with other religions across the globe.

God is back

In Britain, violent Islamism has been a major issue for government for the past fifteen years, as well as a focus of wider public concern. But there is also a minority aggressively antipathetic to all religion. The Catholic Church has been a particular target for this opposition, particularly in the run-up to the visit to the UK of Benedict XVI in 2010. But it is also apparent in the continuing criticism of its schools and the demand that they be mandated to no longer benefit Catholic pupils in their admission policies. The reason for targeting Catholicism might be due to its power, to its visibility, or to it having a clear-cut structure and leadership. But it might also be due to what the sociologist Grace Davie calls 'a residual Protestantism' in Britain that she believes 'explains a certain degree of caution, suspicion even, with respect to some aspects of Roman Catholicism, not least the question of papal authority'.[22]

Education has not been the only neuralgic issue for the Catholic Church in the past thirty years. It has been involved in several political spats that it mostly failed to win, with its hierarchy outmanoeuvred by governments of different stripes. It lost its arguments over homosexuality, taking on first Labour over gay adoption and then the coalition government over same-sex marriage. The Church's opposition to greater rights for gay people was not unique to Britain, indicating that doctrine can consistently influence Vatican relations with public policy-makers across the globe. The Vatican spoke out on the matter on several occasions, as did several bishops' conferences.[23]

But it was apparent in the UK that Catholics in the pew did not share the bishops' views on homosexuality. While the Vatican might have insisted that the siren call of secularism was the cause of this ignoring of doctrine, there are other reasons too. Firstly, the Church's standing on sexual matters, including among Catholics, has been badly damaged by the sex abuse crisis. The incidences of cases across the world, from Australia to the US and to Europe, has shown a common trend: that priests were engaged in the abuse of minors, with many of the victims adolescent boys, and that rather than deal with the problem, perpetrators were moved from parish to parish by their bishops, with little regard for the damage done to victims. Although recent disclosures in the UK of abuse being carried out by powerful individuals in entertainment, politics and the Church of England as well, indicated that the cause is not celibacy but rather an individual's power and standing in society, the damage to the Catholic Church's reputation has been profound. Efforts to tackle abuse and protect children – starting with a report by Lord Nolan in 2001, when he was commissioned by the then Archbishop Murphy-O'Connor to investigate clerical child abuse in the

Catholic Church in England and Wales, and followed by a further enquiry and the subsequent establishment of safeguarding bodies – has not been enough for many people. The Church is still perceived as hypocritical, seemingly lecturing people on what happens in the bedroom, while some of its clerics were abusers and bishops sometimes covered up the scandals. Cardinal Murphy-O'Connor, whose time as Archbishop of Westminster was marred by sex abuse scandals, has expressed his regret regarding the victims. But his regret goes beyond that. As he told me: 'The abuse scandal was an absolute disaster for the Church.'[24]

Second, the Catholic Church's stance on sexual matters, since Paul VI's 1968 encyclical, *Humanae Vitae*, has not been accepted wholesale by many Catholics, with generations rejecting its teaching on contraception. This means that natural law, the bedrock of its sexual teaching, no longer has the full support – or understanding – of educated Catholics. And finally, the experience of many Catholics as the friends, siblings and parents of homosexual people – as well as gay Catholics themselves – means that many people want homosexuals to be more openly accepted by the Church. The problem is that the Church's admonition to treat gay people equally, while still insisting homosexual acts are sinful, is seen as unworkable. Research conducted by the sociologist Professor Linda Woodhead of Lancaster University shows that young Catholics are increasingly liberal on gay marriage while interviews she has conducted reveal that many young people, including practising Catholics, see any prejudice against homosexuals as a moral aberration akin to slavery or racism.[25]

Although there was some indication prior to the Synod on the Family in Rome in 2015 that bishops from the west, including Cardinal Vincent Nichols of Westminster, realize that there is a disconnect between the people and Catholic teaching on morality, their overall view is that the problem lies more with the influence of secularism. Yet this issue is not entirely new. Even thirty years ago there was evidence of the growing secularization of Britain and the attendant declining influence of Christianity. Clifford Longley recalls that in 1982 there was nervousness about the visit of John Paul II and a fear of anti-Catholic protests. A Gallup poll of the time revealed 'a secular opposition that at the time was little known – from what you might call *Guardian* secularists', he said.[26]

Secularists, *Guardian* ones or not, have certainly grown in number in Britain since the time of John Paul's visit. Although 72 per cent of the population identified itself as Christian according to the 2011 Census, just 12 per cent of Britons attend church each week, according to a 2004 Gallup survey. The Catholic Church claims around four million members in England and Wales while Catholic Directory figures estimate that around one million of them are Mass attenders. Recent arrivals from Eastern Europe, Africa and Latin America have helped offset lapsation by British Catholics.[27]

We live in a society whose relationship to religion is complex. It remains a backdrop where there is an established Church, and Christianity is still evident through major national holidays such as Christmas and Easter. Yet there is remarkable ignorance about Christianity. Few people today, for example, know what Good Friday commemorates and why it is so called. According to an Ipsos Mori survey of October 2014, Christian belief was largely underestimated, while the number of Muslim believers was grossly overestimated. Survey respondents thought that 39 per cent of the population was Christian when it is 59 per cent, while they estimated that 21 per cent of British people were Muslim when it is only 5 per cent.[28]

Power and influence

Christianity, including Catholicism, retains a major influence in wider society through its role in charities, faith schools, and parishes, and through its chaplains working in prisons, ships, hospitals, and the forces. Nor should its role in 'hatching, matching and despatching' be forgotten.

In May 1993, the highly respected political commentator Hugo Young, himself a Catholic, wrote:

> The Catholic voice has grown in confidence in 30 years. Some see it as the only reliable beacon. All the same, its interests have still been predominantly inward. It has made the very most of its unestablished status.
>
> What the Anglican overtures make it ask seriously for the first time is what its place should be in national life. Those who once relished outsiderdom now face with some trepidation a life at the centre.[29]

Young was writing at a time when the Church of England was considering allowing women to be ordained, something which would cause tremendous upheaval and cause many Anglican priests to leave and become Catholics.

At this juncture, now over twenty years ago, Clifford Longley advocated a Catholic Church that should make the most of its position as a voluntary organization making its voice heard, while not attempting to be *the* national Church. Longley advocated a Church that could quietly influence public opinion by winning debates through quality of argument, but would have to be cautious 'about pressing for legislation to align English law with Catholic moral teaching on issues where the majority of the population does not share that teaching'.[30]

Longley's remarks echoed a view taken seven years earlier by the sociologist Michael Hornsby-Smith, who argued that British Catholicism had come of age and become acceptable to fellow citizens and would survive if it became a 'domesticated denomination' indistinguishable from other Christian churches and secular morality. Quiet understatement seemed the predicted way forward.[31]

This has not always happened. In the past twenty years, there have been conflicts between Church and State, often pushed by the Vatican, which has clearly been behind a constant effort by bishops in different countries to oppose gay marriage. The then nuncio to the United Kingdom, Archbishop Antonio Mennini, wanted to steer the English bishops this way, urging them to make their voices heard and defend Church teaching on this issue when he spoke to them at their bi-annual meeting in Leeds in 2012.[32]

Were Longley and Hornsby-Smith right about the caution and the quiet helpfulness required in this country? Or has English Catholicism become in the twenty-first century a more confident, challenging and prophetic voice? When they were writing, nobody could have imagined the invention of social media and its use by the papacy, and how a pope such as Francis could transform general perceptions of the Church. By 1989, after a visit to Rome, the then Archbishop of Canterbury, Robert Runcie, spoke of recognizing the pope as the central and leading figure of a united Church. Grace Davie has argued that: 'Reservations do, nonetheless, remain when it comes to any notion of papal authority in this country.'[33]

In the chapters that follow I will examine how the relationship between the papacy and the British in the modern era, which grew out of the background I have just outlined, has grown and developed. There is clear evidence today of British recognition of the Catholic Church's place in the world and I will examine this through an analysis of the diplomatic relations forged between the Catholic Church and the United Kingdom during the pontificates of John Paul II, Benedict XVI and Francis.

The British today have plenty of reasons to continue doing diplomatic business with the Catholic Church due to its size and influence. It has diplomatic relationships with 180 countries and the Church has 1.2 billion members. It is also a superb conduit of information from around the globe; the skills of its diplomats are legendary. It also has a vast network of people on the ground, working in developing nations. Its global social services organization, Caritas, is second only in size to the International Red Cross. I will also pay particular attention to the role that the Catholic Church has played in domestic politics in England and Wales, as well as its role in Scotland and its part in forging peace in Northern Ireland – an issue which has long been of concern in Rome. The parts played in this unique relationship between the kingdom to which Christ gave Peter the keys – the Catholic Church – and the United Kingdom by this trio of popes will be described and analyzed. So will the roles of British politicians, clerics both Catholic and Anglican, and not least, the Queen. There is much here about the influence of a global religion on one nation but the traffic is not one-way. The United Kingdom has due influence in the Vatican too, and I will show how the British were in particular at the heart of Rome during the election of Pope Francis.

Today Francis appears to speak effectively to the world, and not just at Christmas and Easter in his traditional messages, but constantly. The average Briton may not recognize papal authority, but intuits what might be described as spiritual authority through the attractiveness of Francis's character, rather than his office. There is nobody in Britain to match it. In that sense, the country that Henry VIII separated from Rome has come full circle, at least during this particular papacy. Whether that connection will last through another pontificate with a very different person at the helm, is a tantalising question to speculate upon.

Notes

1   *Liverpool Mail*, 18 July 1851, quoted in *The Rise and Fall of Liverpool Sectarianism*, Keith Daniel Roberts, University of Liverpool Repository. Available online: http://repository.liv.ac.uk/2010280/3/RobertsKei_April2015_2010280.pdf

2   Pepinster, C (2010), 'Glastonbury with God', *Mail on Sunday*, 19 September.

3   Farberov, Snejana (2013), 'The touching moment Pope Francis halted his weekly audience to kiss and hold disfigured man with Elephant Man disease', *Daily Mail*, 7 November. http://www.dailymail.co.uk/news/article-2489534/Touching-moment-Pope-Francis-halted-weekly-general-audience-kiss-hold-disfigured-man.html

4   Wiseman, Cardinal Nicholas (1850), *From Out The Flaminian Gate*, 7 October, quoted by Clifford Longley (1994), *The Tablet*, 2 April.

5   Wiseman riposted, quoted by Clifford Longley (1994), *The Tablet*, 2 April.

6   Kerr, Fergus (2011), 'Catholicism in England, Wales and Scotland', in *The Blackwell Companion to Catholicism*, James J Buckley, Frederick Christian Bauerschmidt and Trent Poplum (eds), Chichester: Wiley-Blackwell, 160.

7   M.A. Fitzsimons quoted by Hornsby-Smith, Michael P. (1987), *Roman Catholics in England*, Cambridge: Cambridge University Press.

8   Interview of Cardinal Cormac Murphy-O'Connor (CMO'C) by Catherine Pepinster (CP), February 2015.

9   Interview of Lord (Peter) Hennessy (PH) by Catherine Pepinster (CP), October 2014.

10   Hornsby-Smith, ibid, 50.

11   For an account of Hume's life, see Howard, Anthony (2005), *Basil Hume: The Monk Cardinal*, London: Headline.

12   Paul Vallely (2008), Annual Newman Lecture.

13   Interview of PH by CP, ibid.

14   See Chapter 12 of this book for full details of the House of Lords episode.

15   Interview of Lord (Chris) Patten (CP) by Catherine Pepinster (CP), January 2015.

16   Interview of Clifford Longley (CL) by Catherine Pepinster (CP), October 2014.

17   Interview of CL by CP, ibid.

18   Interview of CL by CP, ibid.

19 Interview of PH by CP.

20 Interview of Eamon Duffy (ED) by Catherine Pepinster, December 2015.

21 Wooldridge, Adrian and Micklethwait, John (2009), *God Is Back: How the Global Rise of Faith Is Changing the World*, London: Penguin.

22 Davie, ibid, 76.

23 See Chapter 12 for a fuller account of the rows over homosexual issues.

24 Interview of CMO'C by CP, ibid.

25 Email dialogue with Professor Linda Woodhead, University of Lancaster, March 2015.

26 Interview of CL by CP, ibid.

27 Statistics from the *Catholic Directory* (2015).

28 Alberto Nardelli, *The Guardian*, 29 October 2014.

29 Hugo Young, *The Guardian*, quoted by Clifford Longley, *The Tablet* (1994), 2 April.

30 Longley, ibid.

31 Hornsby-Smith, ibid, 42.

32 Lamb, Christopher (2012), '"Assert your faith", nuncio tells bishops', *The Tablet*, 28 April, 31.

33 Grace Davie, ibid, 59.

2

Relations restored:

Diplomacy, part one

It has produced four popes, thousands of diplomats and is one of the most elite institutions of the Catholic Church. Yet few people have ever heard of the Pontifical Ecclesiastical Academy, the Catholic Church's own training college for diplomats, even though countless visitors to Rome pass its doors on the Piazza della Minerva every day, their eyes usually trained on the magnificent ancient Roman building of the Pantheon nearby. The graduates of the Academy who become the elite diplomatic corps of the Holy See are key to the Vatican's abiding influence across the globe and to its relationship with governments, including that in Britain.

And diplomacy has been the main means by which this country, once so deeply estranged from Rome, has reconfigured its relationship with the Catholic Church over the past thirty years since the two decided to accord each other full diplomatic status.

Rome's power at the diplomatic level owes much to its previous status as one of the great political forces of Europe. So long established is its commitment to diplomacy that the Pontifical Ecclesiastical Academy first opened its doors in 1701. The papal states had ruled great swathes of Italy until the post-Risorgimento government invaded and overran those states in September 1870. The pope of the time, Pius IX, refused to recognize the new regime and so did his successors until 1929. For all of this period, there was no diplomatic status as such for the Catholic Church but the Holy See did exist as an ecclesiastical jurisdiction and continued to be seen as acting for and on behalf of the Church.

Since 1929 the Holy See has also been recognized as a subject of international law with rights and duties akin to that of nation states, and as a sovereign entity, headed by the pope. It is recognized by the UN as an observer state and is a member state of intergovernmental organizations. It has also built up a strong diplomatic corps with diplomatic relations with 180 countries, and can enter into binding agreements with other states.

Foreign embassies are accredited to the Holy See, rather than the Vatican City, and the Holy See establishes treaties and concordats with other states.

It was in 1914, at the outbreak of war in Europe, that Britain's Foreign Office realized that a resident envoy to the Holy See might be useful in counteracting the influence of the German and Austrian ambassadors on the papacy, and accordingly Sir Henry Howard became His Majesty's Envoy Extraordinary and Minister Plenipotentiary on a Special Mission to His Holiness the Pope. Although full status did not occur until 1981, sending that first envoy was so significant in the warming of relations that its centenary was marked with a Mass at the papal basilica of St Paul's Outside the Walls, concelebrated by the Holy See's secretary of state, Cardinal Pietro Parolin, and Cardinal Vincent Nichols.

In recent years British governments have sought to develop an ally in the Catholic Church, an institution with which Britain, for so much of its history, was in significant conflict. The contemporary relationship has been shaped above all by pragmatism, finding for immediate or short-term gain an ally in an organization that was even once a sworn enemy. This has been evident in dialogue over the situation in Ireland, opposition to communism and the ending of the Cold War, and work on aid in the developing world. Sometimes British politicians have worked out that the Vatican has its uses as a listening ear via its diplomats around the world, and used its knowledge to Britain's advantage.

However, it took considerable time in the modern era before Britain accepted that there should be any diplomatic relationship at all. Although the UK had first established a presence in Rome in 1914, there was no attempt at reciprocity for another twenty-four years, which was contrary to usual diplomatic practice, although the Holy See did not press hard for such representation. Although the Vatican was constituted as a state by the Lateran Pacts in 1929 an apostolic delegate was allowed to be appointed in London only nine years later. It took more than another forty years for the delegate to be given diplomatic privileges and to be upgraded to nuncio in 1982.

Why had Britain been so tardy in its relationship with the Vatican? According to Mark Pellew, the former British ambassador to the Holy See from 1998–2002, it was due to inertia as much as anything else.[1] Things had worked well without upgrading to full status. There was also concern about objections from certain sectors. The set-up required annual parliamentary renewal and there were regular letters of protest to the Foreign Office from the Orange Order and the Protestant Alliance. But Pellew asserts: 'The fact that Britain did not do so was not due to fears of Protestant backlash, but rather to small-mindedness and – frankly – laziness on the part of Foreign Office officials dealing with what they regarded as a not very important issue.'[2]

The abiding matter, as far as the Foreign Office was concerned throughout the first half of the twentieth century, was whether the Catholic Church favoured particular forms of government because it suited her purposes in terms of the society they encouraged. During the 1930s the Foreign Office believed that Pope Pius XI was opposed to Hitler, but there was concern that he was in favour of fascism in Spain and Italy. Sir Charles Wingfield, the British minister responsible for relations with the Holy See, wrote in his annual report in 1935:

> It is true that fascism and popular Catholicism rest upon principles which are to some extent similar. Both admit no questioning of their creed; both insist upon the submission of the individual to the system, encourage large families, attach importance to external ceremonies, and to mass psychology.[3]

Yet other developments showed that the British and the Vatican had found common cause in their opposition to totalitarianism of both fascist and communist varieties.

Mit brennender Sorge, the encyclical published by Pius XI in March 1937, confirmed that the papacy was firmly opposed to Hitler, thus showing there was an opportunity for the British to work with the Holy See in facing the fascist threat in Europe.[4]

During the Second World War itself, the British legate, D'Arcy Osborne, stayed in Rome, a virtual prisoner inside the Vatican from 1940–44 and the only Allied diplomat to remain throughout this time. He knew that his encoded messages, despite being sent by diplomatic bag via neutral Portugal, were probably compromised. According to Owen Chadwick's thesis in his account of *The British And The Vatican During The Second World War*, they were written in such a way as to both keep London informed and also mislead suspected German and Italian readers about the Holy See's support for the fascist cause.[5]

The relationship between Britain and Rome deepened during the Cold War through the common fight against communism. The British legate, Sir Walter Roberts, wrote in October 1953 to Sir Ivone Kirkpatrick, the permanent secretary at the Foreign Office:

> Britain's reputation stands high in the Vatican. She is regarded as the one power in the free world which, during and since the Second World War, has shown exceptional qualities of stability, resilience and political wisdom. The Church in the political field is engaged in a long term fight against the twin evils of communism and nationalism, and since I came to Rome its leaders have often testified to the spirit of co-operation shown in this regard by Her Majesty's Government . . . The Vatican regards the material for exposing communist policies prepared by the research departments in London and passed on by this post to the Secretariat of State and to other centres in Rome as most valuable. I am assured that no such material is received from any other source and that much of it is of higher quality than that compiled by the Church itself.[6]

This shared interest in fighting communism was also evident when Sir Peter Scarlett, the British representative from 1960-65, wrote in his farewell despatch:

In the present situation of nuclear stalemate and struggle of ideologies, I would argue that the importance to us of the influence of the Catholic Church has probably increased. Not only is it doggedly resistant to Communism, it is equipped better than most states to encourage resistance in others.[7]

By the early 1980s, it was apparent that the US also saw Rome as a major ally in the battle with communism, especially Soviet Russia. Ronald Reagan's CIA director, Bill Casey, met John Paul II and his secretary of state, Cardinal Agostino Casaroli, several times for private meetings to discuss these matters. Reagan and John Paul had survived assassination attempts six weeks apart in 1981 and both believed God had saved them for a special mission.[8]

According to Mark Pellew:

the new Pope's willingness to stand up to the Soviet bloc, and particularly his support for Lech Walesa and Solidarity in Poland, helped to create a positive mood in the bilateral relationship between Britain and the Holy See. This was certainly a factor in making it possible to think about a papal visit and the upgrading of diplomatic relations to ambassadorial level in 1982.[9]

By October 1981, the visit of John Paul II to the United Kingdom was being planned. The impetus for this had come from the Catholic Church of England and Wales – Cardinal Basil Hume had invited the pope to visit and he had accepted – and it was not a state visit. The British government, though, was warmly disposed towards it. It was then that the government's attention turned to its relations with the Holy See. The then foreign secretary Lord Carrington – who was to resign on the outbreak of war with Argentina, a war that so nearly scuppered the papal visit – recommended to his Cabinet colleagues that the Vatican should be invited to promote its representative in London to the ambassadorial role of pro-nuncio and that the United Kingdom's representation should be raised to the status of an embassy.

Carrington's analysis gives a useful insight into the pragmatic approach to extending diplomatic relations and also to the impact that John Paul II had on Britain, even before his visit. Britain had moved on from its historic tensions with Rome, said Carrington: 'The present level of relations has become an anomaly', he wrote, 'the historical British conflicts with the papacy have lost most of their legal and political significance', while pointing out that with the impending visit, attention would be drawn to the UK–Holy See relationship. And it was clear Britain was lagging behind her allies:

Carrington pointed out that most European nations, Australia and Canada had full diplomatic relations while at that stage the US sent a personal envoy.[10]

The figure of John Paul loomed large over this argument about relations; Carrington pointed out to colleagues that he 'has influence in areas where important British interests are at stake, including Ireland, Eastern Europe and the Middle East'. Just how important the pope's role was in the then fraught situation in Northern Ireland is apparent in the confidential note made of Cabinet that day; Carrington told colleagues that he made his recommendations, having previously discussed them with the secretary of state for Northern Ireland, and he went on to say that: 'The Vatican has consistently condemned violence in Northern Ireland and avoided being drawn into unhelpful comment.'

What this typically English under-statement did not reveal was the tension that had developed between the Catholic Church and the British government that year and the previous one over Northern Ireland, and that had only begun to be dissipated by the end of the hunger strike in the Maze Prison. Looking back, it is extraordinary that within a fortnight of the Maze strike ending, the Cabinet turned its attention to improving relations with the Holy See.[11]

Carrington did warn that there might be hostility among Northern Ireland Protestants to the growing friendly relationship between the UK and Rome, and there was concern that it might be construed as having any connection to the forthcoming Anglo-Irish summit. It was suggested, though, that Mrs Thatcher should use the summit to tell the Irish prime minister about it.

No pope had ever set foot before on the soil of the country which had rejected Catholicism and made it an illegal religion for hundreds of years. The government recognized what an historic moment it would be. Within weeks of John Paul's acceptance of the invitation of the Catholic Church in England and Wales, Number 10 staff and other senior Whitehall figures were engaged in preparations, with regular dialogue taking place between Archbishop's House and Downing Street. Sir Michael Palliser, a trusted senior civil servant and Roman Catholic, was a regular intermediary.

But in a nation with an established, *Protestant* Church, the first visit of a pope was not without controversy and there was clear evidence of latent English anti-Catholicism. The prime minister, though, was adamant in her support of the papal visit, despite vehement objections to it from fundamentalist Protestants, including Ian Paisley. Mrs Thatcher wrote to Paisley in September 1980 of her desire to see the visit go ahead and made it plain that there were no protocol issues:

The Pope is recognised by the UK Government as a Head of State and we are in diplomatic relations with that State; Her Majesty's Government are represented at the Vatican by a Minister. We do not consider that the

Bill of Rights and Act of Settlement would pose any constitutional barrier to contacts between The Queen and the pope, or between Her Majesty's Government and the pope during his visit to this country. It follows that, while no detailed arrangements have yet been made, it would be natural for The Queen to meet the Pope if she is in the country at the time of his visit. It would also be natural for me to do so.[12]

A week before Mrs Thatcher's letter to Paisley, she had received a no-holds-barred letter of objection to the proposed papal visit from the Protestant Reformation Society, supported by eight other Protestant organizations, including the Protestant Truth Society, the Grand Orange Lodge of England and the Grand Orange Lodge of Scotland.

Signed by twenty officials of these various groups, it warned:

The constitution of this country is such that it forbids the recognition of the claims of the papacy, and the solemn Coronation Oath to uphold the true Gospel and maintain the Protestant Reformed Religion must preclude any involvement by the Queen and Government in a papal visit. This would be quite unacceptable and wholly misleading, since it would appear that the Pope was being accorded general acclaim by the British people as a whole.[13]

Perhaps with these objections in mind, but knowing they were made by a vocal minority, Lord Carrington cautiously warned that the maintenance of a barrier to full diplomatic relations with the Holy See is 'anachronistic in the light of the growing ecumenical mood between the Churches in Britain', but he also advised that the queen should be told of the change in diplomatic relations at her next audience with the prime minister, while the Archbishop of Canterbury and the Moderator of the Church of Scotland, already sounded out, should be informed.[14]

But the visit became complicated by a problem that nobody had envisaged when the visit was first mooted: that Britain would be engaged in military conflict with a predominantly Catholic country. When war broke out following the invasion in April 1982 by Argentina of the British territory of the Falkland Islands, it seemed that the papal visit to Britain would be called off. The Argentinians' expression of anger at the apparent papal favouritism shown to their sworn enemy, the pro-Argentine views of Italian officials in the Vatican and the concern of John Paul II's closest advisers nearly scuppered the trip.

When John Paul sent word to Cardinal Basil Hume, the Archbishop of Westminster, of the need to cancel, it was a bitter moment. Two years of hard work had already gone into preparations, including negotiations by the Church with the British government. The visit was supported by the government and Robert Runcie, the Archbishop of Canterbury, had also given it his backing. Runcie's support particularly mattered to Hume, who saw the visit as key to building bridges with the Church of England. According to Cardinal Cormac Murphy-O'Connor, influential Argentinian people were lobbying the Secretariat of State in Rome, urging John Paul to cancel the trip to the UK.[15] Lord Camoys, a leading Catholic layman from one of England's most ancient recusant families who was a friend of the then nuncio, Bruno Heim, recalls: 'There was panic in the nunciature. For a while the visit was touch and go.'[16]

There is debate about what happened next, with some witnesses suggesting that Cardinal Hume was too ready to accept defeat. But according to Jimmy Burns in *The Land That Lost Its Heroes*, Hume consulted with key Catholics, including his own father, Tom Burns, who was editor of *The Tablet*, and Derek Worlock, Archbishop of Liverpool. Within days, a hastily assembled lobbying team of Worlock, Archbishop Thomas Winning of Glasgow and Professor Henry Chadwick, the noted Church historian and leading figure in the ecumenical Anglican-Roman Catholic International Commission who was representing the Church of England, set out for Rome to urge the pope to continue with the British trip.[17] Others suggest that the initiative came from Archbishop Worlock, willingly assisted by Archbishop Winning.

The rescue mission certainly caught people's attention and when Worlock and Winning set off to Rome from Heathrow on 17 May, they were surrounded by cameras and television crews, while in Rome the BBC's Kate Adie was waiting for them at the airport. The following day Worlock and Winning met the pope for lunch. Also at the gathering were the secretary of state, Cardinal Agostino Casaroli, and the president of the Conference of Latin American bishops, Archbishop Alfonso Trujillo. Trujillo was not a man to mince to his words; he would gain notoriety twenty years later for his claim, made during his time as the highly conservative president of the Pontifical Council for the Family, that condoms were ineffective in preventing the transmission of HIV because they had holes big enough for the virus to pass through.[18] On this occasion, though, the man who would later be the scourge of the World Health Organization proved to be the scourge of the British, pressing for a cancellation of the UK visit on the grounds that it would deeply offend the Argentinian people. Worlock and Winning, meanwhile, indicated how cancellation would offend the United Kingdom and embarrass its Catholic population.

Earlier in the day, Worlock and Winning had spent time with Archbishop Achille Silvestrini, Secretary of the Council for the Public Affairs of the Church, who offered the pair sage advice: it would be worthwhile to promote reconciliation between the bishops of the UK and Argentina. According to their respective biographers, Clifford Longley and Stephen McGinty, Worlock and Winning would both claim responsibility for finding a solution that would suit the Latin Americans. Archbishop Winning suggested the pope should also visit Argentina – a balancing act to which John Paul agreed, and one Lopez Trujillo supported.[19] Worlock, meanwhile, claimed that he put forward the idea of a Mass of reconciliation to be celebrated by the pope, Cardinals Aramburu and Primatesta of Argentina, and Cardinal Hume and Cardinal Gray.[20] It was also agreed that the pope would not meet the British government while he was in the UK and that the visit could still be called off if certain events occurred, chief of which was the death of Prince Andrew, the queen's son who was then serving as a helicopter pilot in the Falklands. The pope's view was that the four cardinals, through their Mass of reconciliation, would show that the papal visit to Britain was for the good of the Church, rather than a display of favour on his part. Both Worlock and Winning noted, however, that John Paul referred to the 'Falkland Islands', while Curial officials called them the 'Malvinas'.

While the two British archbishops around the lunch table – Worlock and Winning – had made an agreement, their cardinals, Hume and Gray, had yet to agree and yet to come to Rome. Hume was the harder to persuade, according to Worlock's notes of the time, because he felt cornered, and that the Foreign Office would object to the conditions. It took Cardinal Casaroli to persuade Hume via Worlock that the pope needed his co-operation to persuade the Argentinians that the visit should take place.[21] In fact, Hume was mistaken: the British government *was* still keen for the papal visit to happen; if it did not, it might look as if the papacy disapproved of the United Kingdom's invasion of the Falklands and its right to defend the sovereignty of its territory.

Whilst the visit was saved, the list of public figures that Pope John Paul would meet was severely curtailed. It was viewed as too provocative for him to meet the prime minister, whereas two years earlier, in the first throes of preparations, Michael Pattison, Mrs Thatcher's private secretary, had written to fellow Whitehall officials about what might occur: '[The Prime Minister] feels that she should plan a reception or dinner or whatever form of entertainment the Pope would find acceptable', thus displaying a certain naïve misunderstanding as to what popes get up to on their travels; entertainment is not usually part of their schedule. Two days earlier Thatcher had scribbled in her own hand: 'We must surely plan a reception or dinner, whatever he [JPII] would find acceptable.'[22]

Mrs Thatcher from the outset showed an enthusiasm for the visit of the pope that may well have stunned her Methodist father, Alderman Roberts, who, as Eliza Filby notes in her volume *God and Mrs Thatcher*,[23] displayed old-style disdain for the papacy. The prime minister certainly shared much with the Polish pope, especially a vehement antipathy to communist Russia. But this was not a question of adulation: Mrs Thatcher was also willing to cross swords with John Paul over Northern Ireland and the treatment of the Maze hunger strikers.[24]

Planning for the visit had been going on for months before the Falklands crisis. A committee was formed to which Cardinal Hume had co-opted his brother-in-law, Lord Hunt, the retired Cabinet Secretary, as well as representatives of Buckingham Palace and the Archbishop of Canterbury.

The visit remained a pastoral one to the Catholic Church in Britain but it was clear there were ecumenical and wider public issues. At that stage, pre-Falklands, Cardinal Hume thought the prime minister might want to meet John Paul for private talks at Archbishop's House on the evening of Saturday 28 May, or might wish to greet the pope on his arrival at Gatwick Airport.

Having a pope visit Britain was still a novel idea which clearly made some people very nervous. When Lord Hailsham, following lobbying from peers including Lord Ingleby and Lord Bessborough, suggested that John Paul address both Houses of Parliament in Westminster Hall, he added that Miles, Duke of Norfolk, the premier Catholic peer, 'advised the greatest caution'. There were fears of Protestant protests, while a memo from Colin Peterson, Number 10's Secretary for Appointments, also intimated that people might interpret an address to Parliament by the pope as a sign of supremacy – not something that could be tolerated in a nation where 300 years earlier, the monarch became the Supreme Governor of the Church.

Peterson wrote of the purported address to both Houses of Parliament: 'I would advise in the strongest possible terms against this proposal.' He went on: 'Include the pomp and ceremony (and symbolism) of an address by the pope to both Houses of Parliament, and the visit will be plunged in controversy.'[25] Clive Whitmore, the prime minister's principal private secretary, argued that this was a pastoral visit and so an address would not be appropriate while the other Churches 'would find it very difficult to take'. The planned visit had always been strongly ecumenical and Whitmore argued that an address would undo the atmosphere in which other Churches wanted to discuss the issue of unity. Mrs Thatcher scribbled on the note that it could be discussed orally in Cabinet, 'but I have no doubt the view will be strongly against'.[26] It was clearly a non-starter and rejected outright at Cabinet on 26 March where the prime minister said it would be wholly inappropriate to the nature of the pope's visit and would only add to the 'already formidable security problems surrounding it'.[27]

To those who later witnessed the address of a pope to Parliament, when Benedict XVI spoke in Westminster Hall in 2010, it is hard to understand the nervousness expressed thirty years earlier, although it has to be said that an address of that kind is more appropriate during a state visit. But back in the early 1980s, the British government was not prepared to test the water and the lobbying of the time did suggest that some Protestants were not ready to see a pope take centre-stage in the public life of the nation.

But the pope was still the pope – a person of international standing – and prior to the Falklands crisis, the British government was keen that John Paul should meet both the prime minister and the queen. However, there was concern that, while Basil Hume held the same view, Rome seemed at best lukewarm about these proposed encounters. While considerable progress had been made in the visit happening at all, given that no pope had ever visited Britain, there were certain boundaries which the Vatican would not cross – even for a monarch. The proposal that both Cardinal Hume and the government put forward – lunch with the queen – was ruled out from the start.

The issue was still rumbling on in December when Clive Whitmore minuted the prime minister:

> Cardinal Hume has throughout been personally in favour of a lunch at the Palace rather than a call by the Pope, but Vatican officials have taken the line that the Pope and his predecessors have never been entertained to a meal by another head of state and that it would therefore be impossible for the Queen to give him lunch . . . Lord Hunt told me this morning that protocol will triumph.[28]

Lord Hunt, Basil Hume's brother-in-law, who had retired as Cabinet Secretary two years earlier, had become a conduit for both sides. Number 10 wanted to lobby him about planning, and the Catholic Church, concerned about the costs that it would bear, asked him to approach his successor as Cabinet Secretary, Sir Robert Armstrong. It was agreed that the Ministry of Defence could supply John Paul with a Queen's Flight helicopter to get him from the garden of Buckingham Palace following his meeting with the queen to a pastoral visit in Cardiff. This, according to Hunt, would help with security.

Until John Paul II arrived in the UK, there was little real understanding in the United Kingdom of the place of the Catholic Church in Britain. Cardinal Cormac Murphy-O'Connor's view is that if the pope had visited Britain fifty years earlier, the Church would have mainly been one of poor Irish migrants: 'The church would have been very much on the periphery of society in Britain, and in a sense, the church would have been content to be so.'[29] In 1982, he said:

> The people of Britain saw for the first time, because this was televised, that this was a community that had a part to play in this country, in a new way. And I thought then as I think now, that this was very significant. We were no longer on the periphery of the social and cultural life of England but also at the centre, with our Christian friends, saying what it means to be a Christian.[30]

The pope's visit was also highly significant for the national minorities of Britain. John Paul visited the UK before the Berlin Wall came down, and he was a man who had experienced oppression himself. He knew how important a nation's identity is. Bishop Emeritus Edwin Regan, one of the few native Welsh speakers to ever be a Catholic bishop, thinks it was important for the Welsh that John Paul's trip took in Wales, with a stop in Cardiff, because it meant that the Welsh were accepted as a special nation in their own right. And the former Archbishop of Glasgow, Mario Conti, also recognized the pope's importance for Scots: 'In the history of our countries, the papacy's attitude has at times helped in that identification of our nations.' In acknowledging these nations, the popes put them at the centre of events, encouraging people not to see them as at the periphery.[31]

But the particular circumstances of the conflict with Argentina surrounding the 1982 visit made John Paul jittery. Cormac Murphy-O'Connor recalls that as Bishop of Arundel and Brighton, he had to meet the pope at Gatwick Airport and John Paul was incredibly nervous, shaking in the plane: 'He was afraid there might be rotten eggs when he arrived because of the Falklands.' Despite this and the fact that there had been an assassination attempt on John Paul's life the year before, the Catholic Church had to pay for the visit's policing because it was a pastoral trip rather than a state visit.[32]

The consequences of the visit were highly significant for relations between Britain and the Holy See. Despite the many small irritations, diplomatic difficulties and crises that befell the planning of the visit, the 1982 papal trip opened the eyes of the UK government to Rome and its diplomatic influence and network. The visit, however limited in scope, meant the government had to think about Rome and focus on its position in the world in a way it had never done before. It consolidated its thinking about the British relationship with the Holy See, which had begun with the decision to extend its relations by installing an ambassador to the Holy See in Rome. Even the rumpus over the Falklands War, and the possibility of the pope's visit being cancelled in the wake of it, highlighted that in the Catholic world at least – of which Argentina was a part – the pope was a leader who truly mattered and was a world figure that Britain should engage with. The British government started to see how useful it would be to hear from this institution with its global network. Murphy-O'Connor believes that since the 1982 visit, Britain has had a special place in Rome; it punches above its weight, 'with its language and history and traditions it has a peculiar and particular importance'.[33]

Given that it is the base of the worldwide Anglican Communion, that it has strong connections to both the United States and the rest of Europe, and it nurtures the Commonwealth network, this interest in the UK is understandable. Relations with the UK therefore mean links to vital networks in the world – and networks undoubtedly matter to a Church that has one of the most impressive diplomatic networks of its own.

Sir Ivor Roberts, a seasoned diplomat whose posts included ambassador to Italy, says that above all it is the UK's influence at the UN that most interests Rome: 'It is seen as important because it is a permanent member of the UN Security Council and so can prevent wars. It has membership of significant institutions such as Nato, the EU and has worldwide reach.'[34]

Historical conflicts between Britain and Rome, although not forgotten, faded more into the background and a more pragmatic approach was taken on both sides. The focus became common values and shared interests, such as concerns about communism and the Cold War. Yet there was caution on both sides, as the decision not to invite the pope to address Parliament in

Westminster Hall showed. Above all, though, the greatest consequence of John Paul's visit was that it was a moment of recognition: Britain and Rome turned to one another, and put history behind them.

Yet within twenty-five years, the progress made in relations would be put in jeopardy by the British. The risk that the United Kingdom took for the sake of saving money, the damage done by its focus on making economies, the repairs eventually made and the surprising turnaround that led to another papal visit and, eventually, a mutually warm working relationship between the UK and the papacy, is the focus of the next chapter.

Notes

1   Pellew, Mark (2013), 'The Diplomatic and Political Relationship', in *Britain and the Holy See: A Celebration of 1982 and the Wider Relationship*, proceedings of the Rome Colloquium, Rome: British Embassy to the Holy See, 59.

2   Ibid.

3   Quoted by Pellew, ibid, 61.

4   *Mit brennender Sorge*, Encyclical of Pope Pius XI on the Church and the German Reich. http://w2.vatican.va/content/pius-xi/en/encyclicals/documents/hf_p-xi_enc_14031937_mit-brennender-sorge.html

5   Chadwick, Owen (1987), *Britain and the Vatican during the Second World War*, Cambridge: Cambridge University Press.

6   Quoted by Pellew, ibid, 64.

7   Quoted by Pellew, ibid, 66.

8   Bernstein, Carl (2001), 'The Holy Alliance', *Time* magazine, New York, 24 June. http://content.time.com/time/magazine/article/0,9171,159069,00.html

9   Pellew, ibid, 66.

10 Carington, Peter (1981), United Kingdom Relations with the Vatican, 22 October. http://www.nationalarchives.gov.uk/details/r/C11920383#

11 See Chapter 9 for details of this tense relationship.

12 Thatcher, Margaret (1980), Letter to Ian Paisley, 8 September. http://www.margaretthatcher.org/document/119849

13 Protestant Reformation Society (1980), Letter to Margaret Thatcher, 1 September. http://www.margaretthatcher.org/archive/results.asp?w=Protestant+Reformation+Society&btn=Search

14 Carington, ibid.

15 Murphy-O'Connor, Cormac (2013), 'The Visit of 1982, its circumstances and its consequences', in *Britain and the Holy See*, ibid.

16 Interview of Lord Camoys by Catherine Pepinster, January 2016.

17 Burns, Jimmy (2012), *The Land That Lost Its Heroes: How Argentina Lost The Falklands War*, London: Bloomsbury.

18 Bradshaw, Steve (2003), 'Vatican – condoms don't stop HIV', BBC online, 10 October. http://news.bbc.co.uk/1/hi/programmes/panorama/3180236.stm

19 McGinty, Stephen (2003), *This Turbulent Priest: The Life of Cardinal Winning*, London: Harper Collins, 234.

20 Longley, Clifford (2000), *The Worlock Archive*, London: Geoffrey Chapman, 302.

21 Longley, ibid, 304–05.

22 Pattison, Michael (1980), Letter to George Walden, Foreign Office, 29 August. http://www.margaretthatcher.org/document/127315

23 Filby, Eliza (2015), *God and Mrs Thatcher*, London: Biteback.

24 See Chapter 9.

25 Peterson, Colin (1981), minute to Margaret Thatcher, 20 March. http://www.margaretthatcher.org/document/127325

26 Thatcher, Margaret (1981), handwritten addenda to Peterson, ibid.

27 Minutes of full Cabinet (1981), 26 March. http://www.margaretthatcher.org/document/127201

28 Whitemore, Clive (1981), minute to the Prime Minister, 1 December. http://www.margaretthatcher.org/document/127396

29 Murphy-O'Connor, ibid, 13.

30 Murphy-O'Connor, ibid, 14.

31 *Britain and the Holy See*, ibid.

32 Murphy-O'Connor, ibid, 13.

33 Murphy-O'Connor, ibid, 14.

34 Interview of Sir Ivor Roberts by Catherine Pepinster, October 2014.

3

From farce to Golden Age:

Diplomacy, part two

Anyone used to the great embassies that the United Kingdom runs in major capital cities – on Massachusetts Avenue in Washington, say, or the rue du Faubourg St Honoré in Paris – is in for a shock when they visit the office of the British embassy to the Holy See in Rome. At first as you walk along the major thoroughfare of the via XX Settembre and arrive at a heavily guarded compound, complete with Union Flag, all seems as one would expect. Here is a building which says 'major country speaking unto major force in the world'. But once through the guardroom and the searches, one is faced with reality. This is in fact the embassy to the Italian Republic, and the office of Britain's representative at the Holy See is tucked away in a tiny annexe.

This has been the set-up in Rome for the last ten years, since the British attempted to end more than eighty years of diplomatic convention and have a co-embassy and a co-ambassadorial residence as part of a cost-saving effort. The Foreign Office's endeavours showed not only an extraordinary lack of understanding as to how the Catholic Church would perceive such matters, but also a lack of historical knowledge. Since the 1982 papal visit and the establishment of full diplomatic status, the Holy See and the United Kingdom had enjoyed good relations. But by the first decade of the twenty-first century, all that effort was jeopardized by a cost-saving exercise.

That the UK keeps a separate embassy to the Holy See – and is obliged to do so – is due to the Lateran Pact of 1929, when the Catholic Church sought to ensure its status and position at a time when Mussolini was on the march. What began to counter 'Il Duce' ended up causing one almighty Whitehall row.

According to the Lateran Pact, no country is allowed by the Vatican to have a co-ambassador to Italy and the Holy See, and no nation can co-locate its two ambassadors. In 2005 the Labour government of Tony Blair decided to end decades of tradition by openly advertising a vacancy for an ambassador to the Holy See rather than make an internal appointment from within the ranks of the Foreign and Commonwealth Office. The person appointed did in fact come from the FCO; he was Francis Campbell, who had also worked for Blair at Number 10. Choosing him did break new ground, though: Campbell was a Catholic, and until then Catholics had not been appointed as British ambassadors to the Holy See, the fear being that they would go native, and be put under undue pressure by the Church. New Labour then decided to push for further change, by relocating the residence of the ambassador to the Holy See to the same place as the main British residence.

The suggestion that the UK's man at the Holy See should move out of the prestigious residence of the Villa Drusiana, which had been home to the British representative for years, and into the gatehouse of the main British residence, outraged Rome. But the UK wanted to save money by getting rid of the villa – an aim that turned into a Whitehall farce. For not only did the gatehouse plan get abandoned, but the replacement building the Foreign Office eventually acquired as the home of the ambassador to the Holy See – the top floors of a city centre palazzo – turned out to be far more expensive than the previous villa on the edge of town.

This saga also caused the end of a great Foreign Office tradition. For centuries, British ambassadors had complete freedom in their valedictory despatch to be frank and speak without reprisal when they made their final comments before retirement. Sir Ivor Roberts, outgoing ambassador to Italy, who had served as a diplomat for forty years, including previous stints as ambassador in Dublin and Belgrade, was particularly candid in his last missive in 2006. Roberts' disillusion had been compounded by witnessing the Holy See fiasco.

His valedictory described a Foreign Office under siege by a management consultants' efficiency drive. 'Can it be', he wrote, 'that in wading through the plethora of business plans, capability reviews, skills audits, zero-based reviews and other excrescences of the management age, we have indeed forgotten what diplomacy is all about?'[1]

Hours after this telegram was sent, ambassadors received word from Whitehall that the practice of distributing valedictories widely around the service was to be discontinued. Sir Ivor's despatch also included reference to the fiasco over the embassy to the Holy See, a topic to which he returned on 17 July 2007, when he was cross-examined by members of the Select Committee on Foreign Affairs, including Andrew Mackinlay, the Labour MP for Thurrock, who happened to be a Catholic himself.

Andrew Mackinlay: 'The first is brief. You were ambassador to the Italian Republic, and to save money the Foreign Office decided effectively to abandon the United Kingdom mission to the Holy See. There was panic about that, a reverse, and then it was decided to locate that mission in the same campus as our embassy to the Italian Republic. I understand that your counsel that this was most inappropriate for a whole variety of constitutional reasons was ignored. Is that correct?'

Sir Ivor Roberts: 'Sure. First, may I slightly correct you? No decision was taken to abolish the mission to the Holy See. The decision was taken to downgrade it and to lower its cost as much as possible. As you rightly said, part of the exercise involved co-location of the Holy See mission inside the residence of my mission to the Italian Republic. I wrote to the then head of the Foreign Office and I said, "This is your baby not mine, but let me say from the perspective of someone who knows Italy well, and is a Catholic and therefore understands the Catholic Church very well, that this is not going to wash. They are not going to put up with co-location of the embassy to the Holy See with the embassy to the Italian Republic because it crosses their fundamental red line—see the Lateran Treaty 1929".'[2]

Later, Sir Ivor expounded further to me what happened when he wrote to Sir Michael Jay, then permanent secretary at the Foreign Office (but perhaps better known to the British public as the man who announced the death of Diana, Princess of Wales, when he served as ambassador to France).

I had been told about the plans for the new ambassador and that he could move into the gatehouse at my villa. I wrote to Michael Jay and said that it would not be acceptable to the Holy See and that they would get [the new ambassador to the Holy See] Francis Campbell's time off to a bad start. There was no reply for five weeks and then Michael Jay's letter said the Holy See was ultra cool about it. Of course they were not. On day two Francis was summoned to a verbal cuffing around the head. The Holy See said it had not been consulted. We then had to go back to the landlord and say, 'Oh dear, we have made a terrible mistake. Can we have our lease [for the residence] back?' He said, 'Of course you can have your lease back, but instead of costing €9,000 a month, it will now cost you €25,000 a month'.[3]

The row over the embassy's location, with little regard for the need to treat the Holy See entirely separately from the Italian Republic, illustrated Whitehall's limited perception of the usefulness of relations with the Holy See. This seems to have been a long-lasting ignorance that had not improved despite the British according it full diplomatic status. The journalist Edward Stourton recalls that when he was diplomatic editor for ITN during the 1990s, 'I got no sense of the Vatican being understood by the Foreign Office'.[4]

It was not just Rome's reach throughout the world through its network of nuncios – the Church's own ambassadors – that was being overlooked, but also its global influence on other bodies and governments. Also ignored were the opportunities the Church offered in Rome itself: the Vatican is a crossroads in Europe from other parts of the world, with people continually visiting for meetings, conferences and other events.

This old-school failure to understand the opportunities Rome offered was highlighted in an infamous moment involving the late Robin Cook, who served as foreign secretary during the first Blair administration. Mark Pellew, the British ambassador to the Holy See during Cook's stint in this role, has recalled that when Cook visited Rome to see Italian ministers he was asked if he would like to visit officials in the Vatican, including Archbishop Jean-Louis Tauran, at that time working in the Secretariat of State; Cook replied that he would rather do some sightseeing. The legend is that what Cook actually said was: 'I'd rather eat ice cream in the Piazza Navona.'[5]

Ironically, Cook's Foreign Office, according to Pellew, later turned to the Vatican for help at a crucial moment for New Labour's ethical foreign policy. The intervention it desired over the situation in Kosovo is a prime example of how the papacy can subtly influence matters with a few words or back-door negotiation, its influence stretching beyond ecclesiastical or doctrinal issues.

In 1999 the British government was keen to secure support for NATO allies during the Kosovo War – the first time in NATO's existence when it mounted a bombing campaign – to stop the Christian Serbs from attacking the Bosnian Muslims. In order to stop this ethnic cleansing, NATO planes had to take off from bases in Italy, and NATO members believed that the Italian government would not wear this if Pope John Paul II condemned the bombing during his 1999 Easter *Urbi et Orbi* message, as he was expected to do.

Mark Pellew has recalled that Number 10, fearing that the campaign against Serb leader Slobodan Milošević would fail and NATO would be damaged as a result, 'called me at home that night – the only time they ever did so – instructing me to tell the Pope not to condemn the bombing'. Mr Pellew 'went round first thing to see the secretary for relations with states, Archbishop [Jean-Louis] Tauran, to explain my instructions. My American and German colleagues took similar action, and whether or not our intervention made a difference, the Pope did not, in the event, condemn the bombing.'[6]

Sir Ivor Roberts also had first-hand experience of the Holy See's influence in the Balkans. Sir Ivor arrived in Belgrade as consul in 1994, becoming ambassador until his departure in 1997. During this time he conducted negotiations on behalf of mediators David Owen and Carl Bildt with the Yugoslav authorities and the Bosnian Serbs. At the time Slobodan Milošević was the president of Serbia and was responsible for onslaughts in Bosnia, Croatia and against the Albanians of Kosovo.

Roberts saw how Bishop Vincenzo Paglia, who had helped found the Catholic religious movement Sant'Egidio that became an influential body in peace negotiations, was able to bring different groups together. Paglia had been the first Catholic priest to enter Albania after free elections in May 1991 and went on to secure the re-opening of the seminary and the cathedral, as well as paving the way for diplomatic relations between the country and the Holy See.

'Paglia negotiated an agreement between the Albanians and Serbs on state education which was a mechanism for bringing them back into the state system,' recalled Roberts. 'Of course, everything later broke down with full war in Kosovo. Paglia was in Belgrade where he mediated between Serbs and Kosovans. Milosovic said he was like the Pope's Kissinger.'[7]

There was a similar incident of Vatican helpfulness in 2007 when Royal Navy personnel were detained by Tehran after their map-reading skills took them into Iranian waters. The Europe minister of the time, Denis MacShane, himself a Catholic, happened to be in Rome and asked Francis Campbell, the British ambassador to the Holy See, to contact the Vatican to see if anything could be done via the Church's diplomatic channels to help the sailors. He recalled:

Campbell came back to say the Vatican had every sympathy with the detained Royal Navy amateur navigators and were on the case. Pope Benedict made an Easter appeal to the ruling Ayatollahs in Iran saying it was a period of peace when families should be re-united. The next day the Royal Navy personnel were released to spend Easter with their nearest and dearest.[8]

In one sense these issues were part of traditional British–Holy See diplomatic engagement, given that its focus, pre-1997, was mostly foreign affairs rather than internal British policy. Rome and the UK, for example, saw one another as allies in the battle against communism. However, on the domestic front, Northern Ireland was also the focus of attention, with anxiety in Rome about the way in which the Catholic community was treated during the Troubles.[9]

In the same way as the British, many governments around the world consider the Holy See to be a useful listening post, with its diplomats picking up information throughout Africa, Latin America, the Middle East, China, Japan and elsewhere, which ambassadors from other nations can then learn about through their Vatican contacts. Yet the UK has not always fully understood the Vatican's possibilities. Given Britain's Commonwealth, its reach through trade, its membership of NATO and standing at the UN, one would expect it to be interested in the work of an institution with similar global reach.

Francis Campbell, who was British ambassador to the Holy See from 2005 to 2011, is damning in his critique of the Foreign and Commonwealth Office. It did not 'get' the Holy See, he says, and what he found was, in effect, ignorance. 'The FCO could not quite accept that the Catholic Church had influence, so they did not know how to use it,' he said. 'I kept saying it was a global opinion former, irrespective of what they thought of it. Britain sees it as an oddity. Yet they [the FCO] pride themselves as pragmatists.'[10]

Campbell found that the lack of interest in the Holy See was particularly noticeable among civil servants, while it seemed to him during his years in Rome that politicians could grasp the potential for engaging with the Catholic Church on the diplomatic level:

> Politicians had more understanding of religion in people's lives. They connected back to their constituents. They could put aside any confessional dimension and see the Holy See as distinctive. Officials were simply too elitist and they did not see how the Holy See mattered. Often civil servants thought that the role of the pope was the same as that of the Archbishop of Canterbury. And they don't understand the role of an office like that of secretary of state.[11]

His view is shared by Denis MacShane, Europe minister at the time of the row over the residence of the ambassador to the Holy See: 'To be honest, I was misled by officials over this. I asked the FCO if the Vatican was OK with the change and they indicated it was but quite rightly Rome was furious. The civil servants just didn't get it.'

In sharp contrast to those in Whitehall, MacShane found on the occasions he had cause to deal with them, that the diplomats of the Holy See were particularly skilful – a crème de la crème of diplomacy:

> I went to see the Vatican diplomatic service once when working on anti-Semitism and found them very smooth. Oh, yes, super smooth, and I have been used to FCO smoothies but the Vatican diplomats made our very clever boys look like country cousins.
>
> To a man – after all, they were all ordained priests – they were often the best informed on the complexities of Colombian or Albanian politics.[12]

Despite the antipathy of Whitehall on recent occasions, there are clear advantages to the British government in having good relationships with the Vatican, not least the pope's power as a global leader and therefore his influence on issues such as human rights, poverty and debt relief. Campbell, with his interest in and knowledge of both religion and diplomacy, understood this. As a Catholic and former seminarian he knew the Church extremely well, and was at ease among clerics. He was also well versed in how Westminster politics works, having been a policy adviser to Prime Minister Tony Blair from 1999–2001, and private secretary to Blair from 2001–2003. His time in office both at Number 10 and as ambassador to the Holy See coincided with prime ministers who also understood the Vatican's potential as an ally.

Successive popes have spoken of world affairs in terms of Catholic Social Teaching, which focuses on the concepts of solidarity, subsidiarity and the preferential option for the poor. During the Blair and Brown years, the Vatican's agenda frequently overlapped with that of a Labour government that used the language of rights and social justice to reflect on similar issues in foreign policy. (This concord, however was not mirrored on the domestic front.[13])

John Paul II made debt relief one of his major projects for the Millennium as the Catholic Church and others celebrated the two thousandth anniversary of the birth of Christ. The Blair government, and particularly Gordon Brown, shared the same ideal of promoting wider debt relief for the world's most heavily indebted countries, such as Mozambique. Mark Pellew, ambassador from 1998 to 2002, recalled this shared aim 'amazed the Vatican' and it helped transform policy towards the developing world.[14]

'This led to a fruitful series of exchanges between HM Treasury and the Vatican', wrote Pellew, 'as a result of which our G7 partners were persuaded, against their initial instincts, to agree a programme of debt relief for the heavily indebted poor countries, that is still in place today.'[15]

This focus on the developing world continued through the Blair and Brown years and was helped by the two politicians' personal commitment to Africa, expressed through their formation of the Africa Commission. Campbell noticed too that not only the Labour premiers, but also some of their key ministers, spotted potential in working with the Holy See.

'Tony Blair and Gordon Brown understood the importance of the Holy See because of their own clear convictions,' he said, 'while [Labour ministers] David Miliband, Shreeti Vadera, Sean Woodward and Jim Murphy all had an interest in the moral sense.'[16]

Yet both diplomatic status and doctrinal issues can get in the way of full co-operation. Some of the tensions between nations and the Holy See have involved diplomatic matters and child abuse. A particularly notable case involved the British archbishop Paul Gallagher during his time in Australia as papal nuncio, when he was asked to hand over documents to an Australian commission convened on this issue. The New South Wales Special Commission of Inquiry into sex abuse, chaired by Deputy Senior Crown Prosecutor Margaret Cunneen, twice requested documents from the then Archbishop Gallagher, but he initially declined to hand them over, despite repeated requests for archival documentation that might assist Cunneen with her inquiry.

The inquiry had been first established in November 2012 to investigate sexual abuse committed by two priests of the Maitland-Newcastle diocese, Fr. Denis McAlinden and Fr. James Fletcher (both deceased), following allegations made by a senior New South Wales police whistleblower, Chief Inspector Peter Fox. Relevant documents from dioceses in Papua New Guinea, New Zealand and the Philippines, where McAlinden also served, were handed over voluntarily to the Crown Solicitor's Office but a similar request sent directly to Cardinal Gerhard Müller, prefect of the Congregation of the Doctrine of the Faith in Rome, has as yet had no reply. The commission also released correspondence with Archbishop Gallagher that included a reminder from the nuncio that his office is protected by international agreements, including the Vienna Convention on Diplomatic Relations. However, Archbishop Gallagher eventually agreed after four months to submit the relevant material.[17]

His first response, stressing that the matter should be addressed in the correct manner, given the Holy See's standing, was reminiscent of the Church's attitude to requests for co-operation from the enquiry headed by Judge Yvonne Murphy over sex abuse of children by priests in Ireland's archdiocese of Dublin. The Murphy enquiry, which reported in 2009, examined not only the abuse, but also the way in which it was covered up as part of an effort by the Church to avoid scandal. Benedict XVI responded to the report, expressing outrage and shame, and the need to address governance of the local church. But he did not mention the issues raised by the Murphy Report regarding the Holy See, which objected to the inquiry writing directly to the pope for information, rather than using diplomatic channels.[18] Everything has to be done by the book, and the Holy See is insistent about its diplomatic status. Its approach to requests from civil authorities for assistance in abuse cases led to the United Nations Committee Against Torture expressing its concern about it in its May 2014 report, although in response the Vatican did say it was giving serious consideration to the criticisms.[19]

Archbishop Gallagher, now secretary for relations with states in the Secretariat of State, continues to this day to insist that the Vatican has every right to protect itself through article 24 of the 1961 Vienna Convention, which stresses the inviolability of documents linked to a diplomatic mission, and this includes issues to do with potentially criminal acts. 'There are certain documents that have a certain confidentiality, that are private,' he said, when I challenged him on the issue at a public lecture on Vatican diplomacy. 'Pope Francis is striving to do more and we are trying to make these digital archives. We are not doing as much as people want but we do what we can.'[20]

Diplomatic archives usually consist of the written documents linked to negotiations and activities of diplomatic officials, such as despatches to headquarters and reports back to them. It seems unlikely that the Vienna Convention authors considered their principles should be used to withhold information about criminal activity. Insisting on diplomatic immunity and inviolability of archives suggests Rome is making a convenience of having a head of a Church who is also the head of a state, as well as a certain rigidity.

Doctrinal issues such as contraception and abortion remain neuralgic issues for the Church and it tends not see eye to eye on these matters with British politicians. This was a clear stumbling block during David Cameron's premierships, with successive International Development Secretaries, Andrew Mitchell and Justine Greening, taking a utilitarian approach to population control. Mitchell recalled to me major tensions with Rome's senior representatives when discussing birth control.[21]

Diplomacy on such matters can sometimes be required of senior clergy back in Britain. The Archbishop of Westminster, Vincent Nichols, for example, understood how sensitive these issues could be when he gave the inaugural Annual George Pinker Memorial Address to the Royal College of Obstetricians and Gynaecologists in October 2011 and he spoke about global maternal health, focusing on the need to help mothers. He saw an opportunity to build bridges with his specialist audience, rather than alienate them over matters such as contraception or specifically abortion where there is unlikely to ever be common accord.[22] It was not a strategy that appealed to all Catholics, however: the Society for the Protection of unborn Children called the speech shameful.

The Vatican similarly focused attention on a matter where accord could be found – child health – rather than the sensitive one of population size during Gordon Brown's administration. Brown was publicly acknowledged by the Vatican as the driving force behind a project to raise money for vaccination of children in the developing world through the issuing of bonds, and Pope Benedict XVI was the first person to purchase one of the bonds. The pope sent Cardinal Renato Martino, president of the Pontifical Council for Justice and Peace, to London to purchase a bond at their launch on 7 November 2006.

The initiative, backed by the World Bank, gets governments that have pledged immunization aid to issue bonds for this purpose. At the time of writing, Britain had pledged the most funds to the programme — £1.38 billion over twenty years. The money lent by bond purchasers goes straight into the vaccination programmes in some seventy-two of the world's poorest countries.

In a brief address delivered in English at the moment of purchasing the first bond, Cardinal Martino said:

People living in poverty are looking forward to the time when corruption at the various levels of government or in the social sector will no longer hinder opportunities for development from reaching all members of society. A government that is truly responsive to the needs of its people is not only a necessity for development, it should also be seen as a right.

Pope Benedict XVI believes that this is the time. This is why he has decided that the Holy See would participate in the International Finance Facility bond programme. His Holiness recognizes the need to quickly provide the funds in order to respond to poverty, hunger, the lack of educational and literacy opportunities and the ongoing fight against the scourge of malaria and the spread of HIV/AIDS and tuberculosis.[23]

To what extent was this understanding of Rome's potential as a diplomatic partner a personal matter? Some may argue that the fact that Tony Blair 'got it' was due to the fact that his wife Cherie was a devout Catholic, and he would accompany her and their Catholic children to Mass every Sunday.

Cherie Blair, like any partner, no doubt had influence on her husband, and a senior source has told me that senior Catholic clerics would sometimes place a call to her when they wanted to make their views known at Number 10. Blair himself was attracted to the Church, and indeed became a Catholic six months after leaving office in 2007. Yet there was always a distance between him and the Church: he had words with Cardinal Basil Hume about receiving Communion years before he converted, and he distressed clerics who helped prepare him for reception into the Church by criticizing it two years later over its views on homosexuality during an interview with the magazine *Attitude*, whose main readership is gay men.[24]

Nevertheless, there had been warmth and understanding of Rome's importance during Blair's tenure at Number 10. This continued after Gordon Brown succeeded him as prime minister. The 'son of the manse' who talked of his moral compass appeared to be comfortable with a Church that during his youth had been on the opposite side of the sectarian divide from his Presbyterian forebears. But Brown spoke a similar language to Rome on development matters, something that was made clear by Cardinal Martino during his trip to London to launch the immunization bonds when he described the then Chancellor of the Exchequer as 'the driving force behind this initiative'. The cardinal described how in 2004 the Treasury had collaborated with the Pontifical Council for Justice and Peace in organizing a meeting on globalization and poverty.

'It was there that he reminded us,' said the cardinal, 'that, "In the absence of finance, the Millennium Development Goals look like another set of promises set, reset and reset again and then only betrayed. So our goals demand urgent action, indeed sacrifice, from the world's richest countries".'[25]

Brown also articulated his shared beliefs in his lecture for the Catholic aid agency Cafod, also given in 2004 when he was Chancellor of the Exchequer. He told his audience:

> It was Pope Paul VI who as early as the 1960s alerted the modern world that the old evil of poverty had to be addressed as an unacceptable scourge of the new global economy. It was Pope Paul VI who in 1967 in his Encyclical 'Populorum Progressio' – 'Development of Peoples' – urged upon the richest countries their sacred duty to help the poorest. And it was Pope Paul VI who set out, for our generation, the obligations that we all have a duty to meet: obligations that arise from – as he said in his own words: 'Our mutual solidarity; the claims of social justice; and universal charity.'[26]

Brown was the second prime minister under whom Francis Campbell served as ambassador to the Holy See, and many argue that it was Campbell who was the key to the success of Labour's relationship with Rome. These years became a golden age for UK–Holy See diplomacy, for all the misunderstandings and the Whitehall farce over the ambassador's residence. By the turn of the century, Foreign Office officials still seemed unused to the Holy See; they were familiar with nation states. Despite the existence of other organizations with global reach, such as the United Nations, some of them struggled to understand not only the workings but also even the point of the Catholic Church as a network, a diplomatic entity and a body with which to do business. Politicians were quicker to understand the Holy See, or at least Tony Blair and Gordon Brown saw opportunities to make use of such a body in order to achieve their goals. The Vatican, too, seemed surprised at times by the new alliances it was making with the British. But sometimes politicians are judged with too much cynicism by their critics. First the Labour governments of Brown and Blair and later, the Conservative–Liberal Democrat coalition government found agreement with the Holy See in areas where the driving goal was a common obligation to humanity, in areas such as child health, education and the environment.

These growing accords were to culminate in the visit of Pope Benedict XVI to Britain, the first ever state visit to the UK by a pope. The story of that visit and all the dramas that befell it in its preparation, are what follows next. The visit was to make clear an acceptance of the papacy by the Establishment and a warm friendship that it now shared with the Church of England. The old enmity in England was gone, but in its place was a new hostility based not on Protestantism but secularism.

Notes

1   Bryson, Andrew (2009), 'Ambassadors going out with a bang', BBC News. Available online: http://news.bbc.co.uk/1/hi/8307273.stm

2   Select Committee on Foreign Affairs (2007), minutes. http://www.publications. parliament.uk/pa/cm200708/cmselect/cmfaff/50/7071706.htm

3   Interview of Sir Ivor Roberts (IR) by Catherine Pepinster (CP), October 2014.

4   Interview of Edward Stourton by CP, January 2014.

5   Pellew, Mark (2013), 'The Diplomatic and Political Relationship', in *Britain and the Holy See: A Celebration of 1982 and the Wider Relationship*, proceedings of the Rome Colloquium, Rome: British Embassy to the Holy See, 69.

6   Pellew, ibid, 67.

7   Interview of IR by CP, ibid.

8   Interview of Denis MacShane (DMacS) by CP, March 2015.

9   See Chapter 9.

10 Interview of Francis Campbell (FC) by CP, October 2014.

11 Interview of FC by CP, ibid.

12 Interview of D MacS by CP, ibid.

13 See Chapter 12 for details of domestic clashes between the Catholic Church and the British government.

14 Pellew, ibid, 69.

15 Pellew, ibid, 60.

16 Interview of FC by CP, ibid.

17 Crittenden, Stephen, 'Australian sex abuse commission gets documents from nuncio', *National Catholic Reporter*, 20 December 2013. http://ncronline.org/news/accountability/australian-sex-abuse-commission-gets-documents-nuncio

18 This was revealed in the Wikileaks files released in 2010, where cables showed diplomats were offended by requests for documents concerning paedophilia. http://www.breakingnews.ie/ireland/vatican-wikileaks-documents-a-matter-of-extreme-gravity-485314.html

19 http://www.bishop-accountability.org/UN/CAT/2013_05_23_CAT_Concluding_Observations_Advance_Unedited_Version.pdf
    See also Davies, Lizzy (2014), 'UN Committee Against Torture criticises Vatican handling of abuse', *The Guardian*, 23 May. http://www.theguardian.com/world/2014/may/23/un-committee-against-torture-vatican-sex-abuse-scandal

20 Archbishop Paul Gallagher in answer to a question from Catherine Pepinster about the Vatican using its diplomatic status in child abuse enquiries, University of Swansea, 7 April 2016.

21 See Chapter 12 for further details.

22 Nichols, Vincent (2011), 'Global challenges of women's health today', Sir George Pinker Memorial Address, 12 October. http://www.rcdow.org.uk/archbishop/default.asp?library_ref=35&content_ref=3532

23 Martino, Cardinal Renato (2006), Declaration on the purchase of the first IFFM bond, 7 November. http://www.vanthuanobservatory.org/notizie-dsc/notizia-dsc.php?lang=en&id=127

24 'Blair questions papal gay policy' (2009), BBC, 8 April. http://news.bbc.co.uk/1/hi/7987566.stm

25 Martino, ibid.

26 Brown, Gordon (2004), Pope Paul VI memorial lecture, Cafod, 8 December. http://webarchive.nationalarchives.gov.uk/20091118103503/http://www.hm-treasury.gov.uk/speech_chex_081204.htm

4

Faith and reason:

Benedict XVI and the British

Westminster Hall has been at the centre of Britain's political and indeed, religious, history for generations. It housed three of the most important courts in the land; it has been the venue for coronation banquets, lyings-in-state of monarchs, addresses to the nation, and the trials of traitors and enemies of the people. King Charles I was tried in the hall; so was Warren Hastings, the first Governor-General of India. In September 2010, an event that once would have seemed unimaginable took place there. In the very spot where Thomas More and John Fisher were tried for their opposition to Henry VIII's divorce from Katherine of Aragon, his break with Rome, and their refusal to sign the oath of supremacy, Pope Benedict XVI addressed the nation, urging that faith and reason should work together. Four surviving prime ministers listened: Margaret Thatcher, John Major, Tony Blair and Gordon Brown. David Cameron, elected to that post just a few weeks earlier, was absent due to the death of his father, and was represented by his deputy, Nick Clegg. So poignant was the moment that many notable Catholics invited to witness the event shed tears as the pope walked past the brass plaque that marked the site of More's trial.

While the pope's words were applauded, the run-up to his state visit to Britain that September had been marred by anti-Catholic feeling which bears comparison with some of the most virulently anti-papal emotions of Britain's Protestant past. Bit by bit, week by week, the focus of attacks on the forthcoming papal visit to Britain sharpened so that they eventually boiled down to one thing: why should it be a state visit? The vitriol expressed early on by critics of Roman Catholicism was so vicious that one sensed that it backfired: those people in Britain who always like fair play started to feel that the condemnatory remarks by the most fervent opponents of Pope Benedict XVI and of his Church were getting too personal.

There was then a noticeable change in gear: the vocal opponents' critique became 'you Catholics should be able to see your pope, but don't bother the rest of us with it'. And it worked: a poll for the Theos think tank ten days before Benedict's arrival indicated that respondents did not approve of it being a state visit, with 76 per cent objecting to taxpayers part-funding it, while a survey for my own publication, *The Tablet*, by Ipsos MORI, showed that most people neither supported nor opposed the actual visit. It was the trip's *status* that stuck in the craw among some non-Catholics. Those most vocal in their opposition tended to be active atheists, rather than members of Protestant denominations, the majority of whom appeared to support the visit.[1]

But it wasn't quite a state visit. Instead it was an official visit, with the status of a state visit. Pope Benedict was not the guest of honour at a vast banquet at Buckingham Palace, nor was there a ride down the Mall with the queen with all the attendant pomp, nor did he stay at the palace, to be waited on by flunkeys. Not only did the pope himself not want that, but it was also impossible practically, given that Her Majesty was resident at Balmoral for her annual Scottish holiday during the trip. The absence of these events made the visit vastly cheaper for the UK taxpayer.

What was noticeable about the protests regarding the papal state visit was that they were much noisier than those made about visits to Britain by other heads of state that some people might find unpalatable. Similar loud cries of disgust did not emerge at the appearance of heads of state from countries like China and Saudi Arabia, for example, despite their track records on human rights issues. Did the pope really deserve to be singled out in this way? Or could there have been some latent 'no popery' here in Britain? Cardinal Vincent Nichols, who accompanied Benedict XVI during his visit, thought that the opposition was 'a different sort of antagonism to the pope than previously in Britain. It was almost a primal opposition to the religious dimension.'[2] As it turned out, the protests fizzled out. A minority had been very vocal but there was little general public support for such aggressive opposition.

The visit was in effect tri-partite: a pastoral one to the Catholics of Britain; an ecumenical and inter-faith one, enabling the pope and his Vatican entourage to engage with other religious leaders; and a diplomatic one. The focus of the government was on the pope as head of state and on the Holy See as a global power player with whom it could do business. As noted in earlier chapters, the Holy See is the central government of the Church, and is recognized in international law as a sovereign entity, and maintains relations with 180 states, including the United Kingdom.

The visit was also a PR exercise for the papacy, and proved to be a greater success than could have been first imagined. The pope's encounters with Catholics drew huge crowds; the meetings with Anglican leaders were full of warmth; and diplomatically too, it went well. As always with papal visits, the pope came to Britain with an entourage of diplomats and other Curial officials. It is known as the *seguito* – Italian for a 'following' – and is made up of people who run Vatican departments. The talks that they held with civil servants and ministers, including a major dinner at Lancaster House, were a chance to discuss some of the most crucial matters affecting the world today, with people who could well make a difference.

Support for a papal visit had first emerged during the Blair and Brown governments, with both prime ministers inviting Pope Benedict to the UK. As noted in Chapter 3, Labour might have had difficulties at the domestic level with the Catholic Church – there were clashes over faith schools and over same-sex couples adopting children – but relations were different at the global level. It was as if the party had a revelation rather akin to Mrs Thatcher's when she encountered Gorbachev: this is someone we can do business with. That business focused on the most pressing global issues: poverty in the developing world, eradication of diseases such as malaria, climate change, sustainability, and the achievement of the Millennium Development Goals.

A series of Labour Cabinet ministers – Gordon Brown, first as chancellor and later as prime minister, David Miliband as environment secretary, Douglas Alexander and Baroness Vadera from international development, as well as Tony Blair on several occasions during his tenure at Number 10 – all flew to Rome to have talks in the Vatican.

Yet the coalition government, elected in May 2010, just four months before Benedict's trip to Britain, did not seem so convinced of the Church's significance, and nor was there the same enthusiasm expressed by the Conservative government elected in 2015 as there was during the Labour years. Alastair Campbell, Blair's press secretary, famously insisted of the Labour government, 'We don't do God': except that Brown and Blair did, at least as far as working with the papacy is concerned. Just two days before the papal visit in 2010, Baroness Warsi, co-chairman of the Conservative Party, made a dig at Campbell with her 'This government does do God' speech, but that did not lead the most senior ministers serving in either the 2010 coalition Cabinet or the subsequent 2015 Conservative administration to visit Rome, with the exception of the then home secretary, Theresa May. At major events – the installation of Archbishop Vincent Nichols as a cardinal, the celebration of 100 years of UK–Holy See diplomacy – the British government was represented only by junior ministers. Although prime minister David Cameron and Benedict XVI met briefly in Britain in 2010, Mr Cameron never went to see the pope in the Vatican. This did not go unnoticed in Rome.[3]

While the coalition government was stalwart in its support for the international aid budget, refusing to cut it despite its pledge of austerity, its relations with Rome regarding aid were nevertheless difficult at times. Andrew Mitchell, for example, the first coalition secretary of state for international development, has recalled that while he admired the Catholic Church greatly for its work in the developing world, he found it extremely difficult to deal with over contraception in developing countries.[4]

By the time that David Cameron came into office in May 2010, preparations had already begun for the visit of Pope Benedict that September. The original invitation had been offered by Gordon Brown, who had spotted that the Vatican shared his commitment to the Millennium Development Goals for combating poverty, inadequate health care and shelter, improving education and environmental sustainability. In 2008, before the United Nations summit on poverty, Pope Benedict issued a message to world leaders, urging them to act, which resulted in US$15 billion being pledged towards combating poverty. 'I do think the pope and the Vatican have played a huge part in making the Millennium Development Goals come alive, not as aspirations that might be one day delivered, but as commitments that have to be honoured,' Brown told me at Number 10 in 2009.[5]

Labour cabinet minister Jim Murphy, a Catholic, had been deputed to co-ordinate the preparations, which meant negotiations with Rome, especially the Secretariat of State, with the Catholic Church in England and Wales, and Scotland, and with Britain's ambassador to the Holy See, Francis Campbell. The civil service were also closely involved in preparations. Soon after Brown had issued the invitation, it occurred to Gus O'Donnell, the cabinet secretary, that the visit had the potential to be more complicated than a normal state visit. This, after all, was not just a head of state, but also a head of a global Church. It would involve not just the government but also the Catholic Church in England and Wales, as well as in Scotland, and the Church of England. This head of state would not only attend events in central London, but around the country too. O'Donnell no doubt had particular insights on the requirements of the visit because he himself was a Catholic. But as cabinet secretary it would have been difficult for him to find the time to co-ordinate preparations. Instead he turned to his fellow Catholic senior civil servant, Helen Ghosh, at the time permanent secretary at the Department of the Environment, Food and Rural Affairs.

O'Donnell thought that both an organizing committee of civil servants and a ministerial committee with Jim Murphy and ministerial representatives from other departments was required. While the Foreign Office was the most important, Ghosh recalled, transport, the security services, the police and the Department for Communities were all involved. 'Moving people about safely was the greatest challenge,' she said.[6]

Yet progress was slow, interrupted for weeks by the 2010 general election campaign and the subsequent negotiations after polling day over the formation of the next administration, given no party had an overall majority. 'The general election caused a definite hiatus and left time short. There was also the issue of the change of personnel,' recalled Ghosh.[7]

One person, though, remained particularly concerned about the visit: the queen. And no wonder. Back in April, before the general election, the visit had become mired in political scandal when the *Sunday Telegraph* reported that the Foreign Office had produced a memo about the visit following a brainstorming session involving young civil servants. The memo, entitled

'The ideal visit would see . . .', included blue-sky thinking such as asking Pope Benedict to open an abortion clinic and launch his own brand of condoms during the visit. The proposals, which appeared to be deliberately controversial rather than serious suggestions, nevertheless caused planning for the visit to be open to ridicule. The Labour foreign secretary, David Miliband, reportedly thought it a colossal failure of judgement and was said to be appalled.[8]

So was the Vatican. Cardinal Renato Martino, the former head of the Pontifical Council for Justice and Peace said: 'The British government has invited the pope as its guest and he should be treated with respect. To make a mockery of his beliefs and the beliefs of millions of Catholics not just in Britain but across the world is very offensive indeed.'[9]

It was a deeply embarrassing moment for those involved in planning the visit. Ghosh can still remember the moment when Sir Peter Ricketts, permanent secretary at the Foreign Office, told her about the story; she hadn't yet read the Sunday papers. 'I was in a garden when I received the call. Whenever I visit it, I always relive that moment,' she said. 'There had certainly been discussions about what the pope might do and what was appropriate and we did talk about how they would link to the messages the government was sending about its policy. But before the memo leak I was not aware of this "blue sky thinking" and those discussions taking place.'[10]

Despite rumours that the visit might be cancelled, apologies appeared to suffice to keep the trip on track, and Francis Campbell was sent to make the government's embarrassment plain to Vatican officials. There was also a public apology made to the papal nuncio to the United Kingdom, Archbishop Faustino Sainz Muñoz, by Helen Ghosh, in full view of other guests as they arrived at Archbishop's House, home of Archbishop Vincent Nichols, for a reception.[11]

At that stage, one of Britain's leading Catholics, Lord (Chris) Patten was leading a relatively quiet life after taking a step back from his many achievements on the public stage. But concern about the visit descending into chaos brought Patten right into the heart of arrangements.

David Cameron, like every prime minister before him, visited the queen to formally accept her invitation to form the next government and then attended weekly audiences with her. She had been observing the problems that were afflicting the papal visit, in which she would play a key role, and quickly raised it with the new premier.

Patten recalled:

After the election David Cameron went to see the queen who said the visit was looking rather shambolic.

Then I got the call from Cameron's chief of staff about getting involved and I said, 'you must be joking'. Then they rang back and said the prime minister has already told the queen that you are doing it. Jim Murphy had had very little help and people to work with. I said 'I need a budget and I can't haggle over every pound'. They delivered on that.[12]

With just three months to go, Patten took overall control, working to bring the Catholic Church and the government together after the embarrassing fiasco of the condom memo. With Helen Ghosh, Patten looked to knock heads together, and work out the co-ordination of the four-day visit, including security.

Cardinal Vincent Nichols saw a major difference in planning once Patten was involved because he wasn't constrained by the Treasury. But he also felt that the fallout from the memo fiasco actually benefited the visit:

It acted as a kind of spur because they were so embarrassed about it. It pinpointed a real level of ignorance about the papacy. People in the Foreign Office, I was told, didn't know if they were dealing with San Marino or China when it came to the Holy See . . . I remember at a really early meeting on the papal visit with Jim Murphy and [Archbishop of Canterbury] Rowan Williams, when the civil servants present were astonished that the pope personally expressed his support for civil government.[13]

The government side had to work out with the Catholic Church who was responsible for what. That, in turn, meant deciding who was paying for which aspects. Security was most definitely the government's responsibility and therefore the taxpayer was liable. 'The most murky issues were the open air events and the extent to which the Church was responsible for the pope in a big park,' said Ghosh.[14]

'I had a good team of civil servants and a Ministry of Defence official in charge of big events,' said Patten. 'It was a question of going back and forth between Archbishop Mamberti [secretary for relations with states] in Rome, Cardinal Keith O'Brien in Scotland, Archbishop Nichols in Westminster and Francis Campbell. It can't have been a big priority for David Cameron. But he's a good delegator.'[15]

While Patten now says that the visit was in some ways relatively easy to organize, he does remember one particularly awkward issue involving the then first minister of Scotland: 'Alex Salmond was a problem because he wanted the pope to speak to the Scottish parliament and complained we weren't making as much effort as we should.'[16]

Patten was firm: the pope was going to speak in Westminster Hall. Salmond was not the first to lobby for Scotland, however. Jim Murphy and Cardinal Keith O'Brien, then Archbishop of St Andrews and Edinburgh, had previously gone to Rome and done the rounds of the Curia, as well as attended a general audience with Benedict XVI, asking that the pope visit Scotland.

Scotland, in the end, received particular honours: after delicate to-and-fro negotiations between Rome and London of the type that diplomats practise continually, it eventually emerged that the queen would leave her Balmoral summer bolthole to travel to the Scottish capital to meet the pope at Holyrood Palace, rather than travel all the way back down to London. It was less inconvenient for the queen, it meant the Vatican could tick off Scotland on the itinerary, and the Salmond/Cardinal Keith O'Brien camp were appeased because Scotland gained special honours because the visit to the UK started there.[17] [18]

When the pope arrived in Edinburgh, it was the culmination of not only months of planning but also followed months of griping by protesters. 'When we travelled from the airport and saw the cheering crowds along the way,' remembered Francis Campbell, then the British ambassador to the Holy See, 'we knew it was going to be alright.'[19]

Despite all the problems in advance of the visit, it was indeed alright, something that organizers put down to the type of nation that the United Kingdom is. 'In some ways it was quite easy to have the visit to Britain because of the Establishment,' said Patten. 'The queen and the Church of England were part of the process and Britain clearly wasn't a heathen, godless land.'[20]

After the first day in Scotland, which culminated in an open-air Mass celebrated in Glasgow, complete with singing star Susan Boyle, Pope Benedict and his entourage flew south to London. Organizers wanted the pope to learn about the contribution the Catholic Church in Britain made to interreligious dialogue, ecumenical relations with the Church of England, the Catholic Church's contribution to society, people's faith and the interplay between the religious and secular world. So there was a multi-faith gathering at St Mary's University, Strawberry Hill, a Mass in Westminster Cathedral, a vigil in Hyde Park, encounters with the Anglican bishops and the Archbishop of Canterbury at Lambeth Palace, evensong at Westminster Abbey, and the major event at Westminster Hall. Church met state there, just as it had earlier at Holyrood, where the pope met the queen – who had, unusually, sent her husband, the Duke of Edinburgh, to greet her visitor when he stepped off the plane at the airport. It was taken by Rome as a sign of particular regard for the pontiff, and went down extremely well.

After all the advance complaints about Benedict XVI coming to Britain, the 'Protest the Pope' march in central London on the Saturday of the visit attracted only a few hundred protesters. In contrast, the crowds flocking to the Mall who wanted to greet the pope reached hundreds of thousands, according to police estimates, something that particularly moved Vincent Nichols. 'One of the most astonishing moments for me was the sight of The Mall, prepared for the visit with the Union and papal flags hung together. I never thought I would see that,' he recalled.[21]

But what particularly took the pope's entourage by surprise was the Anglican liturgy at Westminster Abbey, and even more so the vigil, including a procession, music and silent prayer, in Hyde Park. 'They were amazed by it', said Patten.[22]

What the Vatican also saw were the different strands of Catholicism in Britain: the strongly migrant Church, evidenced by the crowds in the streets, and especially those who attended the Hyde Park Vigil; the work of service of the Church, symbolized by the visit of Pope Benedict to an old people's home run by religious sisters; and the intellectual tradition of the Church, represented by the beatification by Pope Benedict of John Henry Newman during his visit, as well as the pope's own address to parliament in Westminster Hall.

Newman has long been loved by English Catholics as one of the greatest intellectuals of the Catholic Church. It cannot lay claim to having created him, given that he spent the first half of his life as an Anglican, working as a priest and an Oxford academic. After helping to found the Oxford Movement, which urged the return of the Church of England to the liturgy and beliefs of Catholicism, he was received into the Catholic Church in 1845, and ordained a priest. He founded the Oratorian Fathers, served in Birmingham, created the Catholic University of Ireland and was made a cardinal in 1879. His prolific writings, including those describing his careful consideration of the path to Rome, have ensured that his influence on English Catholic thinking has endured. While Newman was regarded by many English Catholics as a liberal – and he was considered a major influence on the reformers of the Second Vatican Council – his work has also been appreciated by more conservative thinkers, not least Benedict XVI, for his concern about the dangers of relativism and religious toleration.[23]

Thus it was that the English Catholic Church and Pope Benedict came together on 19 September 2010 for the beatification of Newman. Years of work by supporters of Newman's cause led to the acceptance by Rome that the healing of a debilitating spinal condition suffered by American deacon Jack Sullivan was due to the intercession of Newman. The healing took place in 2001; Benedict recognized it in July 2009; just over twelve months later he was in a park in Birmingham to personally declare Newman blessed, a stage on the road to full sainthood. The event confirmed the pope's regard for Newman; beatifications do not require the Holy Father to conduct them. It was also one of the major events of the official visit to Britain. Despite an almost day-long downpour, thousands turned out for the event in Birmingham's Cofton Park, not far from Newman's former home in Rednal.[24]

Benedict was lavish in his praise of Newman during his beatification Mass homily, but also set him in the context of English sainthood:

> England has a long tradition of martyr saints, whose courageous witness has sustained and inspired the Catholic community here for centuries. Yet it is right and fitting that we should recognize today the holiness of a confessor, a son of this nation who, while not called to shed his blood for the Lord, nevertheless bore eloquent witness to him in the course of a

long life devoted to the priestly ministry, and especially to preaching, teaching, and writing. He is worthy to take his place in a long line of saints and scholars from these islands, Saint Bede, Saint Hilda, Saint Aelred, Blessed Duns Scotus, to name but a few. In Blessed John Henry, that tradition of gentle scholarship, deep human wisdom and profound love for the Lord has borne rich fruit, as a sign of the abiding presence of the Holy Spirit deep within the heart of God's people, bringing forth abundant gifts of holiness.

Benedict went on to describe Newman's motto *Cor ad cor loquitur*, or 'Heart speaks unto heart', as 'an insight into his understanding of the Christian life as a call to holiness, experienced as the profound desire of the human heart to enter into intimate communion with the Heart of God', and it was the motto chosen for his own visit to Britain.[25]

Yet however moving the Newman celebration was, the standout moment of the visit for a huge number of Catholics was the pope's address in Westminster Hall. It was certainly a major occasion: as Colette Bowe, then chairman of Ofcom, made her way to the hall to take her seat, she was asked by people outside Parliament if she would sell her ticket.[26]

Also attending was Helen Ghosh. After all the dramas and hard work of the previous months, at last the pope was speaking to the nation: 'I was sitting some way back in the hall and two heralds appeared with their trumpets. And then this small white figure appeared, the first time that a pope had ever stepped into that place, where Thomas More had been tried. It sent a shiver down the spine.'[27]

This was a visit then, that reflected the characteristics of Benedict's own papacy while combining them with those of the Catholic Church in Britain and its particular place in the nation: high intellect, a strongly spiritual theme, engagement with the Anglican tradition, a melting pot Church, a commitment to service to people in need, and the need to apologize to victims of sexual abuse by priests (the pope met a group of them during his days in Britain). The concerns of some British Catholics about Benedict's conservatism, particularly regarding the liturgy, were for a few days forgotten.

For all the success of the visit, Lord Patten found during his dealings with Rome while he undertook a review of Vatican communications in 2014–15, that some attitudes to Britain remain entrenched. 'The problem is that a lot of elderly Italians still see us as a godless stamping ground. Things are changing somewhat under Pope Francis and a new generation is coming through.'[28]

Vincent Nichols believes a change in perceptions about the UK started with the papal visit, particularly with the presence of so many former prime ministers in Westminster Hall when Pope Benedict gave his address. 'The Curia noticed; that sets a benchmark,' he said. 'And London is a world stage; what happens here is very important.'[29]

The relationship between the UK and the Holy See was further cemented in 2012 when a 'return visit' took place of government ministers to the Vatican. Led by Baroness Sayeeda Warsi, then Conservative Party co-chairman and Cabinet Office minister with responsibility for faith, the party also included Jeremy Hunt, the culture secretary, Michael Moore, the Scottish secretary, and Alan Duncan, the international development minister. There were talks with officials and round-table discussions on religious freedom, climate change, aid, and trouble spots such as Syria. It was one of the largest British ministerial delegations to ever visit another state. At the time Warsi was pushing hard in government the idea that religion must not be moved to the margins in society, whether that religion was her own Islam or Christianity. 'I'm arguing for faith to have a seat at the table ... People say take faith out of the public sphere and I think, who would come in and do the work: the National Secular Society?' she said to me the day before she left for Rome.[30]

Sayeeda Warsi's comments during her Rome visit certainly made waves at the Vatican. Her views about the role of faith in society, in part a response to Benedict XVI's comments in Westminster Hall in 2010, chimed with those of Vatican officials and were noted approvingly. She was given a front-page slot in the Vatican newspaper *L'Osservatore Romano*, during which she commented on the Holy See's usefulness as a network, and declared that this 'made it an influential voice in today's important moral, ethical and intellectual debates'.[31]

In her major Vatican speech she not only criticized 'militant secularization' but also commented on her Pakistani Muslim parents raising her within the Christian culture of Britain. It was an upbringing, she said, that taught her 'being sure of who you are is the only way in which you will be more accommodating of others'.[32]

This sense of Britain's Christian heritage that still makes space for religion particularly resonated during this pontificate. Benedict XVI came into office after writing his book *Senza Radici*[33] – *Without Roots* – warning of the dangers of losing track of Europe's Christian foundations, and at one time he voiced concern over Turkey's admission to the EU because of its Muslim values. The most controversial speech of his pontificate was given in Regensburg in 2006 when he explored the same topic – faith and reason – that he would discuss in his Westminster Hall Speech four years later. But at Regensburg he unfavourably cast Islam as being linked to violence through invoking the comments of Byzantine Emperor Manuel II: 'Show me just what Muhammed brought that was new and there you will find things only bad and inhuman, such as his command to spread by the sword the faith that he preached.'[34]

While the Vatican finds the United Kingdom of particular interest because of its multi-ethnic, multi-faith make-up, Benedict's speech at Westminster Hall emphasized the Christian heritage he favoured rather than the traditions he feared. After Lady Warsi's speech of 2012, Archbishop Dominique

Mamberti, then secretary for foreign relations, said: 'Her opinions respond to our point of view – they form part of a shared patrimony', a reference more to her status as a British minister than that as a Muslim.[35]

That shared patrimony matters a great deal to Rome in its dealing with the UK, from its relations with the Church of England to those with the government. Yet there is concern in the Vatican that the two governments led by David Cameron until he stepped down in 2016 – first the coalition government of 2010–15, and then the Conservative government elected in 2015 – did not remain so enthusiastic about relations with Rome. At one time there was optimism that the British would continue to pursue close relations with Rome – during the 2012 delegation to the Vatican, Cardinal Nichols recalls Foreign Office minister Lord Howell saying the reason the British ministers had come to Rome was because the government perceived foreign policy as a series of multilateral networks.[36]

So what has shifted in the last three or four years? A change in personnel could be one key factor. Nigel Baker, the British ambassador to the Holy See from 2011 to 2016, believed that Baroness Warsi particularly, was an advocate of strong relations with the Vatican. 'Afterwards we lacked a little bit a champion in government for the embassy's work here in Rome,' he said.[37]

The sophisticated diplomats of the Holy See do not perceive the issue as antagonism from the United Kingdom towards the Catholic Church; there has been no return to the days of Robin Cook. Instead they perceive a lack of profound interest in foreign affairs, and a retreat into domestic matters, with overtones of Euroscepticism affecting thinking. The Holy See's concern about this was evident when Archbishop Paul Gallagher, the Briton serving as the secretary for relations with states in the Secretariat of State, told ITN's Julie Etchingham some months before the EU referendum vote of June 2016, that while any decision on leaving the EU was down to the British people, 'Britain would be better in than out'. Rome has long believed that the EU, whose roots are in Catholic Social Teaching that so influenced the Community's Catholic founders such as Jean Monnet and Robert Schuman, is a valuable organization. If the UK left, said Archbishop Gallagher, 'We would see it as being something that is not going to make a stronger Europe.'[38]

One senior Holy See figure said: 'It seems as if the UK is withdrawing from the international scene. It does not look outward. Neither the [then] prime minister David Cameron nor the foreign secretary Philip Hammond visited the Holy See and I am not sure they understand it. Although the policy was changed by another government [enabling a Catholic to be the UK ambassador] they still think the ambassador should be an Anglican.'[39]

And yet this senior figure was not entirely negative and recognized that there are common interests. The relationship, he said, 'is very positive on matters such as human rights, the defence of Christians, and the environment,' he said.[40]

Seven years after the papal state visit to Britain, it does seem as if the UK government cannot always work out what the Holy See is. It does not fit into an obvious region within the Foreign and Commonwealth Office. At one time the embassy to the Holy See came under global economic affairs, then it was nearly moved to multilateral policy. Now it falls under the purview of the European directorate. Much of what it deals with is of little interest to Whitehall or Westminster. Internal arguments over moral theology, aired at the Synod on the Family, for example, in October 2014 and 2015, were of minor relevance, but its relationship with the Church of England does matter. The British ambassador to the Holy See is expected to report back on matters affecting the Church of England.

And yet for all Rome's concerns, Britain still does sense something of the Holy See's worth in the modern world. When the centenary of the restoration of diplomatic relations between Britain and the Holy See was marked in December 2014, Nigel Baker, the then UK ambassador to the Holy See, wrote in *L'Osservatore Romano* of the usefulness of the Holy See in a world of soft power:

> We have an embassy to the Holy See because of the extent of the Holy See soft power network, the influence of the pope, and the global reach and perspective of papal diplomacy focused on preserving and achieving peace, on the protection of the planet, and on bringing people out of poverty.[41]

The standout comment here is about network. This is an organization built on and exercising soft power; it does not exist to provide technical solutions to problems, but rather to exert its influence, as Nigel Baker says, 'with no tool other than the ultimate arm of diplomacy: persuasion'.[42]

One network that mirrors the Holy See in terms of effective use of soft power and diplomacy, of maintaining traditional friendships while also engaging in the modern world, is the British Commonwealth. Yet surprisingly the parallels have not yet been exploited by either side in their relationship.

While Rome maintains its networks not only through its episcopal and parish structures, it also makes use of its diplomatic relationships with 180 countries around the world, putting it at the centre of a vast global population of more than 1 billion people, as noted in earlier chapters. The British Commonwealth's own network consists of fifty-three countries, 2.2 billion citizens, and common values as expressed in its charter focusing on democracy, equitable economic development, good governance, young people, human rights and social progress. Both could be termed 'transversal' organizations, cutting across ethnicity, gender, social and class divisions, age, national borders and political affiliation.

As Nigel Baker points out:

> There should be real synergies. Pope Francis is focused on mission to the world beyond Europe. The Commonwealth Secretary General has called

on the organisation to raise its global profile. However, it appears that the two organisations do not know each other, and have little formal or even informal contact across their networks. Yet over 140 million Commonwealth citizens are Catholic, there are resident papal ambassadors in many Commonwealth countries, and around a fifth of the voting members of the College of Cardinals are from Commonwealth countries, as well as many important senior Holy See officials ... We believe that it's about time the two networks started to know each other better.[43]

The years of Pope Benedict's pontificate were a time of consolidation for the relationship between the British and the papacy. The papal visit of 2010 emphasized the pastoral, ecumenical, inter-faith and diplomatic aspects of the relationship. The visit played to Benedict XVI's strengths: the quiet, somewhat introverted and intellectual pope gave homilies, addresses and talks that offered food for thought, particularly about the role of religion in the public arena of the twenty-first century. While there were none of the difficulties that beset the planning of the previous visit in 1982, due to the Falklands War, there was clear evidence of secular hostility to the pope prior to his arrival in the UK. Given that hostility, it was apposite that Benedict should speak about the place of religion in Britain and the visit also served as a reminder that the Catholic Church was no longer beset by its traditional foe, Protestantism, in this country but rather by those who disapproved of *any* place for religion in public life. Indeed the papal visit confirmed that relations between Catholicism and Anglicanism had entered a new era of mature friendship, and this helped convince the Roman Curia in 2010 of the merits of a warm relationship with the UK.

That growing connection between the papacy and the United Kingdom was in many ways a recognition of the usefulness of the two entities' own global networks. It is worth examining next how, in March 2013, one occasion did bring these networks together to such dramatic and significant effect that it would change the Catholic Church's course of history. Perhaps it was that sense of global reach, that idea that Rome could help sometimes to join up the dots of the world map, that led Britain to play its own particular role in the election of the successor to Pope Benedict – the man who was to shake up not only the Catholic Church but its relations with the world, and who would try to reshape the institution of the papacy itself.

Notes

1   *The Tablet* (2010), issues throughout July and August.

2   Interview of Cardinal Vincent Nichols (VN) by Catherine Pepinster (CP), March 2015.

3   Prime Minister David Cameron never visited the pope in Rome during his premiership.

4   See Mitchell's account in Chapter 12.

5   Pepinster, Catherine (2009), 'Our common cause', *The Tablet*, 28 February, 4.

6   Interview of Dame Helen Ghosh (HG) by Catherine Pepinster (CP), July 2015.

7   Interview of HG by CP, ibid.

8   Wynne Jones, Jonathan (2010), 'Ministers apologise for insult to Pope', *Daily Telegraph*, 24 April. http://www.telegraph.co.uk/news/religion/7628752/Ministers-apologise-for-insult-to-Pope.html

9   Rayner, Gordon and Nick Pisa (2010), 'Pope "could cancel UK visit" over "offensive" Foreign Office memo', *Daily Telegraph*, 24 April. http://www.telegraph.co.uk/news/worldnews/europe/vaticancityandholysee/7632259/Pope-could-cancel-UK-visit-over-offensive-Foreign-Office-memo.html

10 Interview of HG by CP, ibid.

11 Witnessed by the author.

12 Interview of Lord Patten (LP) by Catherine Pepinster (CP), January 2015.

13 Interview of VN by CP, ibid.

14 Interview of HG by CP, ibid.

15 Interview of LP by CP, ibid.

16 Interview of LP by CP, ibid.

17 According to a Holy See source.

18 For further details of the Scottish visit, see Chapter 10.

19 Interview of Francis Campbell by CP, October 2014.

20 Interview of LP by CP, ibid.

21 Interview of VN by CP, ibid.

22 Interview of LP by CP, ibid.

23 For an account of Newman's life and work, see Cornwell, John (2010), *Newman's Unquiet Grave: The Reluctant Saint*, London: Bloomsbury Continuum.

24 Burns, Jimmy (2015), *Francis: Pope of Good Promise*, London: Constable, 30.

25 Benedict XVI (2010), Homily at the Mass with the beatification of Venerable Cardinal John Henry Newman, Cofton Park, Birmingham, 19 September. www.vatican.va/content/benedict-xvi/en/homilies/2010/documents/hf_ben-xvi_hom_20100919_beatif-newman.html

26 Recalled to the author.

27 Interview of HG by CP, ibid.

28 Interview of LP by CP, ibid.

29 Interview of VN by CP, ibid.

30 Pepinster, Catherine (2012), 'Slaying the secular dragon', *The Tablet*, 18 February, 4.

31 Kington, Tom (2014), 'Vatican welcomes Lady Warsi's comments on "intolerant secularisation"', *The Guardian*, 14 February. http://www.

theguardian.com/politics/2012/feb/14/vatican-lady-warsi-intolerant-secularisation

32 Kington, Tom (2012), 'Lady Warsi gets rapturous reception at Vatican for speech on faith', *The Guardian*, 14 February. http://www.theguardian.com/politics/2012/feb/14/warsi-reception-vatican-speech-faith

33 Pera, Marcello and Joseph Ratzinger (2005), *Senza Radici*, Milan: Mondadori.

34 Benedict XVI (2006), Regensburg Address, http://w2.vatican.va/content/benedict-xvi/en/speeches/2006/september/documents/hf_ben-xvi_spe_20060912_university-regensburg.html

35 Tom Kington, ibid.

36 Interview of VN by CP.

37 Interview of Nigel Baker (NB) by Catherine Pepinster (CP) October 2015.

38 Etchingham, Julie (2015), Interview with Archbishop Paul Gallagher, 20 January, http://www.itv.com/news/update/2016-01-20/vatican-tells-itv-news-britain-better-in-than-out-of-eu/

39 Interview with an unnamed Holy See source.

40 Ibid.

41 Baker, Nigel (2014), *L'Osservatore Romano*.

42 Interview of NB by CP, ibid.

43 Baker, Nigel (2014), blog 30 September. http://blogs.fco.gov.uk/nigelbaker/page/6

5

The Franciscan age:

A very British coup

Nothing compares to the drama surrounding the election of a new pope. There is the anticipation of the crowds who gather each day in St Peter's Square, waiting for news; the princes of the Church who make up the College of Cardinals being locked away in the Sistine Chapel until they finally make a majority decision; the black smoke from the chapel's tiny chimney indicating that their latest vote was not decisive; and finally the white smoke that shows a pope has been chosen.

Then the bells of St Peter's ring out across Rome, and thousands more run to the square from across the city. Finally, one of the officials of the election process, the *camerlengo*, steps on to the balcony of the basilica and announces to the city and the world: *Habemus papam* – 'we have a pope'.

A papal election usually follows a more sombre drama, that of a death. But when Pope Francis was elected in 2013 the Church and the world had been rocked by the unexpected resignation of his predecessor, Benedict XVI. At eighty-five, Benedict had indicated that he was worn out, too tired to deal with the scandals that had so riven his pontificate. From child sex abuse to financial mismanagement, the Vatican seemed dysfunctional and mired in controversy. So the next pope would need to be strong in mind and spirit, and ready to take on huge difficulties.

That the cardinals believed that Cardinal Jorge Bergoglio of Argentina was the man for the job at first stunned the crowds. Despite the fact that he had effectively been 'runner-up' when Cardinal Joseph Ratzinger was elected pope in 2005, Bergoglio was little known outside his native Argentina and few had predicted that he would be chosen this time round. Much of that was to do with his age: at seventy-six, it was thought his time had been and gone, especially as Pope Benedict had indicated that stamina was an issue.

With Jorge Bergoglio, the cardinals had chosen someone very different: the first Jesuit pope, the first pontiff to dare call himself Francis after the much-loved saint of Assisi, and the first Latin American pope. The new pope was quite clear in his first words to the crowds that his fellow cardinals had made a defining decision about the Catholic Church. 'You know that it was the duty of the conclave to give Rome a bishop,' he said. 'It seems that my brother bishops have gone to the ends of the earth to get one . . . I thank you for your welcome.'[1]

But what had made the bishops reach across the globe to Jorge Bergoglio? While the members of the College of Cardinals make the choice via an election, Catholics believe that the Holy Spirit inspires them. The idea that the Spirit might need a helping hand is not new. The princes of the Church are not averse to politicking and lobbying in the days leading up to the moment when they are locked in the Sistine Chapel to vote by secret ballot for the man who will lead the world's Catholics.

It was evident in the days before the election of Joseph Ratzinger as Benedict XVI in 2005 that certain groups of cardinals were well organized. They arranged unofficial gatherings where they would talk about the likely candidates to be *pontifex*, thus ensuring their man – Joseph Ratzinger, in this case – would be elected. Although formal talks, known as 'general congregations', are held for voting cardinals and non-voting elderly cardinals during the days in the run-up to a conclave, it is the informal lunch and evening get-togethers where deal-making and deal-breaking really takes place.

In 2005, one group of people in particular were left out of discussions – cardinals from the developing world. Reporters at the time described how many of these cardinals were seen wandering around Rome before the 2005 conclave, looking bemused, unsure where to go, unaware of unofficial gatherings taking place in the city where they would have been able to discuss who might be the right man to be pope.

As *The Tablet* reported at the time:

> Some, especially from the developing world, were living on the outskirts of the city and had no entourage, let alone press secretaries, like many Western cardinals. They would have been unaware of the intimate gatherings of cardinals over whiskies or quiet lunches to discuss strategies for the forthcoming election. They did not know many other cardinals and some did not even speak Italian, even though it was the only language used in the first days of the general congregations.[2]

When it came to the election of the next pope eight years later, following the surprise resignation of Benedict XVI, there was concern that the developing world cardinals could be left on the sidelines again. Many of them come from countries with little representation in Rome, while other – richer – nations, such as the US and the UK, have a substantial presence there by way of a resident ambassador with an office and a residence where receptions and dinners are held, often attended by cardinals and archbishops. The seminaries, or national colleges, are also used for such events prior to conclaves, as well some of the cardinals' favourite Rome *trattorie*.

Within the first few days of the cardinals arriving from across the world for the 2013 conclave, factions had already opened up among them. Those who served in Rome – the Curial officials – were split between two groups. One was of the followers of Cardinal Angelo Sodano, a former secretary of state, while the other backed his successor in that office, Cardinal Tarcisio Bertone. They were united in one aim: to stop Cardinal Angelo Scola of Milan from being elected. Scola was not popular with his fellow Italians but had support elsewhere. The Sodano faction preferred Cardinal Scherer of Brazil, who they believed would maintain the status quo.

Meanwhile four leading European cardinal reformers – Cormac Murphy-O'Connor, Walter Kasper, Godfried Danneels and Karl Lehmann, all of whom were thought to have backed Jorge Bergoglio in the 2005 conclave – realized that these splits afforded them an opportunity. They could rely on many Latin American voters, as well as several influential Europeans. Then there were others. As Austen Ivereigh puts it in his biography of Pope Francis: 'There were 11 African and 10 Asian cardinals. For the ones from historically English-speaking nations, the British cardinal, Murphy-O'Connor, was a reference point, and key to bringing them onside.'[3]

This is where the UK made a substantial contribution to the run-up to the 2013 conclave. Conversations among people in senior positions in the Church in London and Rome led to the realization that there was a major overlap between the developing world and the British Commonwealth. Where better to host a gathering for the cardinals who had no real base than the UK embassy to the Holy See?[4]

The idea that the British could provide a meeting place for the cardinals from emerging nations and also use such an event as a networking opportunity for people from the Commonweath was put to the UK ambassador Nigel Baker, who then discussed it with Cardinal Cormac Murphy-O'Connor. It led to a reception on behalf of the British government for cardinals from Commonwealth nations that took place at the ambassador's residence at the Palazzo Pallavicini. The residence, just around the corner from the Quirinale, the Italian government's buildings, is the place that the Foreign Office bought after it sold the Villa Drusiana, home to British ambassadors for generations. While it is in reality a loft apartment, it has proved a highly popular venue in Rome for receptions, with a rooftop terrace where cardinals can sip pre-dinner cocktails as they enjoy a spectacular view of St Peter's across the rooftops of Rome. In the reception rooms, silver-framed photographs of the queen and various prime ministers meeting different popes adorn the side tables. There is Harold Macmillan, accompanied by Edward Heath, meeting John XXIII in 1963; Harold Wilson with Paul VI in April 1965; Margaret Thatcher with John Paul II in November 1980, and separate photographs of Benedict XVI with Tony Blair, Gordon Brown and David Cameron.

As usual at the British embassy, the host that night was the British ambassador, Nigel Baker. But the most significant guest was Cormac

Murphy-O'Connor. The cardinal was in Rome to participate in the general congregations – a series of discussions – in the run-up to the conclave which began on 12 March, but did not vote himself, as he was over the voting age of eighty. His successor as Archbishop of Westminster, Vincent Nichols, did not yet have a red hat in 2013, and the Scottish cardinal, Keith O'Brien, had become embroiled in controversy over inappropriate relationships by the time of the conclave, so he did not attend. That left Cardinal Sean Brady of Armagh as the only cardinal representing any part of the British Isles who would vote in the conclave that elected Pope Francis.

Cormac Murphy-O'Connor had a highly significant role to play that night at the Palazzo Pallavicini. Rome is a place of gossip and networking and the cardinal, through his time in the city as rector of the English College, and the many meetings of Curial congregations he has attended over the years, knows how it functions better than most. An affable man, he has always found it easy to get on with people of all kinds, and among those with whom he struck up a friendship was the Archbishop of Buenos Aires after the two of them were installed as cardinals on the same day in February 2001. Murphy-O'Connor had been a voting cardinal in 2005 and he once let it slip that he had not voted for Joseph Ratzinger. It was more than likely that he had voted for his friend from Buenos Aires, Cardinal Jorge Bergoglio, the man who came second at the 2005 conclave.

By 2013, the majority of commentators had forgotten about Bergoglio. After Benedict had indicated that his age and health were major reasons for his decision to stand down, pundits declared that the voting cardinals would opt for a much younger man. With the Argentine cardinal already seventy-six, few saw him in the fallout from the papal resignation as *papabile*. Cormac Murphy-O'Connor, however, was one who did.

That night, as Commonwealth cardinals gathered from around the globe at the ambassador's home, they were warmly welcomed to the Eternal City by the British ambassador and by the English cardinal. Murphy-O'Connor had always been respectfully loyal to Pope Benedict, but his own coat of arms indicates that he is more of a Vatican II man than the Bavarian pope. He chose for it the motto *Gaudium et Spes* – 'joy and hope', the opening words of the Vatican II pastoral constitution on the Church in the modern world, that embraces contemporary society and reflects on the plight of the poor and afflicted. The motto suggests a particular form of Catholicism that Jorge Bergoglio had made his own in Argentina.

While the guests were from Commonwealth countries, high-profile cardinals George Pell of Australia and Marc Ouellet of Canada were not among them. The focus was on those from the poorer nations. Quite what Cormac Murphy-O'Connor said to the cardinals that night is not known. Even the ambassador and his waiting staff do not know; at one point, Nigel Baker told me, they left the cardinal to it. The ambassador's ecclesiastical adviser, Mgr Charlie Burns from Scotland, who is a regular at embassy gatherings, was not there that night either. Staff from the embassy told friends that there was one moment when none of them at all were present. It left the cardinal able to have a few minutes of totally confidential chat with the red hats from the south.[5]

On 13 March, 2013, after two days of deliberation and five ballots, white smoke – the sign that a new pope has been chosen – billowed from the chimney of the Sistine Chapel, and bells rang across the city of Rome. At first Cardinals Ouellet and Scola had seemed to be in favour, although neither secured the vital two-thirds majority and their candidacies stalled. Ouellet made it known he was putting his support behind Bergoglio. By the fourth ballot it became clear that Bergoglio would be chosen and on the fifth the cardinals voted overwhelmingly for him. Cardinal Brady later said that applause broke out as it became clear the Buenos Aires cardinal had achieved the required majority. There were 115 voters in all, of which eighty came from Europe and North America. The other thirty-five were from the rest of the world; left out in the cold during the lobbying in 2005, a sizeable number had been drawn into the process far more effectively in 2013, thanks to the Foreign Office and an English cardinal who understood both Rome and Jorge Bergoglio.[6]

In the days running up to the conclave, the United Kingdom had seemed, due to the age and misdemeanours of its cardinals, banished to the sidelines. Instead, a nation that thirty years earlier had been at war with his country, played a crucial role in the election of the Argentinian destined to shake up the Catholic Church with his drive for reform and his peacemaking. As Tim Fischer, former Australian ambassador to the Holy See and that country's former deputy prime minister put it: 'The British influence on the conclave was against all the odds, yet it happened. That was down to one of the most capable cardinals I've ever met – Cormac Murphy-O'Connor – playing the most powerful non-voting role in the choosing of a pope I've ever known.'[7]

It was quickly apparent to not only the officials of the Roman Curia but also to the diplomats based in Rome and their governments that in choosing Francis, the Catholic Church was changing course. His election began a new era of engagement with the world, perhaps greater than it had been since John Paul II's involvement in the ending of the Cold War and the *ostpolitik* of the Vatican twenty-five years earlier. It told the world that the Vatican was a global player, focusing not so much on the old powers of Europe but on the emerging nations of the developing south. In other words, its attention was located where the Catholic Church's own membership was stronger, as well as where there was population growth and new industry and opportunities were nascent.

Despite the UK's involvement in the election of the new Pope, this was a time when Rome was noticing a reduced interest on the part of the UK government. This seems particularly strange given that under Pope Francis, Holy See diplomacy has been having a profound influence on international relations. Quite how influential the Holy See can be was evident at the end of 2014 with the extraordinary thawing in the last, lingering theatre of the

Cold War – the decades-old clash between the US and Cuba. A simultaneous announcement by Raoul Castro, the island's president, and US president Barack Obama that diplomatic relations would resume between the two nations was quickly followed by credit being given by both of them to the peacemaking role of the Holy See.

The role of the Catholic Church in Cuba during the difficult years has rarely been mentioned, but it proved a useful institution for the British as they tried to work amid an atmosphere of *froideur*. Nigel Baker has given an intriguing insight into it with his recollections of his time there as a British diplomat in Havana during what became known as the 'cocktail wars' of 2003. In order to show its objection to European embassies inviting dissidents to their official receptions, the Cuban government vetoed the events and cut off diplomatic relations with the EU. Nigel Baker decided that if the Cubans would not come to him, he would go to the Cubans, working out that he would still meet them through their work and membership of the Catholic Church.[8]

The Church, throughout fifty-six years of Castro rule, has maintained strong ties with Cuba, as evinced by a record held by Cardinal Daniel Ortega of Havana. He is the only archbishop to have received visits to his diocese from three successive popes: John Paul in 1998, Benedict XVI in 2012, and Francis in 2015.

Francis's major intervention came before he visited Cuba, when Barack Obama visited him in Rome in March 2014. An hour and a half closeted in the Vatican library with the pope gave Obama a clear idea of Francis's thinking: that he believed that the US had isolated itself with its attempts to isolate Cuba and that an upcoming summit of the Americas would leave just the US and Panama attending it, while all the other Latin American nations boycotted.

Cardinal Ortega recounted this story later to the French ambassador to Cuba, explaining that the pope's efforts continued with letters urging reconciliation to both Castro and Obama, missives that he asked Ortega to hand-deliver. He also offered to host talks in October 2014. There has been little further disclosure about what Francis sought, other than urging the two sides to resolve humanitarian questions such as the release of political prisoners. Being a Latin American pope, and one on good terms with the cardinal in Havana, will no doubt have helped negotiations. Links with the White House, through American cardinals, were also brought into play. The author of a French study of Vatican diplomacy has revealed that a conference was organized at the Jesuit university of Georgetown in order to provide Ortega with a cover story for visiting Washington.[9]

The role of Cardinal Pietro Parolin, secretary of state, who was one of Pope Francis's first appointments, should not be underestimated either. After years spent in Rome in the Secretariat of State, Parolin was appointed nuncio in Venezuela; at the time, this was regarded as his being sent into exile because his face did not fit in the Secretariat as it was run by Cardinal

Bertone during the previous papacy. But Venezuela proved useful, for there Parolin dealt with Castro's ally, President Hugo Chávez, and would have been part of the essential groundwork for understanding the Cuban leader's mindset over tensions with the US. He had also worked on the normalization of relations between the Church and Mexico.[10]

This, then, is one of the most effective uses of Vatican diplomacy. Rather than an armoury of technical solutions to problems or the threat of force, it uses diplomatic persuasion. In other words, soft power is the Holy See's art form.[11]

Nigel Baker has commented more than once on the way in which the Vatican and the British Commonwealth – both soft powers – might, to their mutual benefit, do business. And as highlighted above, the Commonwealth came into its own during the 2013 conclave that elected Pope Francis. But could they work more closely together? The fifth secretary-general of the Commonwealth, Kamaleesh Sharma, never visited the Vatican, and indicated that he was anxious not to favour any particular religion in his work. His successor, Baroness (Patricia) Scotland, a former British attorney-general, was elected in November 2015 after her nomination for election by Dominica, the Caribbean island where she was born. Scotland is a keen Catholic, which has been noted in the Holy See. She indicated shortly before her election that faith has particular importance for her, and noted: 'If you go round the Commonwealth, lots and lots of the countries are deeply committed to God . . . what seems to have resonated is that I am a person of faith and I am not ashamed of being a person of faith.'[12] Within two months of being elected, and three months before she took up her Commonwealth position, Patricia Scotland did travel to the Vatican as part of the entourage of the President of Dominica. The visit included meeting Pope Francis and discussions were held on subjects such as climate change and the natural disasters that have caused severe damage to Dominica. She has indicated that her own priorities as secretary-general would be shared projects on climate change, healthcare and organized crime.[13]

Meanwhile, the most successful shared project between the United Kingdom and the Catholic Church since the election of Pope Francis has had global reach. Work on human trafficking has brought the British government, the Catholic Church in Britain and the Vatican together in the Santa Marta project.

Named after the residence where Pope Francis lives, the project has developed following an international conference held in Rome in April 2014. Senior police officers from twenty countries as well as the heads of Interpol and Europol, together with the then home secretary Theresa May and Metropolitan Police commissioner Bernard Hogan-Howe, joined Vatican officials and cardinals from around the globe to discuss the problems of human trafficking and modern slavery.

The event was a signal from the Church that it felt a combined effort is needed to tackle the problem, but also that it could help, particularly through the work of nuns offering safe houses to women who have been trafficked for sex and who are often so traumatized that they do not trust men. The invitation to so many leading figures from the UK confirmed Rome's approval of the co-operation of Church and government on the issue, including the Metropolitan Police's human trafficking unit working closely with Church charities to help victims and encourage them to give evidence against organized criminals.

The victims, wrote Theresa May and Cardinal Vincent Nichols in a co-authored piece, all tend to have in common 'that they are socially and economically vulnerable, on the margins of society. Organised criminal gangs deliberately prey on and exploit people they perceive to have no voice. That is why we must all become their voice and speak loudly for them.'[14]

The anti-trafficking project is a prime example of how years of work at the grassroots in Britain combined with the power of the Vatican's global platform could lead to an effective, international project. Since the April 2014 gathering, safe houses run by nuns have been set up, further conferences have taken place, a research centre has been established at St Mary's University – a Catholic institution with strong links to the Church in Britain, and a growing network is taking shape. The Church was praised by Bernard Hogan-Howe for its close collaboration with the state.[15] With Theresa May's appointment as Prime Minister, the issue of human trafficking looked set to stay high on the British agenda and to remain a matter which would benefit from further Church–state partnership; within three weeks of entering Number 10, Mrs May authored her first newspaper article as premier, saying that 'My government will lead the way in defeating modern slavery'.[16]

While a cordial relationship with Britain was thriving in one sector of the Vatican's work, there was another issue which raised its head again in papal dialogue with the UK during the Franciscan pontificate: the Falklands. Thirty years after the war with Argentina nearly scuppered the first visit by a pope to the UK, British diplomats again made representations to the Holy See regarding the United Kingdom's overseas territory of the Falklands.

From the moment that Pope Francis was elected in 2013, the then president of Argentina, the Peronist Christina Fernandez de Kirchner, visited her fellow Argentinian regularly. The relationship between the two had often been strained in Argentina, with Cardinal Bergoglio ready to criticize her government and its treatment of the poor. But perhaps in an effort to win support in Rome, the president continually sought to meet Pope Francis, even turning up in Cuba during his visit there. Her remarks about ownership of the Falklands were also frequent, with regular appearances at the United Nations General Assembly where she denounced British ownership of the islands and asked the UN to call on the UK to discuss sovereignty of what Argentinians call the 'Malvinas'.[17]

Kirchner is believed to have asked Francis to intervene over the Malvinas. Then in August 2015, after an Argentinian gave him a poster to hold urging in Spanish 'It's time for dialogue between Argentina and the United Kingdom' during a general audience at St Peter's, Kirchner tweeted the picture to her four million followers.[18]

This is the kind of publicity stunt that alarms Whitehall, particularly as Pope Francis, when Cardinal Jorge Bergoglio, spoke in passionate terms about the fallen of the war, and at a thirtieth anniversary Mass to mark the end of the conflict, urged the congregations to 'pray for those who have fallen, sons of the fatherland who went out to defend the fatherland, to claims as theirs what had been usurped [by the British]'.[19]

With concern rising in Whitehall, the British ambassador to the Holy See visited the secretary of state regarding the Falkland Islands to discuss the UK's view, Rome's view and, as the ambassador put it 'to make sure they restrain the Argentinians' efforts to misrepresent the Pope'.[20]

As well as the propaganda coup for the Argentinians if the pope were to make his personal views about the Malvinas known, the UK on this occasion had another headache: there were different diplomatic languages being spoken. The Holy See likes nothing better than dialogue when there is a conflict. However, as Baker put it: 'To the Argentinians, dialogue means sovereignty and nothing else. So if they say they want dialogue they mean they want to discuss sovereignty but for us it is non-negotiable.'[21]

This struggle to find common ground with the Holy See's diplomats may well continue. Mrs Kirchner's successor as president, Mauricio Macri, has also insisted on Argentinian sovereignty for the Malvinas while wanting dialogue. Britain's relationship with Rome has over the years ebbed and flowed, depending on who has political power in the UK and who holds the office of pope. Time and time again, this relationship has made headway through pragmatism and compromise on both sides. But on the Falklands there seems little chance of finding common ground.

It is ironic that the nationality of the pope that the British did their bit to help get elected has caused this particular anxiety for the Foreign Office. In other ways, the Francis pontificate has provided opportunities to consolidate the relationship between the United Kingdom and the Vatican: Pope Francis's priorities regarding climate change, poverty and exploitation, and peace, particularly in the Middle East, chime well with the British government's global aims. And yet there has not been quite the synchronicity this suggests. The Holy See remains concerned that the United Kingdom has turned somewhat inward in its focus of attention, and was deeply concerned by its vote to leave the EU. As noted in Chapter 4, the values of Catholic Social Teaching – solidarity and subsidiarity – were of profound influence on the Catholic founders of the European project, and the EU flag – with its twelve stars nodding to the twelve stars of the Virgin Mary's crown – also hints at its Catholic roots. It was no surprise, then, when the EU leaders returned to Rome for the sixtieth anniversary of the treaties that led to its creation, that the leaders of its remaining twenty-seven nations – the UK was markedly absent – should gather with the pope in the Vatican. There, Francis warned

them of the dangers of looking inward and not being so open to migrants
– a hint at criticism of the UK vote to leave:

> 'Where generations longed to see the fall of those signs of forced hostility,'
> he said, 'these days we debate how to keep out the "dangers" of our time:
> beginning with the long file of women, men and children fleeing war and
> poverty, seeking only a future for themselves and their loved ones.[22]

This more introverted British approach to the world has occurred just
when the Holy See itself has become a more substantial global player,
evidenced by Pope Francis's engagement in Cuba and in the refugee crisis
besetting Europe as a result of the ongoing civil war in Syria.

Diplomacy may well be about ideas, policies, ideologies and beliefs, but
it depends always on relationships and networks. With the British – and
Catholic – Baroness Scotland appointed as Secretary-General of the
Commonwealth, the opportunity is there for greater communication
between the United Kingdom and the Holy See. She will find several people
in the Secretariat of State, the Vatican's key department for relations with
the world, who will understand the British Commonwealth.

Its secretary for relations with states – in other words, the foreign minister
– is a Briton, Paul Gallagher, while his deputy, Antoine Camilleri, is Maltese.
The head of protocol, Mgr Jose Avelino Bettencourt, is Canadian, and the
private secretary of Secretary of State Parolin is Fr Robert Murphy, a priest
from Birmingham.

Britons today have more influence in Rome than they have ever done
before in the last 100 years. The way in which the British operate at the
heart of the Church, and how this enables Rome to understand the British
at large but also the pastoral needs of British Catholics, is my next focus, as
is the extent to which this substantial presence helps the British understand
Rome too.

Notes

1   *Crux* (2013), Pope Francis: https://cruxnow.com/tag/pope-francis

2   Curti, Elena (2005), 'How to win – and lose', *The Tablet*, 30 April 2005, 8.

3   Ivereigh, Austen (2015), *The Great Reformer: Francis and the Making of a
    Radical Pope*, London: Allen and Unwin, 357.

4   These conversations were reported to the author at the time.

5   This account is based on off-the-record conversations with several sources.

6   Allen, John L. (2013), 'Path to the papacy: "Not him, not him, therefore him,"
    National Catholic Reporter, 17 March. http://ncronline.org/news/global/
    path-papacy-not-him-not-him-therefore-him

7   Interview of Tim Fischer by Catherine Pepinster, October 2015.

8   Baker, Nigel (2015), 'Cuba and the Church: from cocktail wars to a common
    future', blog, 21 September. http://blogs.fco.gov.uk/nigelbaker/2015/09/21/
    cuba-and-the-church-from-cocktail-wars-to-a-common-future/

9   Colonna Cesari, Constance and John Laurenson (2015), 'One pope, two letters,
    three cardinals – the Vatican's crucial contribution to the end of the US/Cuba
    cold war', *The Tablet*, 19 September, 8.

10 *The Tablet* (2015), 3 January, 21.

11 Interview of Nigel Baker (NB) by Catherine Pepinster (CP), October 2015.

12 Peter Stanford (2015), 'In God she trusts', *The Tablet*, 21 November, 10.

13 http://www.patriciascotland.com/#!commonwealthvision/chgo

14 May, Theresa and Vincent Nichols (2014), 'We must all play a part in
    abolishing slavery', *The Telegraph*, 8 April. http://www.telegraph.co.uk/news/
    worldnews/europe/vaticancityandholysee/10752750/We-must-all-play-a-part-
    in-abolishing-slavery.html

15 Hogan-Howe, Bernard (2014), 'Prevent, rescue, support', *The Tablet*,
    12 April, 4.

16 May, Theresa (2016), 'My government will lead the way in defeating modern
    slavery', *Sunday Telegraph*, 30 July, 1. http://www.telegraph.co.uk/
    news/2016/07/30/we-will-lead-the-way-in-defeating-modern-slavery/

17 Kirchner, Christina (2014), Address at UN General Assembly, 24 September
    http://www.cfkargentina.com/address-by-cristina-kirchner-at-un-general-
    assembly-2014/

18 Khomani, Nadia (2015), 'Pope Francis "tricked" into calling for Falklands
    talks', *The Guardian*, 20 August. http://www.theguardian.com/world/2015/
    aug/20/pope-francis-falklands-argentina-britain-talks

19 Burns, Jimmy (2015), *Francis: Pope of Good Promise*, London: Constable, 185.

20 Interview of NB by CP.

21 Ibid.

22 Canter, James and Gaia Piangiani (2017), 'On eve of EU anniversary, Pope
    warns of bloc's fragility', *New York Times*, 24 March. https://www.nytimes.
    com/2017/03/24/world/europe/pope-francis-european-union.html?_r=0

6

The British at the heart of Rome

If English Catholics were asked to name the most important priest from the Archdiocese of Liverpool, the vast majority would suggest Cardinal Vincent Nichols, Archbishop of Westminster. But eight years after Nichols took holy orders, another Englishman was ordained in that diocese who today holds one of the most influential posts in the Vatican, wielding influence across the globe.

Until November 2014, Paul Gallagher was little known in Britain. After ordination by Archbishop Derek Worlock, who was an influential mentor of Vincent Nichols, Fr Gallagher's first post was as a curate in Fazakerley, in the Archdiocese of Liverpool. He then trained as a diplomat at the elite Pontifical Ecclesiastical Academy and entered the service of the Holy See in 1984. After thirty years working in nunciatures across the world, he returned to the heart of the Catholic Church when, that November, he was appointed the Holy See's secretary for relations with states, within the Secretariat of State – effectively becoming the pope's foreign minister.[1] This makes Archbishop Gallagher arguably the highest English office holder in Rome since Nicholas Breakspear – another diplomat – became Pope Adrian IV in the twelfth century.

The Curia, the central governing body of the Holy See, has always been an Italian preserve. Despite Paul VI's intentions that it should change after the Second Vatican Council, this has largely not happened – at least not at the very top. In 2014, out of twenty-five secretariats, congregations, pontifical councils, and tribunals, nearly half were headed by Italians.[2]

When it comes to the Byzantine ways in which Rome works, Italians have a distinct advantage: they understand how the place operates, given how similar it is to other aspects of public administration in Italy. The use of Italian as the working language of the Vatican is also advantageous to them. There have been longstanding accusations of cronyism and nepotism in the Vatican, issues that Pope Benedict was unable to combat, as the revelations about Vatican governance, known as 'Vatileaks', were published, and many hoped Pope Francis's reforms would combat them. Cardinal George Pell, the tough-talking former Archbishop of Sydney who was entrusted by Francis to run the newly created Secretariat for the Economy, which is responsible for the annual budget for the Holy See and the Vatican City State, and is also on the pontiff's key reform committee of nine cardinal advisers, told one eminent British Catholic that the Church's governance had to change because: 'It's the rest of us versus the Italians.'[3]

The dominance of Italians has continued despite a run of Polish, German and Argentinian pontiffs. So where does it leave the English and Welsh, and the Scots? If any English-speakers have made headway in recent years, it would seem to be Americans. Certainly, some of them have played key roles in the Vatican as Curial cardinals in the past fifteen years: James Stafford headed the Apostolic Penitentiary; Edmund Szoka was president of the Commission that governs the Vatican City State; William Levada ran the Congregation for the Doctrine of the Faith; and Raymond Burke headed the Apostolic Signatura. At the time of writing, though, the only American was Cardinal Kevin Farrell, prefect of the newly established Dicastery for Laity, Family and Life.

So what about the British? Are England and Wales, and Scotland (given they are dealt with as separate jurisdictions by Rome, although the same nuncio covers the UK, as he is assigned to the Court of St James, rather than the Church's own areas), well represented by their personnel in Rome?

In the last few years under Pope Francis, the British have certainly become more prominent. Apart from Archbishop Gallagher, there is Archbishop Arthur Roche, the secretary of the Congregation for Divine Worship, while others serve at more junior levels within the Curia. Britons who have served in the Secretariat of State in recent years include Mgr Philip Whitmore, now the rector of the English College, and Archbishop Leo Cushley, now Archbishop of St Andrews and Edinburgh.

Cardinal Vincent Nichols believes that there is now a higher profile of Britons in the Curia than there has been for a hundred years, something he puts down to Rome appreciating more how the Catholic Church has had to negotiate its role in British secular society, and realizing that the Church will have to do more of this elsewhere in coming years. 'Some of the stances and the ways of working that we use are becoming more important and that is partly why there is a higher profile of our people in the Curia today,' he said. 'Rome understands this is the way things are going with government relations and churches in Europe generally.'[4]

But a full-time post in the Curia is not the only way in which the British make their presence felt in Rome: they also exercise influence through the diocesan bishops' membership of Curial bodies, through more junior administrative posts, including non-diplomatic posts, and also through the networks in Rome involving staff of seminaries and universities, not to mention the diocesan bishops themselves attending 'ad limina' visits. These take place every five years and are undertaken by the diocesan bishops of each country to Rome to visit the tombs of St Peter and Paul and the pope.

Most people would assume air miles are clocked up in large numbers by businessmen. But bishops and cardinals of the Catholic Church collect air miles like the rest of us collect supermarket points. And most of the flights they take are to Rome to participate in the congregations and councils that effectively run the Church.

Who is chosen to be on the congregations and councils depends on the pope but names can also be recommended by the prefect or president of a congregation and the Secretariat of State. One area where senior English bishops have acquired clout in recent times is on the powerful Congregation for Bishops, which helps sets the tone for the way the Church is run, and on which both Cormac Murphy-O'Connor and his successor as Archbishop of Westminster have both served. This is the 'Thursday table' gathering in Rome held around twice a month, when between twenty and thirty cardinals gather to decide who will win episcopal appointments around the world (but always subject to the pope's final approval).

The importance of this congregation was highlighted in the run-up to the appointment of Cormac Murphy-O'Connor's successor, when there was significant debate over the leading candidate, Vincent Nichols. At one point in 2008 it appeared that he would be rejected and interest among those on the Congregation of Bishops turned towards Bernard Longley, then a Westminster auxiliary bishop. It is understood that Longley himself let it be known to Rome that he did not feel ready for the onerous duties of effectively being leader of English Catholics. On the day he was appointed in 2009, Nichols indicated that he had perceived the post at one point 'drifted away' from him. Then, presumably after Longley ruled himself out, interest turned back toward Nichols.[5]

Nichols's difficult moment, before his appointment was eventually confirmed, came during the pontificate of Benedict XVI. Since Pope Francis's election, Nichols's star has been in the ascendant with appointment to several congregations, including the Congregation of Bishops. As Thomas Reese, Jesuit author and former editor of *America* magazine, wrote: 'The number of congregations and councils of which a cardinal is a member is a crude measure of his influence in the Vatican.'[6]

On average, according to Thomas Reese, around 35 per cent of members of congregations and 24 per cent of those serving on councils are based in the Vatican full-time. Vatican officials will naturally always find it much easier to attend meetings as they are in Rome already, so they have a greater influence on outcomes. Congregation members from dioceses such as Vincent Nichols's, and particularly those beyond Europe, have to juggle collecting those air miles with their responsibilities on the home front.

Discussing and choosing bishops is a major part of the work of Rome; sometimes up to 200 new appointments per year are made around the world. The nuncio of a country requiring a new diocesan bishop submits a 'terna', a list of three names of priests he is recommending for the post, after he has consulted with favoured Catholics, including laity. The Congregation for Bishops then studies the list and can also make its own recommendation.

The prefect of the Congregation will keep the pope apprised of any disagreements over candidates. Ultimately, it is the pope who decides: he can select who he wants when there are a variety of opinions, such as the nuncio's choice, the Congregation's pick or even a dissenting minority's nomination. If he finds that he is consistently rejecting the Congregation's choices, he has an easy solution: change the membership of the Congregation. Pope Francis moved swiftly to do just that within nine months of his election. Out went Cardinals Justin Rigali, archbishop emeritus of Philadelphia, and Raymond Burke, who was also prefect of the Apostolic Signatura, (and was moved from his Signatura post too a year later), in a move interpreted by many as cutting the most conservative voices. In came Cardinal Donald Wuerl of Washington DC, a far more liberal prelate, who was later joined on the congregation in July 2016 by the like-minded Cardinal Blase Cupich of Chicago.

Reform of the Congregation for Bishops was also on Pope Francis's mind when he asked his new advisory body, the International Council for Cardinals, otherwise known as C9, to study the way the Church vets and chooses bishops and consider the qualities needed for episcopal office today.

Some sense of how the tone of the Congregation has changed in the years since Francis's election can be seen by examining the comments made by cardinals regarding the two Synods on the Family, set up by Pope Francis in 2014 and 2015. The ousted Cardinal Burke was highly vocal during the first Synod in October 2014, when a midterm report was published, written in conciliatory language about those in same-sex relationships and difficult non-marital heterosexual relationships. Cardinal Burke told a reporter that a statement from the pope reaffirming traditional Catholic teaching was 'long overdue'. Some time later he told another journalist that the ship of the Church 'had lost its compass'.[7]

In sharp contrast Cardinal Wuerl had the following to say on the second Synod, held in October 2015:

> The real takeaway from this synod is that Pope Francis has changed the way the Church goes about reflecting on her pastoral ministry. That's no small thing ... teaching includes the mercy of God and the care of the individual believer. Those two elements of the same reality are what the pope has lifted up and made visible in a way they haven't been in a long time.[8]

Vincent Nichols indicated he was on the same page as Cardinal Wuerl when he spoke on his return from the Synod of 'voices that found it difficult to build on the notion that in a person's life which, overall, might be irregular in terms of how our lives should be, and therefore in an unacceptable framework, there might be real signs of goodness'.[9]

The consequences of this changing membership of the Congregation for Bishops – highlighted by these comments – will be long-lasting, for these members will influence the choice of bishops in short to medium term. That influence, of course, depends on Congregation members turning up in Rome for the meetings. They are not required to attend every meeting, and indeed only the plenary meetings that are usually held every three years are obligatory. But the members know that if they are to be involved in making the choices that are sent on to the pope, frequent attendance and voting is important.

Being involved also means that the needs, pressing issues and priorities of a particular country are recognized. They are also more likely to be understood if more of its priests work in Rome, seconded to Curial offices. This was something that Cardinal Cormac Murphy-O'Connor, who understands Rome well, was keen to see developed. Certain congregations are, for example, organized according to language so that English-speaking officials deal with the Catholic Church's work in the English-speaking world. In practice this could mean that Americans would have considerable influence over affairs in the Church in England and Wales. If Vincent Nichols had not joined the Congregation for Bishops, and both Rigali and Burke had stayed on when Wuerl came in, then the Americans would have played a key role in choices about English appointments.

Absorbing the Roman atmosphere is also supremely useful for any future diocesan bishop. Cardinal Murphy-O'Connor not only trained for the priesthood himself at the English College in Rome but was later its rector – a time that provided him with rich experience and understanding of how Rome works, how to press your point and how not to overstep the mark, where charm and humour will work, and when to be more restrained in what you ask for.

Even Cardinal Basil Hume's greatest admirers would admit that he did not understand Rome as well as bishops and cardinals who were educated and worked there. As noted in Chapter 1, Basil Hume was educated at the Benedictine school of Ampleforth before joining the monastery there. Later his education took him to Fribourg rather than the Eternal City.

The puzzlement worked both ways. Rome also didn't quite 'get' the very English Basil Hume. Charles Wookey, Hume's former public affairs assistant, who has also worked for Cormac Murphy-O'Connor and Vincent Nichols during their time as cardinal archbishops of Westminster, recalled:

I always felt that Rome did not know how to deal with Basil Hume because he was not educated in Rome. He had not attended the English College and so he was an unknown quantity. He had not been on the circuit before he was appointed. He was also incredibly popular because very quickly his reputation spread beyond this country because of his writing and his holiness. He stood for a distinctly English Catholicism but he was taken to the heart of people in Northern Ireland and Scotland as well as England and Wales.[10]

In his memoirs, Cormac Murphy-O'Connor recalls that making vaguely sympathetic comments about married priests led both Hume and himself to receive letters from Rome. Hume's response was to suggest that they go to Rome together and confront the Curial officials. It didn't happen. Murphy-O'Connor doesn't explain why; perhaps he persuaded Hume it was a bad idea. Outright confrontation certainly isn't the Murphy-O'Connor approach; he is more circumspect about how to deal with the upper echelons of the Church.[11]

Like other bishops and archbishops across the globe, the Archbishop of Westminster will, from time to time, engage with the Congregation for the Doctrine of the Faith, the Vatican body charged with ensuring orthodoxy, over any matters in their diocese causing particular concern in Rome. Some cower; some refuse to do so; others try to head the CDF off at the pass.

Basil Hume tried this tactic on various occasions. When Graham Leonard, the former Anglican Bishop of London wanted to be received into the Catholic Church – the most senior Anglican prelate to do so since the Reformation – Hume was asked by the Congregation for the Doctrine of the Faith to prepare a dossier and took it to its prefect, Cardinal Joseph Ratzinger. It was very thorough in addressing concerns that Rome might have, said Wookey. 'He was very organized about that sort of thing.'[12]

Hume's most difficult time with the CDF was over homosexuality. In 1992, Cardinal Ratzinger wrote 'Some Considerations Concerning The Response To Legislative Proposals On The Non-Discrimination Of Homosexual Persons', a document that suggested that it was right for the law to discriminate against gay people in certain instances. While it reiterated that 'It is deplorable that homosexual persons have been and are the object of violent malice in speech or in action', the document also said that 'rights are not absolute. They can be legitimately limited for objectively disordered external conduct. This is sometimes not only licit but obligatory.' Its remarks that 'The passage from the recognition of homosexuality as a factor on which basis it is illegal to discriminate can easily lead, if not automatically, to the legislative protection and promotion of homosexuality. A person's homosexuality would be invoked in opposition to alleged discrimination, and thus the exercise of rights would be defended precisely via the affirmation of the homosexual condition instead of in terms of a violation of basic human rights' also deeply hurt Catholic homosexuals.[13]

As Charles Wookey put it, 'There was a degree of friction there with elements of the Curia' for Basil Hume. After being approached by gay Catholics he decided to do something about it and so produced his own document. Hume himself had not had an easy time over matters concerning homosexuals. The campaign group, Outrage!, had on occasion disrupted liturgies in Westminster Cathedral, and he had fallen out with the Catholic gay lobby group Quest, having its inclusion in the Catholic Directory withdrawn because he believed their reference to relationships implied sexual ones. But on this occasion Hume was sympathetic, and wrote his own document.[14]

His English sensibility was evident. Rome's documents on homosexuality frequently described it as 'objectively disordered'. 'The word "disordered" is a harsh one in our English language,' wrote Hume. 'It immediately suggests a sinful situation, or at least implies a demeaning of the person or even a sickness. It should not be so interpreted.'

Hume then went further, using the pastoral skill which had endeared him to the British nation: 'In whatever context it arises, and always respecting the appropriate manner of its expression, love between two persons, whether of the same sex or of a different sex, is to be treasured and respected.'[15]

But there was more to this episode than sensitively worded writing. Hume's document first appeared three years after the CDF's, and was then revised again in 1997. The cause of the delay was two-fold. Hume had not only spent a great deal of time writing it, but he had consulted his fellow-bishops, as Charles Wookey described:

He didn't want to get other bishops embroiled in any row so he wrote the document in his own name. But then he sent it to the four most conservative bishops and asked them what was wrong with it and for their help. It was a very clever move and they were very helpful, so that when there was a flurry in Rome over the press coverage of it and the CDF undertook a detailed critique, there was nothing in it that contradicted Catholic teaching. He deeply thought about it and prayed over it. He had the courage to do it: to reframe the teaching, but not to change it.[16]

Hume was not the last Archbishop of Westminster to encounter difficulties with Rome over this issue. Cardinal Cormac Murphy-O'Connor, a man much more at ease in Rome than his predecessor, had made an effort to deal with Rome by making himself known there. During his time at Westminster, he recalled, he would go round the various congregations in Rome at least once a year so that they knew who he was. This approach would pay dividends when tensions developed over what became known colloquially as the 'Gay Masses'. The Masses, held in Soho since 1999, were gatherings that enabled homosexual Catholics to come together for worship. Those involved said they were about solidarity rather than the challenging of Church teaching which ruled out homosexual relationships (although there has been a softening of this approach in recent years by some Church leaders, most notably Pope Francis with his 'who am I to judge?' remark, made about gay people).

Cardinal Murphy-O'Connor was both aware that the Masses were opposed by certain Catholics for existing at all, and that others were concerned about the services depending on Anglican goodwill, as they were held in a Church of England church in Soho. He worked out that the situation was so sensitive that it was worth gaining the tacit approval of Rome first, although it was essentially a pastoral issue in his diocese. He pre-empted any intervention by the doctrinal custodians of the Congregation for the Doctrine of the Faith by approaching them first. Fortunately the prefect of the CDF at this time was William Levada, who as Archbishop of San Francisco had dealt with similar situations. The solution was to bring the Masses into a Catholic church in Soho, and later the group was integrated into regular parish worship at the Jesuit church in London's Farm Street.[17]

Another Englishman who is in a useful position to understand how Rome works is Philip Whitmore, current rector of the English College, the ancient seminary for Englishmen, at the heart of Rome. Mgr Whitmore was appointed in 2013 after a stint as an official in the Secretariat of State. Just how close Mgr Whitmore was to the centre of power during the previous papacy is clear from his role in providing the well-regarded English translation of Benedict XVI's 2007 book, *Jesus of Nazareth*. He was also a key official during the *sede vacante* between Benedict and Francis, when he was one of seven prelates of the Apostolic Chamber assisting the *camerlengo*, keeping the Church going during the papal interregnum. Like Cardinal Murphy-O'Connor, Mgr Whitmore believes that having Englishmen present in Rome is immensely beneficial, saying:

> I would say it is very important for the well-being of the Church at home to have men in Rome in order to help Britain be more au fait with Rome. There is a widespread expectation in Britain, that Rome ought to be more Anglo-Saxon. It is not the kind of attitude that wins us friends internationally.
>
> The Roman Curia is well informed about the situation of the Church in Britain and indeed everywhere else through the extensive and efficient network that is the diplomatic service as well as the constant stream of 'ad limina' visits from all over the world, to say nothing of consistories and synods. Yes, it does help to have people on the spot, who can act as 'interpreters' when aspects of the culture are not immediately understood – and our culture is particularly impenetrable to foreigners, even to many Americans. But the benefit of having English clergy working in Rome works at least as much in the other direction – serving to correct one-sided perceptions of Rome and to open up the often insular concerns of the British to a more global perspective.[18]

The importance of the crossover between Rome and Britain became particularly evident during the preparations for the visit of Benedict XVI to Britain in 2010, when British officials in the Secretariat of State played a major role in the writing of the pope's speeches. They included Mgr Whitmore and Mgr Leo Cushley, later to become Archbishop of St Andrews and Edinburgh. Benedict's speeches revealed an understanding of how Britain is both steeped in religion, given its Established Church, and also a nation not given to appreciating overtly religious sentiment but preferring a more rational way of framing argument. The speech in Westminster Hall given by Benedict XVI particularly mastered this aspect of British cultural life. It was also evidence of the importance of the team working behind the scenes to get the speech right; people who could both negotiate the pitfalls of Rome and with Foreign Office officials in London, who were shown drafts of the speech.[19]

Archbishop Leo Cushley said of the Westminster Hall speech: 'It was drafted and checked several times. There is an attempt to understand the audience. You have to make that conscious effort and be appraised of the subtleties. By the time it is finished no one person working on it owns it and once the Holy Father has spoken, it is his.'[20]

So how do people – and these are mostly men, given the majority are Catholic priests – end up in positions of influence in Rome?

Staffing of the various bodies and organizations in Rome depend on word of mouth and personal recommendation rather than appointment through fair competition, the advertising of vacancies and interview. There are effectively two forms of appointment: via diocesan bishops, seminary rectors or religious superiors; or through a career in the diplomatic service.

Some bishops' conferences have made it a policy to ensure their own people are in Curial offices, in order to help their country's interests, while others prefer to keep the best at home. But seasoned hierarchs who understand Rome have realized that it is worth having your own people in post – or even that Rome might be a useful place to put a member of the 'awkward squad'. Germany has long had a bishops' conference keen to fill places in Rome. What of the British?

There are currently four alumni of the English College in the diplomatic service, all of whom were ordained within the last forty years. According to Mgr Philip Whitmore, there have been at least ten diocesan priests from England alone in non-diplomatic posts in the Holy See during the time he has known it.

Archbishop Michael Fitzgerald's Vatican career – he was first secretary and then president of the Pontifical Council for Interreligious Dialogue for four years from 2002, and later nuncio to Egypt and the Arab League – began in a different way to that of diocesan priests. As a White Father, it was his order, the Missionaries of Africa, which was asked to release him.

'I was already in Rome, having worked in the Pontifical Institute of Arabic And Islamic Studies, where I already had contact with the Secretariat for Non-Christians as a consultor, and then in the General Council of the Missionaries of Africa. The Vatican asked for me, and my society made me available. I did not feel in any way that I was representing the Catholic Church in England and Wales,' he explained.

'However, some time after I had been ordained a bishop by John Paul II, his secretary Stanislaw Dziwisz let it slip that one of the reasons for being appointed bishop was that there was no one of this rank from England and

Wales. I was disappointed to hear that, as I had thought the appointment
was not a matter of nationality, but a sign that importance was given to
interreligious dialogue.'[21]

Fitzgerald believes that some bishops definitely do not want to release
priests to work in Rome and sometimes the Vatican has to insist. The
reluctance is often due to a very basic concern with manpower.

'The Church in England and Wales is small, and it does not have the
personnel available in comparison with the USA,' he said. 'I remember when
we were trying to recruit someone for the Council for Interreligious Dialogue
and the bishop refused. Cardinal Arinze [his predecessor as president at
interreligious dialogue] said this was a good sign, since if the bishop released
the man too easily it would be suspicious. He said we should not give up,
and we kept pressurizing the bishop until he agreed, with some negotiation
in the first years. The priest was allowed to return to the seminary to teach
his course until a successor had been found for him.'[22]

It is not always easy to find people who want to be based in Rome. Most
men, considering a vocation to the priesthood first think of serving Christ in
the way that is most familiar to them: being a parish priest. However,
according to one unnamed source cited by Thomas Reese, this is just how
many see their work in Rome. 'People are happy to do this kind of service to
the Church. I don't want to idealize everything but you're working for Jesus
Christ who is working through the Pope,' a formal council secretary told
him.[23]

But Mgr Whitmore said that young seminarians tend to prefer pastoral
ministry than, say, teaching in a seminary themselves:

> Curial jobs, and desk jobs in general, are even less popular. So the pool of
> candidates who might be attracted to this kind of work is already limited.
> It is also the case, naturally enough, that bishops and religious superiors
> are reluctant to release gifted young priests for work outside their own
> diocese or province ... They frequently have difficulty covering all the
> requirements of their own territory with the manpower available to them,
> and if they have already released one or two priests for work outside,
> they often feel constrained to decline when asked to release more.[24]

Archbishop Cushley recalled how he came to be chosen to train as a
diplomat and therefore work in Rome, rather than in Scotland: 'I was
working in Lanarkshire and out of the blue I was asked to see the bishop.
There was a letter from the secretary of state. I had seen these men in Rome
and they were preparing to spend the rest of their lives away from home. It
took me a long time to say yes. The bishops are not sitting around thinking
about diplomacy (for their diocesan priests). Someone said to me we don't
want Ferraris, we want Volvos.'[25]

Rome often requires highly specialist knowledge too so the pool of
candidates is not necessarily large. And it can be a difficult, isolated life in

the Curia. 'You were given a grace period of about six months when you would be able to use your own language,' said Fitzgerald, 'but after that you would be expected to operate in Italian. I think that most of the British working in the Curia had studied in Rome and so this was no real difficulty. But even if you spoke Italian well, you always felt, and perhaps sometimes were made to feel, that you were an outsider.'[26]

The men who work in the Secretariat of State are mostly diplomats who have trained at the elite Pontifical Ecclesiastical Academy, which has just over thirty places a year for trainees. It is not a question of applying for a vacancy; people are invited and those who enquire themselves tend to be rejected. Nuncios and bishops are also asked to recommend somebody when an individual from a particular country is needed. Intellectual skills are needed and Rome insists it is essential to be an ordained priest.

The training lasts four years, including two spent gaining a licentiate in canon law in one of Rome's universities, unless the candidate already possesses a doctorate. Internships are also organized in both the Secretariat of State and in a nunciature. There is plenty of contact with existing staff via not only placements but lectures to help provide a practical understanding of the Holy See's diplomatic work. Students also need a talent for learning foreign languages as well as writing skills for providing diplomatic reports and correspondence. Once the course is over, the students take oral and written exams that test their aptitude and skills for problem-solving. Anyone who has been through the Whitehall fast stream for senior civil servants would find the system familiar.

Those joining the diplomatic service move from post to post, starting as an attaché, then six years as a secretary, and then as an *uditore*, and on to be a counsellor. It can be a daunting, lonely life, but for someone like Archbishop Paul Gallagher, who travelled this route and made it back to head office, the early years help develop a network of contacts across the globe and an understanding of the finer workings of Rome at the international level. But there is something else essential too: loyalty to the Holy See. As Thomas J Reese puts it: 'Anyone who is known to question decisions or theological views coming from the Vatican would not be invited to the academy.'[27]

Once the priest-official is working in the Vatican, this loyalty is shown regularly by total support for papal and Curial statements. A new encyclical is a reason for statement of praise and loyalty to the pontiff. Much of this devotion is due to the belief that the pope is the successor to Peter, chosen by Christ to found his Church. But the fact that the working environment is still a court emphasizes this approach, with the most senior cardinals and officials closest to the throne.

Yet it would be wrong to conclude that this means Rome is entirely hidebound by rules and rigidity. Rather, when one dips into the world of the Vatican, it is obvious that what is most effective are the relationships conducted both within and without the Vatican walls. There are a remarkable series of interlocking networks, where officials of the Church, diplomats, university staff and students make connections, some of them lasting a lifetime.

Some of these contacts are strictly businesslike: meetings are held with representatives from different Curial offices attending meetings of other councils and congregations. Diplomats will attend meetings and ceremonies at the Holy See. Others are social, such as receptions at foreign embassies, or lunches at the favoured *trattorie* around the Vatican. As Archbishop Paul Marcinkus, the one-time head of the Vatican Bank, famously told John Cornwell, the Vatican is like a village of washerwomen: 'When you're in an enclosed place like this, there's nothing else to do, nowhere to go, nothing else to talk about.'[28]

Michael Fitzgerald acknowledges this hothouse atmosphere too, where those in charge like to keep hold of their teams, fending off competition. 'If you have a good man, you like to keep him. In some positions, such as in Christian Unity, it takes some time to get the feel of the work, and to build up the contacts. The superiors do not like having to break in a new man. Nevertheless, I think it is very healthy for the persons concerned, and perhaps even for the office, to have change.'[29]

One way in which Rome makes use of people from abroad is to ask the staff of universities there to help by acting as 'consultors', providing expertise and advice to the Curial offices. These are not paid roles, nor are the academics given additional time for the work but they are encouraged to do so for the prestige it brings to their institutions. Over the years various British citizens have worked in Rome at university level – Sr Helen Alford, for example, teaches at the Angelicum University, and has become a notable authority on Catholic Social Teaching. Sr Helen is exceptional for obvious reasons – the vast majority of contributors to the Church in Rome are priests. It is even rarer for the laity to contribute, rather than a member of a religious order, but it does happen, and one British woman has risen higher than any other in Pope Francis's papacy. Margaret Archer, a professor of sociology, has long been engaged in advising the Vatican on social sciences and in 2014 she became the president of the Pontifical Academy of Social Sciences.

Another example of non-clerical advisers are the lay consultors on Vatican finances. The influential committee, the Administration of the Patrimony of the Holy See (APSA), is replete with experts in banking and finance, whose purpose is to advise on investments and property holdings used to ensure the security of the Church. Just what the holdings are is kept strictly secret, although it is known that they include properties in London and Paris. In London, the properties are managed by British Grolux Investments which looks after houses and shops with, according to Gianluigi Nuzzi's most recent investigative book on the Vatican, a market value of 73 million euros, but entered in the books at 38.8 million.[30]

An insight into the financial side of the Vatican came with the 'Vatileaks' episode, when confidential documents were taken on two occasion and handed over to journalists. Gianluigi Nuzzi's first book of Vatileaks revelations, *Benedict Was Afraid*, was based on documents taken from the pope's desk by his butler, who was later jailed for the theft. They revealed financial mismanagement which has long been thought to have led to Pope Benedict's resignation as he struggled to cope with the clean-up required. Nuzzi's second book on Vatican finances, *Merchants in the Temple*, revealed details from a document that the British banker Lord Camoys had produced during his time as a consultor to APSA in the 1990s. He concluded that reforms were essential to the way the Vatican conducted its business. But despite his expert opinion, nothing changed: his careful report had been set to one side. The way in which it had been ignored indicates particular problems in the Vatican: people in power keep their grip on it and despite seeking external feedback from what the Vatican would surely consider an ideal background – in Lord Camoys' case, being a loyal English Catholic with extensive banking experience in the City of London – they do not act on it. This long legacy has yet to be fully challenged, even by a pope as keen on reform as Francis. The ancient institution of the Vatican remains difficult to penetrate and remains mysterious to outsiders.[31]

That mystery pervades Rome and it takes time to understand Vatican institutions and how they exercise influence within the larger institution of the Church. Another key sphere of influence are the colleges of the various countries which train men for the priesthood; being sent to Rome as a seminarian is often perceived as sign that the individual is a candidate for advancement. The seminaries may not be as difficult to grasp as the labyrinthine workings of the Vatican's finances, but they are nevertheless a rather enclosed world to outsiders.

In the via Monserrato, just off Rome's major highway, the Via Vittorio Emmanuele, lies the Venerable English College (VEC). The English seminary was founded as a pilgrims' hospice by King Edward III in 1362. From the time of Henry VII to the Reformation, it was known as the King's Hospice and was akin to an ambassadorial presence in Rome. Despite Elizabeth I's long reign, which consolidated the success of the Protestant Reformation, a significant minority of English people still stayed loyal to the 'old faith' and thus required priests. From 1579, the King's Hospice was used as a seminary for English priests with forty-four of them martyred at a time when Roman Catholicism was feared in England.[32]

Today the VEC remains the premier seminary of the English Church and its graduates include the last two cardinal archbishops of Westminster, a sure sign of the importance of the national colleges in Rome. The pride of the college in these archbishops was evident in February 2014 when Archbishop Vincent Nichols gained his cardinal's red hat and the VEC threw a party for hundreds of guests, serving champagne and its own English College gin cocktail.

Although the main role of the seminaries is to provide priests for their home nations, they are also crucial in spotting high-flyers who could be candidates for diplomatic office. As Thomas J Reese says: 'Having lived in Roman colleges, these students already know some Italian and have absorbed some of the Roman atmosphere. Having watched them for three or four years, their rectors would know whether they have the qualities necessary for Vatican service.'[33]

Yet however prestigious your national college, and however many people you have in Rome, there is no clear-cut policy on who is consulted, by language, nationality or opinion about the running of the Church and its relations with each country. It is up to Rome, and Rome only, not the country concerned. The only right, as it were, is for the bishops to be spoken to through their ad limina visits.

The term comes from the Latin *ad limina apostolorum* – 'to the threshold of the apostles' – and it brings the Church around the world to the city of Rome and the pope. The visits are part of a tradition begun by Pope Zachary in 743 and then confirmed as a universal obligation on bishops by Pope Sixtus in 1585. They are now set in canon law with the bishops of each country visiting together every five years.

For most Catholics back home, the most they know of ad limina visits is the photo-opportunity – the picture of the pope with all the country's bishops. But there is much more to it than that, although the one-to-one meetings each individual bishop has with the pontiff is limited in scope given they last only fifteen minutes, and the larger gatherings are often a question of trying to make the pope familiar with a country he may not even have visited or know where to locate on the map.

Far more time-consuming are lengthy sessions with Curial officials. Before arriving in Rome, each bishop and his team will have submitted detailed questionnaires about their diocese, covering issues from education and Mass attendance to finances, ecumenism and seminarians, and use of marriage tribunals. It suggests that Rome desires detailed information about every corner of every country.

The Secretariat of State is a vital department for these visits, with its second section playing a particular role. The Secretariat is divided into two, with the *sostituto* heading the first section for general affairs, caring for the universal Church and with eight language desks answerable to him. In the second section, the secretary for relations with states (currently Archbishop Gallagher) is responsible for country desks which deal with civil governments, concordats and international organizations such as the United Nations. When the ad limina visits take place, the second section is a vital stopping-off point as it is concerned with the national Churches' standing in their respective countries.

But when it comes to other matters, the Secretariat of State's first section also plays a prominent part. It contains the protocol office that deals with ambassadors to the Holy See and also manages details for a papal visit to a country, or for that country to send their head of state to the Vatican. In this way the Holy See uses the two sections to deal with first, pastoral matters, and second, diplomatic ones – but it sees the links that can be made between them.

The ad limina process is two-way: Curial offices will make presentations to the bishops about their own work, but with so many offices to visit, there may be little time for questions. And in a world where obedience and loyalty matter so much, many hierarchs are wary of questioning the status quo.

The ad limina visit also takes the bishops of a country as a group to visit the pope. In the past this has often involved bishops effectively listening to a statement from the pontiff; Pope Francis, however, prefers to be more discursive. For England and Wales, there is just one visit; a country like the United States has to send its bishops in batches, given how numerous they are. Indeed so numerous are the bishops of the world that despite these visits supposedly being five-yearly, it usually takes seven years for a pope to complete his encounters with all the countries; Pope Benedict completed his and then started again in 2013 by meeting Italy's own 227 diocesan bishops – only to resign in February that year.

The visits are more than just juridical or administrative. With their emphasis on the apostles – there are pilgrimages to the tombs of Peter and Paul – they stress the apostolic succession and the binding links between popes and consecrated bishops.

They also reinforce the sense that Rome remains the centre of the Church. With the growth of social media, Philip Whitmore believes that younger Catholics are far more aware of the pope as leader of the Church than their predecessors, although over the past fifty years television had already played a significant role in increasing the profile of the papacy among Catholics and non-Catholics. Meanwhile they would find Rome is well aware of Britain's significance in the world. In the past it has lost out to its Anglophone competitor, the United States, although the British influence has increased during Francis's pontificate.

'It is known [in Rome] that Britain punches above its weight in terms of international and cultural influence. Americans are extraordinarily generous, as well as numerous, and this inevitably means that they get more attention in the Vatican than we do. But there is a great respect for Britain and its venerable traditions, an enthusiasm for London, a recognition that the UK is a key player in global politics,' said Whitmore.

But Whitmore acknowledged that despite the respect that the United Kingdom has garnered, it has its critics. 'Not everyone is Anglophile. Like many nations that have exercised great influence in the world, we have made enemies. But we have many friends too. Overall, as you've probably gathered, I tend to the view that Rome understands Britain better than Britain understands Rome.'[34]

Is Mgr Whitmore correct in his analysis? The relationship between the Catholic Church and the United Kingdom has made great advances since 1982, the year of John Paul II's visit, with greater understanding on both sides. The visit of Benedict XVI was an opportunity for both to learn even more about one another. In Britain, individual Catholics have made huge strides in society, while the Church in England and Wales at times exerts its influence but at others remains deeply cautious. Incidents over the years involving government departments, and charted in this book, particularly involving the Foreign Office, indicate a certain ignorance and lack of understanding of the Catholic Church.[35]

In February 2010, the English bishops met Pope Benedict during their ad limina visit, just seven months before his own visit to the United Kingdom. Among the matters that seemed uppermost in his mind was the need for the Church to remain strong and united in its encounters with the secular, and at one point he told the bishops:

> In a social milieu that encourages the expression of a variety of opinions on every question that arises, it is important to recognize dissent for what it is, and not to mistake it for a mature contribution to a balanced and wide-ranging debate. It is the truth revealed through Scripture and Tradition and articulated by the Church's Magisterium that sets us free.[36]

It was a time when the bishops were facing increasing secular calls for more tolerance on homosexuality and ideas about marriage and the family were being increasingly questioned. Although the Church has since undergone its own self-examination of these issues at the Synods on the Family in 2014 and 2015, the sticking points between Britain and Rome are likely to increase in the future if a more strident, more strongly secularist agenda takes hold, particularly if this has implications for what the Church holds most dear in England and Wales, such as its role in education. But with greater numbers of Catholics at the heart of public life in Britain, and greater numbers of Britons at the heart of Rome, the potential for further dialogue remains. Lord Camoys, who first became a consultor to the Vatican in 1992 but whose more informal engagement with Vatican officials goes back as far as the 1970s, says he has watched British influence noticeably grow in recent years as Rome has become more aware of the skills and talents not only of priests and bishops but also of the laity. But even more use could be made of laypeople, he believes.[37]

The influence of the British at the heart of Rome is manifested in many ways, through service in the various Curial departments, in the diplomatic service, through colleges and universities and through the to-ing and fro-ing to Rome of bishops, archbishops and cardinals. The Catholic Church is often perceived from the outside as an organization that dominates the lives of those who serve it, that demands utter loyalty, and is unbending in its requirement that individuals stick to its teaching. But that is not an accurate portrayal. This account of the British emphasizes the importance of relationships, of negotiation, of the need to understand a system and how to use it to advantage. Rome has a hothouse atmosphere; it is gossipy and intense. It does not suit everyone. What is constantly reinforced there is the belief that Rome remains the centre of the Church, and any hint of innate English superiority is not appreciated.

So far the Briton who has risen highest in the Vatican is Archbishop Gallagher. Could anyone rise higher, even right to the top? At the time of writing, the conversations in the *ristoranti* frequented by cardinals are turning to the papal succession, given Pope Francis's age, and who is *papabile* – looking papal. There has not been an Englishman since the twelfth century, but some are not ruling this out next time round, given Cardinal Nichols's growing standing in Rome. Whether that happens or not, when it comes to the relationship between Britain and Rome, as Benedict XVI said so clearly in his address in Westminster Hall, there can be a mature and wide-ranging debate if faith and reason work together.

Notes

1   O'Connell, Gerard (2014), 'Pope appoints Gallagher as Secretary for Relations with States, replaces Burke with Mamberti', *Vatican Insider, La Stampa*, 8 November. http://vaticaninsider.lastampa.it/en/the-vatican/detail/articolo/37391/

2   Figures collected from the annuario of 2014.

3   Recollected by an unnamed source.

4   Interview of Cardinal Vincent Nichols (VN) by Catherine Pepinster (CP), March 2015.

5   Curti, Elena (2009), 'Pastor with a political touch', *The Tablet*, 11 April, 6.

6   Reese SJ, Thomas J. (1997), *Inside The Vatican: The Politics and Organization of the Catholic Church*, Cambridge, MA: Harvard University Press.

7   Rocca, Francis X. (2014) 'Pope removes Cardinal Burke from Vatican post', Catholic News Service, November 10. http://ncronline.org/news/vatican/pope-removes-cardinal-burke-vatican-post

8   Gibson, David (2015) 'Cardinal Wuerl: The Catholic Church is moving from legalism to mercy', *Crux*, 28 October. http://www.cruxnow.com/church/2015/10/28/cardinal-wuerl-the-catholic-church-is-moving-from-legalism-to-mercy/

9   *The Tablet* (2015), 'Elation, but compromise too', 31 October, 8.

10 Interview of Charles Wookey (CW) by Catherine Pepinster (CP), October 2015.

11 Murphy-O'Connor, Cormac (2015), *An English Spring*, London: Continuum, 193.

12 Interview of CW by CP, ibid.

13 Congregation for the Doctrine of the Faith (1992), *Some Considerations Concerning The Response To Legislative Proposals On The Non-Discrimination Of Homosexual Persons, Congregation for the Doctrine of the Faith*, Rome, 24 July. http://www.vatican.va/roman_curia/congregations/cfaith/documents/rc_con_cfaith_doc_19920724_homosexual-persons_en.html

14 Interview of CW by CP, ibid.

15 Hume, Cardinal Basil (1997), A *Note on the teaching of the Catholic Church regarding homosexuality*, April. http://www.catholic-ew.org.uk/Catholic-News-Media-Library/Archive-Media-Assets/Files/Department-of-Christian-Responsibility-and-Citizenship-files/Briefing-Papers/Homosexuality-a-note-on-the-teaching-of-the-Catholic-Church-by-Cardinal-Basil-Hume

16 As recalled by Charles Wookey.

17 Murphy-O'Connor, ibid, 196.

18 Email interview of Philip Whitmore (PW) by Catherine Pepinster (CP), January 2015.

19 For details of Benedict XVI's speeches during the papal visit, see www.thepapalvisit.org.uk.

20 Interview of Archbishop Leo Cushley (LC) by Catherine Pepinster (CP), March 2016.

21 Email interview of Archbishop Michael Fitzgerald (MW) by Catherine Pepinster (CP), January 2015.

22 Ibid.

23 Reese, ibid, 150.

24 Interview of PW by CP, ibid.

25 Interview of LC by CP, ibid.

26 Interview of MF by CP, ibid.

27 Reese, ibid, 150.

28 Cornwell, John (1989), *A Thief in the Night: The Mysterious Death of John Paul I*, New York: Simon and Schuster, 142–3.

29 Interview of MF by CP, ibid.

30 Nuzzi, Gianluigi (2015) *Merchants in the Temple: Inside Pope Francis' Secret Battle Against Corruption in the Vatican*, New York: Henry Holt and Co, 124.

31 Nuzzi, ibid.

32 *Diplomacy and the Holy See*, ibid, 6.

33 Reese, ibid, 150.

34 Email interview of PW by CP, ibid.

35 See Chapter 3.

36 Address to the bishops of England and Wales by Benedict XVI, 1 February 2010. https://w2.vatican.va/content/benedict-xvi/en/speeches/2010/february/documents/hf_ben-xvi_spe_20100201_bishops-england-wales.html

37 Interview of Lord Camoys by Catherine Pepinster, January 2016.

CARDINAL WISEMAN'S "LAMBS."

PLATE 1 *'Cardinal Wiseman's lambs' by John Tenniel, from* Punch *or* The London Charivari, *25 October 1862. (Getty Images.)*

PLATE 2 *Cardinal Consalvi, Secretary of State at the Holy See, from the Waterloo Chamber. (Royal Collection Trust/ © Her Majesty Queen Elizabeth II 2017.)*

PLATE 3 *Pope Pius VII, pope at the time of Napoleon, from the Waterloo Chamber. (Royal Collection Trust/ © Her Majesty Queen Elizabeth II 2017.)*

PLATE 4 *Michael Ramsey (1904–88), the Archbishop of Canterbury, bids farewell to Pope Paul VI (1897–1978) outside St Peter's Basilica during his visit to Rome, 26 March 1966. The Pope presents Ramsey with his episcopal ring as a sign of friendship. (Photo by Keystone/Hulton Archive/Getty Images.)*

PLATE 5 *HM Queen Elizabeth II meets Pope John Paul II, 1980. (Photo by Anwar Hussein/WireImage. Getty Images.)*

PLATE 6 *HM the Queen presenting Cardinal Basil Hume with the Order of Merit in Buckingham Palace on 2 June 1999 (Photo by © Pool Photograph/Corbis/Corbis via Getty Images.)*

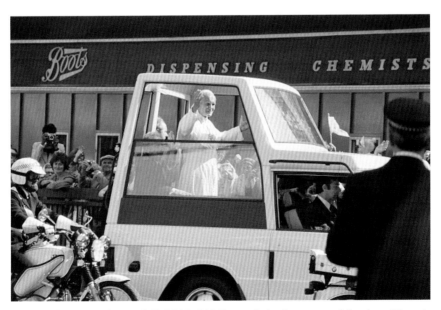

PLATE 7 *Pope John Paul II (1920–2005) travels in the popemobile along Victoria Street in London en route to Westminster Cathedral during the papal tour of the United Kingdom, 28 May 1982. (Photo by United News/Popperfoto/Getty Images. Getty 541951759.)*

PLATE 8 *Pope Benedict XVI meets Archbishop of Canterbury Rowan Williams in Vatican City, Rome, 23 November 2006. (Photo by Eric Vandeville/Gamma-Rapho via Getty Images.)*

PLATE 9 *Photograph taken from the plane of Pope Benedict XVI arriving in Scotland. Reproduced by kind permission of Archbishop Leo Cushley.*

PLATE 10 *Former British prime ministers Gordon Brown (L), Tony Blair (2nd L), John Major (C), Margaret Thatcher (3rd R), former foreign secretary, William Hague (4th L), and former deputy prime minister Nick Clegg (3rd R), watch as Speaker of the House of Commons John Bercow (obscured by Black Rod) guides Pope Benedict XVI to his seat before his address at Westminster Hall in the Houses of Parliament, 17 September 2010. (Photo credit: Tim Ireland/AFP/Getty Images.)*

PLATE 11 *Demonstrators hold banners before a march protesting against Pope Benedict XVI's visit to Britain, in Piccadilly, central London, 18 September 2010. (Photo credit: Carl Court/AFP/Getty Images.)*

PLATE 12 *Cherie and Tony Blair arriving for a memorial service for Pope John Paul II at Westminster Cathedral, London on 4 April 2005. (Photo by Niki Nikolova/ FilmMagic. Getty Images.)*

PLATE 13 *Theresa May, when home secretary, with Pope Francis in April 2014. Photo reproduced courtesy of catholicnews.org.uk.*

PLATE 14 *A special Mass for migrants held in St George's Cathedral, Southwark, on the Feast of St Joseph the Worker, 4 May 2015. The chief celebrant is Archbishop Peter Smith, Archbishop of Southwark.* (© *Mazur/catholicnews.org.uk*)

PLATE 15 *Troubled cardinals: Cardinal Cormac Murphy-O'Connor, Cardinal Sean Brady, Cardinal Keith O'Brien, at the British Embassy to the Holy See in November 2007. Reproduced by kind permission of Francis Campbell.*

PLATE 16 *Mary McAleese, president of Ireland, with Cardinal William Levada, prefect of the Congregation for the Doctrine of the Faith, and Bishop William Walsh of Down and Connor, at a reception in the British Embassy to the Holy See in November 2007. Reproduced by kind permission of Francis Campbell.*

PLATE 17 *The author with Pope Francis. Reproduced courtesy of catholicnews. org.uk.*

PART TWO

Introduction to Part Two:

Taking a look at specifics

The first part of this book has set the scene of the relationship between the British and the papacy, focusing on the Catholics who have played such a significant role in normalizing Catholicism in the UK and therefore making possible a warm and mutually useful relationship between Britain and Rome. It has then examined in detail how the UK and the papacy work together in practice in areas such as diplomacy, and dealt with the key events of that relationship, particularly the two papal visits to the UK of 1982 and 2010. It examined, too, the way in which the relationship has changed during the pontificate of Francis, and how the British played their part in his election. The role of the British in Rome itself and the contribution they make to the life of the Catholic Church was also studied.

It is clear that while the relationship has much improved in the past thirty years since full diplomatic status was agreed, there is still a sense that Rome and Britain do not entirely know what to make of one another. The UK in particular cannot seem to make up its mind, as Cardinal Vincent Nichols so memorably said, whether it should treat Rome as San Marino or China in terms of its significance and influence.[1] It is clearly not San Marino. But the Foreign Office's puzzlement is evident in the way it keeps changing its mind over how the Holy See should be classified in terms of which desk should be responsible for it. It has shunted it from global economic affairs to multilateral policy and then to the Europe desk. One must wonder whether senior British civil servants, many of whom are nominally Anglican and increasingly secular in outlook, perceive the Catholic Church through their view of it in Britain itself as a lesser Christian denomination to the Church of England, and that therefore they underestimate its global reach. This is a particularly out-dated perception, for since Pope Francis was elected, Rome has become a more significant player on the world stage, as evidenced by papal comments on Syria, refugees and climate change, as well as by visits to Cuba and the United States.

But what sort of player is the papacy in Britain? Are those FCO officials correct? Is it a minor concern? In the second half of this book, I am now turning my gaze to the Catholic Church on the domestic front.

The complexities of the relationship between Church and state, and between the individual citizen's conscience, shaped by faith and the state, have been of great significance in Britain's history and were one of the major themes of Pope Benedict XVI's visit to the UK in 2010. When Benedict spoke in Westminster Hall, scene of the trial of St Thomas More, it led many Catholics to ponder how More, and indeed Thomas Becket before him, took on the most mighty in the land. In both cases their refusal to back down saw them fall foul of the sovereign power of the monarchy. Pope Benedict made the connection with More's time and contemporary mores as he challenged Britain to ponder:

> The fundamental questions at stake in Thomas More's trial continue to present themselves in ever-changing terms as new social conditions emerge. Each generation, as it seeks to advance the common good, must ask anew: what are the requirements that governments may reasonably impose upon citizens, and how far do they extend? By appeal to what authority can moral dilemmas be resolved? These questions take us directly to the ethical foundations of civil discourse. If the moral principles underpinning the democratic process are themselves determined by nothing more solid than social consensus, then the fragility of the process becomes all too evident – herein lies the real challenge for democracy.[2]

In effect, Pope Benedict was setting a task for not only individuals but also the Catholic Church in its discourse with society, particularly with government. Here it has a role to play, challenging the foundations of policies and the paths chosen. In this section of the book I shall examine how the papacy, via the domestic Church, has taken on that role in areas such as welfare and education. At times this has meant it has fought hard to defend its own corner, such as in preserving its schools. But at others it has formed strong partnerships with government, such as its recent endeavours to combat human trafficking. It is noticeable, however, that the partnerships between the Catholic Church and the government have not been as strong on the home front as they are at the global level. During the early days of David Cameron's premiership, the policy of the 'Big Society' promised much in terms of advocating greater partnerships between the state and other agencies, and the Bishops' Conference of England and Wales appeared to fully embrace it. Its April 2011 conference on Building A New Culture of Social Responsibility, with keynote speakers Archbishop Vincent Nichols and Conservative Party co-chair Baroness Warsi, indicated the common denominators in government thinking on civic energy and the role of faith communities, and Pope Benedict's on solidarity. Baroness Warsi, whose speeches regularly paid tribute to the work of faith communities, spoke of the Catholic Church's work in welfare, education and urban regeneration. But as Cameron's focus turned to Conservative infighting and the UK's future in Europe, his interest in the Big Society waned, and Church–state partnerships dropped from the agenda.[3]

In the coming chapters I am also turning my attention to specific parts of the United Kingdom and their relationship with Rome. One of the most notable aspects of the relationship between the United Kingdom and the Holy See is that Rome sees clearly the different countries that make up Britain. Scotland has its own bishops' conference while Northern Ireland is treated as part of the island of Ireland in terms of ecclesiastical structure. In both these nations religious affiliation plays a much more notable role than in England and Wales and the place of the papacy and the domestic Catholic Church is analyzed in two separate chapters, including the way in which Rome has responded to nationalist ideals within the Catholic communities.

One of the key players in keeping the United Kingdom united is the queen, and her longevity and her religious faith have played a profound role in developing the relationship between the British and the papacy. This too is examined in detail, as is the relationship between the Church of England, of which she is head, and the Catholic Church. During the quincentenary of the Reformation 2017, the attention of many churchgoers turned to the achievements of ecumenism across Europe. In Britain, ecumenical relations between the Catholic Church and the Church of England are strong, but achieving the ideal of full unity seems as far away as ever.

Few leaders play such a notable role on the world stage as the monarch of the United Kingdom but without doubt another is the pope. In the era of Twitter and Facebook, the pope's place in people's lives, whether Catholic or Protestant, believer or non-believer, has changed markedly, and this too is examined. Papal authority depends on office, status and tradition but the charisma of the individual plays a fundamental role as well. I use the political and sociological theories of leadership, outlined by Weber, Ann Ruth Wilner, Robert Nye and Sidney Hook to analyze and compare and contrast the papacies of John Paul II, Benedict XVI and Francis in order to fully understand the status of the pope in Britain, a country once completely estranged from Rome. For government, the importance of the papacy is in its soft power and its global status. For British Catholics, the pope is by tradition a unifying figure, but with the pontificates covered by this volume, he has also become a controversial one, depending on individuals' particular strand of Catholicism and interpretations of their faith, as well as the individuals who have held papal office. It was noticeable, however, that Catholics did come together for each of the two papal visits to the UK, regardless of people's usual critiques of their leaders. Not all Catholics approve of the contemporary image of the pope as a superstar, preferring the Bishop of Rome to be *primus inter pares*, and desiring the collegiality of bishops to be the dominant characteristic of their Church's governance. But as I will show, for the British as a whole, the pope, the once-feared enemy of these islands, is now an international celebrity.

This status confirms that in the age of globalization, the pope is well placed to bestride the globe, and the papacy has adapted to this era as a major force of soft power. In this next section, I will explore the extent to which the United Kingdom has understood the Catholic Church's role and how this in turn might benefit the UK's own global aims and ambitions. The relationship between the nation and the Church has, over the years, waxed and waned, influenced on both sides for a desire for pragmatism and on occasion, a stubborn insistence on sticking to principle. As I will show, the opportunities for collaboration have been taken up increasingly at the global level but less so in Britain itself. But for a Church and a nation that were once so bitterly at odds, the relationship forged since Catholic emancipation, and particularly in the last thirty years, is a quite remarkable one.

Notes

1 Interview of Cardinal Vincent Nichols by Catherine Pepinster, March 2015.

2 Benedict XVI (2010), Address in Westminster Hall, 17 September 2010. https://w2.vatican.va/content/benedict-xvi/en/speeches/2010/september/documents/hf_ben-xvi_spe_20100917_societa-civile.html

3 Slocock, Caroline (2015), what happened to David Cameron's Big Society? Huffington Post, 20 January www.huffingtonpost.co.uk/caroline-slocock/big-society_b_6505902.html

7

Every picture tells a story:

Ecumenism

The recent relationship between the papacy and the mother Church of Anglicanism, the Church of England, is a story of difficulties that once seemed impossible to overcome. It is also a story of reconciliation, expressed through four key images featuring four separate popes and four archbishops of Canterbury: Michael Ramsey and Paul VI; Robert Runcie and John Paul II; Rowan Williams and Benedict XVI; Justin Welby and Francis.

As anyone belonging to a visually rich institution such as the Catholic Church knows, images can transform history, transform people, and transform relationships. There was the meeting between Michael Ramsey and Paul VI, the first *official* encounter between a pope and an Archbishop of Canterbury (the first meeting between a pope and an Archbishop of Canterbury had taken place in 1960, when Geoffrey Fisher met John XXIII at a private audience). Perhaps even more historic was the moment that Robert Runcie escorted John Paul II through Canterbury Cathedral, the place of Thomas Becket's martyrdom, in a country that broke with Rome after another Englishman was martyred when his king took on the Church. Twenty-eight years later, during the first state visit of a pope to Britain, Rowan Williams was pictured with Benedict XVI in Westminster Abbey after the two cerebral religious leaders prayed together at the tomb of Edward the Confessor, one of the only Catholic shrines left intact after the Reformation. And just a few years later in 2013, two very different leaders, Francis and Justin Welby, met together in Rome after being installed as leaders of their Churches within a week of one another, and making similar calls for societies to change to help migrants, refugees and the dispossessed. All these images of two Church leaders, seen in the context of history, are so dramatic, so symbolic, and so culture-changing that a Catholic might see them almost as sacramental or as relics.

Yet according to Mgr Mark Langham, former secretary to the Anglican and Methodist Dialogues at the Pontifical Council for Promoting Christian

Unity, there has been too much emphasis on the superficial in the coverage of these events and he asks: 'Has the period of our formal relationship really moved the ecumenical agenda forwards, or are we too polite to admit that we are doing little more than smile for the camera?'[1]

So regular have the visits of archbishops of Canterbury been to Rome to meet the pope that it has become a rite of passage, almost a special form of pilgrimage. Robert Runcie visited five times, George Carey six, Rowan Williams a remarkable eight, and Justin Welby three times in his first years as archbishop.

It is difficult today to conceive just how impossible those encounters would once have seemed in the years after England's break with Rome and how traumatized the Vatican must once have been by the actions of Henry VIII. The king to whom it had once awarded the title of Defender of the Faith for his defence of the seven sacraments in the face of Lutheran opposition, then divorced his wife Katherine of Aragon, and went on to execute a cardinal – John Fisher – who refused to accept Henry as supreme head of the Church of England.

In the Vatican archives, they still have letters from Anne Boleyn and Henry to one another, intercepted and stolen by spies acting for officials in Rome. The letters confirmed that Henry was engaging in adultery and deceiving his queen; her nephew, Charles V, the Holy Roman Emperor, was one of the pope's great allies. In 2006, at a dinner held in Rowan Williams' honour at the residence of the UK ambassador to the Holy See, these letters were discussed by a Vatican historian, and the long memory of the Vatican was all too evident. Yet Rome is also pragmatic; relations with the Church of England also mean relations with the Anglican Communion, which has an estimated 85 million members in forty-four different Churches worldwide in thirty-eight provinces and six national or local Churches. It is a substantial organization and is relatively easy to deal with, for its clear episcopal hierarchy mirrors the Catholic model.

The way in which it differs matters a good deal, of course. Rowan Williams acknowledges that the Church of England's split from Rome still affects relations today between the two, given that the impetus for the division was contesting the authority of the pope, and authority for the Archbishop of Canterbury is not juridical. Certainly, issues about authority – how the Church teaches doctrinal decisions – remain central to ecumenical dialogue. 'It is something that is still there underneath the surface, though I would not say it is constantly in the mindset of Anglicans,' said Williams. 'The specific shape of the English Reformation matters in England. The great debate was over the ultimate court of appeal in canon law. It's up close and personal. We were not about reshaping the structure, whereas there was the issue of the chief magistrate.'[2]

And yet today there is a paradox in this relationship. Alongside this sign of the lingering, wounded relationship between Britain and Rome, there is evidence of reconciliation too. The English College was the seminary where

Catholic priests were trained and sent back to England, prepared to be martyred for the faith and staunchly opposed to Anglicanism. It remains England's seminary but now it is the very place where the Archbishop of Canterbury always stays, ever since Michael Ramsey became the first Anglican archbishop to use it. The building, once a hostel for pilgrims and a sanctuary for outlawed priests, is used today as a hostel by the 'pilgrim' Archbishop of Canterbury.

Rowan Williams recollected staying there on his visits to Rome, during his ten years in the role from 2002 to 2012, as deeply affecting. 'When you are surrounded by the memory of the martyrs at the English College it is very powerful,' he said. 'But it is also a hostel for the Archbishop of Canterbury when he visits Rome. It is a real paradox – it is a place of pilgrimage as well as this reminder of past conflict.'[3]

One hundred and fifty years ago, the likelihood of a fraternal relationship between Anglicanism and Catholicism would have seemed highly unlikely. At the time of the restoration of the Catholic hierarchy, Cardinal Nicholas Wiseman inflamed relations with the Church of England through his triumphalist talk, 'From Out The Flaminian Gate', of the return of Catholicism to England. John Henry Newman, convert to Roman Catholicism from the Church of England, called his former Church 'the veriest of nonentities'. In the appendix to his *Apologia Pro Vita Sua,* he suggested that it was 'a mere national institution'.[4]

Newman clearly thought that the Church of England was useful – but only so far:

'Not for its own sake but for the sake of the many congregations to which it ministers, I will do nothing against it. While Catholics are so weak in England, it is doing our work; and though it does us harm in a measure, at present the balance is in our favour. What our duty would be at another time and in other circumstances, supposing for instance that the Establishment lost its dogmatic faith, or at least did not preach it, is another matter altogether ... Doubtless the national Church has been a serviceable breakwater against doctrinal errors more fundamental than its own. How long this will last in the years now before us is impossible to say, for the nation drags down its Church to its own level.[5]

Newman's attitude has been replaced by increasing ecumenical warmth, encouraged by the teachings of the Second Vatican Council, which singled out the Anglican Communion as having a particular place within ecumenical relations. The second half of the twentieth century was an era of optimism, a time when reunion of the Anglican Church with Rome seemed a possibility; it was no longer seen as an enemy, a competitor or a rival. A sense of unity, based on a history going back even further than the Reformation, was evident when Archbishop Geoffrey Fisher visited John XXIII in 1960, the first such visit to Rome by an Archbishop of Canterbury since the

Reformation. The pope told him that it was a joy for the successor of Peter to be brought into contact with the Church of St Augustine.

This sense of common fellowship was evident in the famous encounter between Pope Paul VI and Michael Ramsey when, just three months after the end of Vatican II, Paul VI took off his ring as they said goodbye to one another outside the basilica of St Paul's Outside the Walls, and gave it to Ramsey. The archbishop promptly burst into tears. (The ring – a large, square green stone divided by a gold cross and studded with four diamonds – is still worn today whenever an Archbishop of Canterbury visits the pope, as happened in 2016 when the present incumbent, Justin Welby, went to see Pope Francis to mark fifty years of ecumenical relations between Catholics and Anglicans).

Ramsey and Pope Paul spent four hours in talks that day and signed a commitment to work together towards the unity of the Anglican Communion with the Catholic Church. The groundwork for future endeavour was laid out through the Common Declaration of 1966 with a goal of the restoration of complete communion.[6]

Such optimism now seems highly idealistic. While there have been long friendships between hierarchs and friendliness too at the local level, unity today seems a long way off. Indeed it seems for many people to have been supplanted by a feeling of 'live and let live' while great ecclesiological difficulties remain unresolved. The current situation, with the quest for unity hampered by major theological differences over the ordination of women and occasional spats over tactless behaviour – such as the way Rome treated Canterbury over the introduction of the canonical structure of the Anglican Ordinariate for Anglicans within the Catholic Church – seems to suggest not so much a goal of complete unity but, at best, what could be called reconciled diversity.

And yet for Rome and Canterbury, unity *does* remain the goal. 'At one time we were burning one another at the stake. Now you ask one another to your carol services. Is that enough? No, says Rome, it is unity that we seek, not reconciled diversity,' said Mark Langham.[7]

Rowan Williams agreed: 'Ecumenism is an ideal and we still need to pray for it. It is a tragedy that we cannot be together for the Eucharist. We work for a proper understanding of our baptismal unity and evangelization.'[8]

That separation at Communion is experienced by mixed-marriage families all the time but those engaged in ecumenical dialogue are affected by it too. After Mass celebrated in St Peter's during Archbishop Welby's visit to Rome in October 2016, when Catholics received Communion but the many Anglicans present did not, Welby said: 'We live with this, and every single day we feel the pain. And that is good – because the moment these wounds stop hurting, we have really lost the plot. They stop hurting when we are dead and we are emphatically not dead.'[9]

Efforts at unity characterized the relationship between Anglicans and Catholics in the 1970s with the setting up of the Anglican-Roman Catholic

International Commission (ARCIC), sponsored by the Anglican Consultative Council and the Vatican's Pontifical Council for Promoting Christian Unity. This was originally a decade-long project designed to establish areas of common ground and to bring the two Churches closer together in worship and doctrine but continues to this day. Ecumenical initiatives were not confined to central organizations but extended (and in many ways proved more fruitful) at the grassroots, with the uniting of charitable and welfare activities, the sharing of church buildings, and in some cases, joint worship. The involvement of leading figures from Britain's Christian Churches at national religious services had become the norm by the 1980s. The participation of the General Secretary of the World Council of Churches and the Catholic cardinal at the enthronement ceremony for Archbishop Runcie in 1980 was testimony to the strength of ecumenism and the acceptance that all Christian denominations, including the Roman Catholic Church, were an important facet of British religious life.

Yet there were problems and often they were to do with a certain high-handedness on the part of Rome. In 1977 Archbishop Donald Coggan of Canterbury went to see Paul VI, out of which emerged another Common Declaration which recognized aspects of common faith including: baptism, the Trinity, scripture, the creeds and the desert fathers. Coggan made a stronger bid the night before for Eucharistic hospitality, during a sermon at the Anglican All Saints. It did not appear in the Declaration itself. Bishop Christopher Hill, who was co-secretary of ARCIC from 1974 to 1981, has suggested that the Congregation for the Doctrine of the Faith went through this declaration unilaterally.[10]

Whatever the irritations caused by officials, the bigger picture throughout this time was of two once-estranged family members making strides to reconcile – and be in the family photos together. Never was this truer than on the occasion of John Paul's visit to Canterbury Cathedral as part of his pastoral visit to Britain in 1982.

The Third Common Declaration was made in Canterbury during this visit, highlighting the need for full visible unity while the two hierarchs together presided over a service where people renewed their baptismal vows. There were prayers, too, at the tomb of Thomas Becket while candles were lit to the Polish Catholic martyr St Maximilian Kolbe and a murdered Anglican archbishop from Kampala, Janani Luwum, killed by Idi Amin's thugs. John Paul also met Lord Cecil in a moment of reconciliation; he was descended from the Cecil family that had run the teams of Elizabethan officials who tracked down and executed Catholic priests.

The lasting image is of John Paul and Runcie walking in Canterbury Cathedral and kneeling in prayer together. It was a landmark moment – so much so that Cardinal Cormac Murphy-O'Connor, who had greeted the pope at Gatwick Airport in his then office of Bishop of Arundel and Brighton, but was watching this moment at home on TV, says that he wept.[11]

The Canterbury visit had not always seemed so promising. The Church historian Henry Chadwick was sent on Archbishop Runcie's behalf to discuss the Canterbury visit with officials in Rome and with John Paul II himself. During his encounter with Chadwick, which the historian reported back in detail to Robert Runcie, the pope wanted to know whether Anglican clerics read Catholic medieval theologians, whether honour was given in Anglican churches to the saints, and about the role of the queen as head of the Church of England. But while the pope himself seemed encouraged by some of what he heard, Chadwick wrote on his return that his conversations with the Curia had given him the impression that Anglicans 'have come to seem a bore to the top administrators of the Roman Catholic Church', and that they feared the Church of England is 'at heart simply Liberal Protestants in our ecclesiology'.[12]

It is a sentiment that Rowan Williams does not recognize. However, he does accept the source of this perception by Chadwick: 'I think Rome saw us as wanting to have a special relationship ever since the Malines Conversations [of 1921–27, focusing on corporate union]. There would be wistful Anglicans lounging round the door. But at least the papal visit brought to an end expectations that we were just Swiss Calvinists.'[13]

In 1989 came another Runcie–John Paul meeting, this time in Rome, with a further Common Declaration which talked about 'that certain yet imperfect communion we already share'.[14] If there is any issue that causes the relationship to remain imperfect, it is women's ordination. But here again there are contradictions. On the one hand, there are comments made, such as in the 1989 Common Declaration from Runcie and John Paul II, which says of the ordination of women that it is 'preventing reconciliation between us even where there is otherwise progress towards agreement'. Yet seven years later, and two years after the first women were ordained in the Church of England, another Common Declaration was signed, this time by George Carey and John Paul II, with talk of full visible unity.

As women take on more substantial roles within the Anglican Communion, there are going to be more encounters between them and officials in Rome. For example, the members of ARCIC 3, the latest phase of dialogue of the Anglican–Roman Catholic Commission, which began in May 2011, include Bishop Linda Nicholls, suffragan Bishop of Trent-Durham, Toronto.

Archbishop Sir David Moxon, co-chairman of ARCIC 3, former director of the Anglican Centre in Rome and former Archbishop of New Zealand, said that: 'The Vatican's response [to Bishop Nicholls' appointment] was that the Anglican Communion must choose its own people. It is not an obstacle to dialogue.'[15]

As director of the Anglican Centre, Moxon was also the Archbishop of Canterbury's personal representative to the Holy See, a post which confirms the importance of ecumenical relations to Anglicans. This was re-emphasized by the appointment of Anglican primates – first Moxon, and subsequently his successor, Archbishop Bernard Ntahoturi of Burundi – to the post.

Moxon also witnessed Justin Welby's visit to Rome when he brought two women priests with him during his visit to Pope Francis, 'not to make a point,' said Moxon, 'but because of the posts they hold. They wore collars and were treated with great courtesy.'

There have certainly been occasions when ordained Anglican women have been on the altar in Rome with Catholic priests: I myself witnessed this in 2006 when Cardinal Cormac Murphy-O'Connor presided over vespers at his titular church of Santa Maria Sopra Minerva during the Archbishop of Canterbury's visit to Rome. The same occurred in October 2016 when Justin Welby visited Rome, accompanied by his chaplain, the Revd Julia Pickles, who was on the altar for vespers at San Gregorio al Cielo with Pope Francis and again the following day, when Secretary of State Cardinal Pietro Parolin presided at vespers at St Francis Xavier Oratory.

Yet Murphy-O'Connor maintains that the issue of women's ordination has made unity impossible. 'There is no doubt that it has made it difficult to have Communion with the Anglicans,' he said.[16]

Sometimes it is lower-rank officials rather the pope and his most senior colleagues who have the strongest objections to women in orders. According to one individual engaged closely in ecumenism in Rome, the female Bishop of Indianapolis, Cate Waynick, attempted to visit the Vatican with other members of the governing body of the Anglican Centre, the Rome base of the Anglican Communion, and was stopped by guards. A phone call to a Curial official led to them being told she could enter in her capacity as a governor but the situation would be different if she were there in her capacity as a woman bishop.[17]

The difficulty is not just with women. Well before women's ordination was ever considered, the Catholic Church dismissed Anglican orders. *Apostolicae Curae*, Leo XIII's papal bull of 1896, declared them null and void. Yet as Murphy-O'Connor, himself a former chairman of ARCIC, explains, there is something about Anglicanism that Rome does recognize. 'In some ways I thought at one time that we would be able to recognize Anglican orders and then there would have been inter-Communion,' he said. 'We have so many aspects of our faith that are the same: we believe in the Bible, apostolic succession. So when an Anglican priest is ordained we can't say he is nothing.'[18]

So there is some kind of recognition of Anglican orders on the part of Rome, even though *Apostolicae Curae* is unambiguous. The standing of priests is noted, as is the authority of Anglican hierarchs. Rowan Williams would like to see developments in thinking on this: 'With Vatican II and Paul VI there was a feeling that we are not in the outer darkness. There is something going on in the Church of England which is more like than unlike the Catholic Church. But this needs in some way to be acknowledged.'[19]

The sticking point of women priests highlights just how important the Church of England is for Rome. Other Protestant denominations have ordained women, such as the Episcopal Church in the United States, and it did not bother Rome in the same way that it did when the Church of England did so for the first time in 1994. The reason why it cared so much owes much to history and to Britain's standing in the world. As Cardinal Murphy-O'Connor explained:

> Britain has major significance for Rome. There is our history, the language, the Anglican Communion, the monarchy. They regard us in a particular way. The popes coming here, first John Paul and later Benedict, given that the Church had been outlawed – it had major significance. It was seen as healing the wounds. The Church of England really matters. Rome saw the English as soft Protestants, particularly since Newman. They saw the importance of the Archbishop of Canterbury, although sometimes they wish he was a bit more like a pope.[20]

As Mark Langham pointed out, the path to unity is not as simple as Anglicans sometimes might think. 'The Anglicans think Rome will come round on women's ordination and where they go Rome will follow. But it really did knock the wind out of ecumenism's sails,' he said. 'It pulled the rug from under the business of unity, removing it effectively as a goal.'[21]

What Anglicans often forget is that Rome does not discuss ecumenical relations only with the Church of England and the Anglican Communion. It has a bond with other Churches too, such as the Orthodox, which Pope Francis is working hard to improve, and they strongly oppose women's ordination. Today, however much unity with the Church of England might in theory remain the aim, it is not so apparent in the public statements made by the pope's representatives. A shift has occurred in the relationship. Take, for instance, the comments made about the consequences of the ordination of women by Cardinal Walter Kasper, the then president of the Pontifical Council for Promoting Christian Unity at the Lambeth Conference in 2008. 'Dialogue could still lead to good results but would no longer be sustained by the dynamism which arises from the realistic possibility of unity,' he said.[22] Cardinal Kurt Koch, Kasper's successor, has also indicated that dialogue can no longer concern itself with the goal of full visible unity but with how two communities, one that ordains women, one that does not, can relate to each other.[23]

Despite substantial ARCIC discussions on priesthood and authority, the gulf between the two Churches remains: for the Church of England it is about who you ordain; Rome's Congregation for the Doctrine of the Faith says it is bound up with what ordination is. Once women were ordained, it was quite apparent that the Church of England focused on the person in a very different way from Rome.

And yet there is evidence that efforts are being made to develop a relationship regardless of this vast obstacle. The antagonism towards Rome from Protestants in Britain has largely gone. The kind of opposition to the 1982 papal visit expressed by people like Ian Paisley and Scottish anti-Papist

Presbyterians now seems unthinkable. While the relationship today is cordial, one senses that Rome does not accept it is about equals, nor is it about institutions that fully understand one another.

'Rome doesn't understand the Anglicans,' said Langham. 'There is a very big misconception because they don't get Anglican ecclesiology. When Rowan Williams went out to Rome and addressed the cardinals and talked about the need to look at our Eucharistic origins, their jaws dropped. What the Vatican does not get is that the Anglican Communion was founded to have a very broad range of positions. That is what has bedevilled ARCIC. You can always make agreements with some but can you carry all the Anglican Communion? Rome finds that very difficult to get its head round.'[24]

Nor could the Church of England be blamed for feeling disgruntled about its treatment sometimes by Rome and the varying messages that emerge from it. On the one hand John Paul II's 1995 encyclical, *Ut Unum Sint*, confirmed the importance of unity, stating: 'The call for Christian unity made by the Second Vatican Ecumenical Council with such impassioned commitment is finding an ever greater echo in the hearts of believers'. The importance of this was stressed in the run-up to the Millennium. But on the other hand it was followed in 2000 by *Dominus Iesus*, one of the most controversial documents of his pontificate. The declaration from the Congregation of the Doctrine of the Faith was written by its prefect Cardinal Joseph Ratzinger, later Benedict XVI, and stated that certain Churches were not in fact Churches but ecclesial communities, and were in imperfect communion with the Catholic Church. It did suggest that Anglicanism could be a possible exception to this but it nevertheless deeply upset many members of that Church.[25] [26]

Even a senior Catholic cleric with as sure a touch as Basil Hume was capable of making surprising judgments in his relations with the Church of England. As Cardinal Archbishop of Westminster, Basil Hume became one of the most popular clerics in Britain but also managed to successfully negotiate his way around Whitehall, evidenced in his dealing with the government over the case of the Guildford Four. His acute antennae did not stretch as far as the sensitivities of dealing with the Church of England, though. Cardinal Cormac Murphy-O'Connor recollects that when Cardinal Hume visited Anglican monasteries and cathedrals, 'he would be thinking, "shouldn't this be ours?" His heart wasn't entirely in it really'.[27]

In 1993, Basil Hume celebrated his seventieth birthday and to mark the occasion, he was interviewed by the then editor of *The Tablet*, John Wilkins. The interview coincided with the decision of the Church of England to ordain women to the priesthood. Hume had arranged with Rome to welcome Anglican priests into the Catholic fold who in all conscience could not accept the reform.

To Hume, the crossing of the Tiber by the disaffected Anglicans was a welcome, even providential moment. He had been encouraged by both Graham Leonard, Anglican Bishop of London, who was to 'pope' himself, and by John Paul II, who told him to be generous. Clergy were fast-tracked for ordination, sometimes becoming Catholic priests after just a few weeks' preparation.

'This could be a big moment of grace,' Hume told *The Tablet*. 'It could be the conversion of England for which we have prayed all these years.'[28]

Cormac Murphy-O'Connor was so horrified at this use of language that he recalled telephoning Basil Hume immediately to check that he had not been misquoted. Hume, he remembered, was mystified by Murphy-O'Connor's alarm. 'Yes, I said it, what do you mean?,' he asked. Basil Hume, Murphy-O'Connor went on to explain, was like his own father: 'he thought Catholics had the truth, and that Protestants were in the wrong.'[29]

To other more ecumenical Catholic churchmen, the Hume view was distinctly out of date by 1993. After Vatican II, the more usual approach was to no longer claim a monopoly on truth and rather than pray for the conversion of England, the emphasis was on praying for the conversion of one's own heart. That said, even the most ecumenically minded Catholics almost unconsciously retain a belief in the Catholic Church being number one in the Christian league of Churches, as it were. According to Rowan Williams, Anglicans have noted that even the ecumenical Cormac Murphy-O'Connor's memoir is titled *English Spring*, which they perceive to be an allusion to John Henry Newman's famous 'Second Spring' sermon of 13 July 1852, following the restoration of the Catholic hierarchy two years earlier when he said: 'The English Church was, and the English Church was not, and the English Church is once again.'[30] [31]

Yet throughout the past three decades there has been clear recognition by Rome of the links with Canterbury, and signs that Rome sees a grace-giving priesthood in the Church of England. Above all there is some recognition of authority. The gifts given to Anglicans – the ring to Michael Ramsey, a pectoral cross to Rowan Williams, the blessing that Pope Francis asked Justin Welby to bestow on him when they first met – suggests that Rome believes these men are doing a whole lot more than play-acting. And in 2003 Cardinal Kasper said that the Archbishop of Canterbury is not considered a layman in the presence of the pope. So while ordination is still not officially recognized, it seems episcopal leadership is, in one-to-one encounters.

This does not mean that Rome fully understands the Church of England. Despite the talk and the friendships there is sometimes a lack of knowledge of the other, particularly in the area of authority. There is some evidence that Rome overestimates the authority of the Archbishop of Canterbury, as if he were some kind of Anglican pope. Mark Langham recalls that at the Lambeth Conference of 2008, Catholic delegates were amazed that Rowan Williams didn't simply direct people. 'They think the Archbishop of Canterbury should just tell people what to do,' said Langham.[32]

Rowan Williams' ten years in office as Archbishop of Canterbury and head of the Anglican Communion overlapped with the end of John Paul II's reign as well as most of Benedict XVI's papacy. It was a difficult time to be primate, given the issues of homosexual priesthood and the Gene Robinson affair, when the openly homosexual American cleric was elected bishop in the Episcopal Church in the United States of America, a member church of the Anglican Communion. Williams discussed at the 2003 meeting with John Paul II the issue of primacy – he must have felt a tad envious of papal authority at times. Later he told me that he wasn't sure how much John Paul took in, given his chronic health problems at this time.

> In Rome I was treated as if I were a bishop, quite visibly and extravagantly. It would happen elsewhere too. In Monte Cassino [the Benedictine monastery] I was asked to give the pontifical blessing and it really is very pontifical. My sense is that most people in the Vatican world acknowledge at some level that there is a very deep anomaly here but it is not being sorted out very well.
>
> I think they see the Archbishopric of Canterbury as the patriarchate. Sometimes [in meetings with Vatican officials] I would have to explain our canon law, why I could not interfere in processes, that I could not get my own way but that I have an historic role in advising. For them, having us side by side was very neat but I had to explain I was not the ecumenical patriarch.

Williams recalled that Cardinal Walter Kasper, when he was in charge of the Pontifical Council for Promoting Christian Unity, had once been asked who did the pope think the Archbishop of Canterbury was. 'He said that when the Pope sent him to see me, he sent him with a pectoral cross, not a book token, so that gives some idea of what he thinks. The attitude in Rome was very clear over the gay issue. Why don't you just excommunicate him [Gene Robinson], they would think. But as Archbishop of Canterbury I can't just invade the Falklands, as it were.'[33]

Authority certainly bedevilled the discussions of ARCIC. Cormac Murphy-O'Connor, who chaired ARCIC for sixteen years, has described how Anglicans were asked if they had any means by which decisions could be reached that would bind all the Churches of the Anglican Communion, and how could Anglicans look for an answer when new questions arise that require a united response. 'Anglicans hope', wrote Murphy-O'Connor, 'with each succeeding Archbishop of Canterbury that he'll be the one who will lead them out of captivity and heal its divisions over doctrinal questions. But I don't think anyone can.'[34]

There is little evidence that Anglicans, used to a broad Church, yearn for this in the way he suggests, although its divisions over issues such as homosexuality or women bishops must at times be exhausting. What is clear is that for all the discussions about authority and doctrine, the success of relations between the Church of England and the Catholic Church depends to a great extent on personal relations – between the two men at the top.

Rowan Williams and Benedict XVI were both highly intellectual individuals and excellent linguists, able to converse together in several languages. Cormac Murphy-O'Connor, as Archbishop of Westminster and therefore considered in this country as the leader of the Catholics of England and Wales, regularly witnessed the encounters between the two because tradition has it that the Archbishop of Westminster accompanies the Archbishop of Canterbury on his visits to Rome.

'Personal relationships between Anglican leaders and the popes are vitally important. Robert Runcie, Rowan Williams and Justin Welby have been key in developing relations with the Church of England,' said the cardinal. 'This was particularly the case with Rowan and Pope Benedict. They got on well, they were both thinkers, both highly respected theologians.'[35]

Rowan Williams himself agrees that the relationship between pope and primate matters profoundly. 'There is an expectation now of a double act,' he said. 'When Archbishop Fisher first went to Rome it was extraordinary and with Michael Ramsey and Paul VI it felt like they were on the same page, there was the same sense of a Catholic identity. I would call that a golden age of communion with Rome, symbolized by the giving of the ring. Robert Runcie and John Paul II had something of that too but they were very different personalities.

'I would not compare my meetings with Benedict with those between Ramsey and Paul VI for a moment, but we did speak each other's language. There were long conversations over meals about theology. Sometimes we spoke in English, French and German. I felt I knew Benedict XVI well enough that there was trust there, rather than tanks on the lawn [over the Ordinariate]. Over the years we had a warm relationship. There was an ease of communication.'[36]

This was apparent in the Common Declaration published after Rowan Williams' visit to Rome in 2006 which spoke of 'a real but incomplete communion' being rediscovered and affirmed and the discovery of 'significant elements of shared faith'. However, new developments (presumably issues like female priesthood and episcopacy and homosexuality) are noted as presenting serious obstacles for ecumenism. For the first time there was reference to 'the important issues involved in the emerging ecclesiological and ethical questions between us' – in other words issues of human sexuality. There was a significant development, though, indicating a way forward; the two leaders wanted to look beyond the basic difficulties to issues of common concern and to witness to the world, something that has continued in the latest ecumenical partnership between Francis and Justin Welby.[37]

Welby has described his relationship with Pope Francis as 'very personal'. 'At every conversation I seek his advice on something – because he's wise and very experienced. He has a breadth of view I can't get close to, and a depth of thinking, a spirituality which is profoundly moving – so I will sometimes seek his advice in personal terms – and sometimes in the things that we do.'[38]

Meanwhile, as Cardinal Vincent Nichols points out, others both in Rome and Lambeth are working away on the issues affecting ecumenism. 'The personal relationship [between pope and primate] is important as a signal,' he said. 'It is a reassurance to people. But the ongoing relationship is with the Pontifical Council for Promoting Christian Unity: that is where the work goes on.'[39]

The work is not entirely about meetings between learned clerics. Ecumenical relationships develop through gestures and symbols both at the top and at the bottom. Bishop Christopher Hill has recalled that Rowan Williams' visits to Rome had an almost 'ad limina' feel to them, as he not only visited the pope but also the major dicasteries or departments of the Vatican, just as Catholic bishops of different countries do when they make their ad limina visits to Rome. The Catholic bishops' visits emphasize the pilgrimage origins of the ad limina, something which was apparent in Rowan Williams' visits too. This sense of pilgrimage is not only about Rome's importance as an historical site for Christianity, with St Peter's tomb believed to be beneath the site of the basilica named for him. It is about pilgrimage to Christianity's contemporary HQ.[40]

The importance of Rome as part of the Christian heritage of the Church of England for not only the hierarchy but all Anglicans is also increasingly evident, given the numbers of pilgrims who visit Rome from Anglican parishes. Yet this too can be a problem, according to Mark Langham, with people's hopes about pilgrimage getting caught up in theological difficulties.

The Diocese of Rome used to allow the Church of England to celebrate communion for pilgrims in Catholic churches but it has stopped doing so. Archbishop Sir David Moxon, who as director of the Anglican Centre in Rome was responsible for welcoming many pilgrims from Britain to Rome, does not believe that Communion is such a difficult problem as this suggests. 'Pilgrims who come to Rome have a great interest in and understanding of the connection with the papacy. That is what draws them. As to Communion, I say to them that they don't need to think they are out of Communion. They can make a spiritual Communion. What is important is that we have 80 per cent of our core doctrines in common.'[41]

There is also growing interest among Anglicans in the rituals and practices of Roman Catholicism and a sense of their connectedness with them despite the break with Rome 500 years ago. Typical of this is praying at shrines, something lost when so many tombs and relics were destroyed in the sixteenth century, but is now being revived by many Anglican cathedrals. At St Alban's, for example, the old shrine of St Alban has become a major focus for visitors, now that a part of his body, brought back from abroad, is again housed there in a reliquary. And at Ely, a contemporary statue of the Virgin Mary has been placed in the Lady Chapel. Whether it is a return to an older form of faith, or a tourist endeavour encouraged by clergy who have realized candles can be a source of revenue, these holy places today often remind the English of their Catholic roots.

Discoveries are being made by both sides in this religious relationship, for the extent to which the Anglican tradition owes so much to Rome was little known until recently by the Vatican. As noted above, in 2010, Benedict XVI and Rowan Williams knelt together in Westminster Abbey at the tomb of Edward the Confessor. Their common devotion was the climax of the Anglican service of evensong, a liturgy that not only did Benedict XVI love so much that the Abbey sent him a collection of its choir's performances on CD, but which also enthralled his Vatican colleagues. Most of them had been entirely unaware of the Anglican liturgical and musical heritage.

There was similar astonishment in March 2012, during Rowan Williams' last visit to Rome when he requested that he pray before the Blessed Sacrament with the pope. Many Vatican officials assume that all Anglicans do not believe in the Real Presence. But there is poignancy in all these encounters between the two denominations: that the relationship is expressed through communal experience which highlights similarities but at the same time shows how impaired it is.

Benedict XVI's speech at Lambeth Palace to the Catholic and Anglican bishops during his 2010 visit to the UK spoke of both 'the difficulties that the ecumenical path has encountered and continues to encounter' and also the deep friendship and remarkable progress of ecumenism. During the same visit, the Catholic and Anglican bishops prayed the Lord's Prayer together. There was a pause, recalled Mark Langham, and it was Pope Benedict who added 'for thine is the kingdom, the power and the glory' – the words that end the Anglican but not the Catholic version.[42]

Anglicans have also grappled with the matter of the person of the pope over the years, moving from hostility to developing an understanding of him being the head of the mother Church. Robert Runcie indicated that the very nature of the Catholic Church's structure and the character of the man holding papal office caused problems for unity and primacy. During an interview with his biographer Humphrey Carpenter he suggested that Rome's inherent conservatism – something which Pope Francis, more than thirty years later, is trying to address – was problematic:

> If you are going to be a world evangelist, you can't really mind the shop. I think the people [John Paul II] has had to leave to mind the shop are very often Mediterranean male conservatives. But he goes along with them . . . But when you realize that these are the people who are laying down ethical standards for Polynesian women and so on, then you pause and think it can't be right. But I still stand by my view that you need a focus for the Christian community – and therefore an ecumenical primate. The present pope has never taken that seriously; his ecumenism is strong on rhetoric, but not very good on substantial steps.[43]

However, Robert Runcie did recognize the importance of the Petrine ministry, referring during vespers at San Gregorio al Celio in 1989 to

'Gregory's example of primacy for the sake of unity and mission, which we also see embodied in the ministry of his successor John Paul II, begins to find a place in Anglican thinking'.[44]

Rowan Williams, during his first visit to Rome as Archbishop of Canterbury in 2003, showed a similar line of thought, speaking of a possible 'sharing of the Primacy of love and service'. Meanwhile George Carey in 2002 during an interview on Vatican Radio, had recognized the pope as 'the spiritual leader of the whole of Christianity'.[45]

This approach reflects the landmark document 'The Gift of Authority', published by ARCIC in 1999, which concludes that it is right that there should be some recognition of the primacy of the Bishop of Rome over all Christian Churches. In other words, there is an authority figure in Christendom and that is the pope – something that was reflected in the comments of Robert Runcie after John Paul II's Assisi gathering in 1986 when he brought together religious leaders from around the world for the first World Day of Prayer for Peace. The archbishop commented that nobody else but the pope could have done it. It is a convening power that nobody else has. And yet, opposition to centralization is so deep in the Anglican DNA, that this always remains a neuralgic point.[46]

With full visible unity now so difficult, what else is there? Benedict XVI thought that the answer is Christian common ground when grappling with the world's problems. This was highlighted during Rowan Williams' visit to Rome in 2006 when he said that there was a need to seek common purpose, such as defending life from conception to natural death, the sanctity of marriage and the wellbeing of children in the family. The Common Declaration following that visit spoke of 'witness and service in which we can stand together'.[47] A similar appeal to all Christians to work together to proclaim faith to society was made during Pope Benedict's address in Westminster Abbey during his 2010 visit to the UK. This approach is now evident in the work of ARCIC 3, which decided in 2011 that its focus of discussions would be 'Church as Communion – Local and Universal' and 'How in Communion the Local and Universal Church Comes to Discern Right Ethical Teaching'.

The 2010 papal visit to Britain was markedly different to the previous one in 1982, which had been marred by the Falklands troubles, and fears of assassination. Concerns were raised prior to Benedict's visit about potential secular protest and a godless nation ignoring his arrival. In fact huge crowds turned out. The tension had moved from other faiths to those of no faith. Yet there was one major ecumenical difficulty caused by Benedict: his creation of the Anglican Ordinariate. The ecumenists at the first gathering of ARCIC 3, held eight months after the UK papal visit, officially noted the tensions created by the establishment of the Ordinariate, although they diplomatically urged attention to be focused on what the two Churches had in common.[48]

The Anglican Ordinariate is a canonical structure in the Catholic Church set up by the apostolic constitution *Anglicanorum Coetibus*, published by the Vatican on 4 November 2009 to enable groups of Anglicans to join the Catholic Church while retaining what was described as their 'liturgical and spiritual patrimony'. It was not very clear what Benedict XVI meant by this, but perhaps a simple way of analyzing the ordinariate would be to say that it enables Christians to remain cultural Anglicans while becoming ecclesiological Catholics. In other words, they accept the pope's authority while still attending evensong.

There was little indication that ordinary Church of England parishes were queuing up to join the Catholic Church. Instead the drive was coming from already disaffected organizations such as Continuing Anglicans, and to a lesser extent bodies within the Anglican Communion such as Forward in Faith. Their disgruntlement usually focused on threats to tradition, whether in liturgical matters or women's ordination.

The decision to set up ordinariates for Anglicans was announced simultaneously on 20 October 2009 in both Rome and London, where Vincent Nichols, who had been appointed as Archbishop of Westminster six months earlier, and Rowan Williams put on a display of unity. The reality, though, was that the Anglicans were irritated, feeling that Rome had ridden roughshod over them. Rome gave Williams barely any warning – in fact, just a week.

To Anglicans this seemed like discourtesy at best, if not arrogance – but not as any threat to the Church of England or wider Anglican Communion. Rather, it was poor judgement on the part of the ill-informed. 'I would say that there were a couple of people in high office who had so little knowledge of how the Anglican Communion works that they misunderstood the situation,' said Williams. 'I would have said, "don't hold your breath". I did not lose much sleep if any over the impact.'[49]

It was certainly an endeavour that mattered considerably to Pope Benedict. Twice in 2010, during the visit of the English bishops to Rome, and later in September when he addressed them again at the end of his visit to Britain, he urged them to be generous in implementing his personal initiative, the Anglican Ordinariate:

> I would ask you to be generous in implementing the provisions of the apostolic constitution *Anglicanorum Coetibus*, so as to assist those groups of Anglicans who wish to enter into full communion with the Catholic Church. I am convinced that, if given a warm and open-hearted welcome, such groups will be a blessing for the entire Church.[50]

Yet for all this, the Ordinariate has stubbornly refused to grow. It now seems a project left on the shore of the Benedictine pontificate, while the Catholic Church, its latest pope and the Church of England have moved on.

With Pope Francis and Archbishop Welby, that other desire of Benedict XVI – the sense of a common bond between the Catholic Church and the Church of England being forged in service to people of the wider world – is being continued, with work to help migrants and counter human trafficking. This was particularly evident during Archbishop Welby's visit to Rome in October 2016 when there was recognition of the obstacles to unity that still remain but also emphasis on common witness and service. Their Common Declaration said:

> The world must see us witnessing to this common faith in Jesus by acting together. We can, and must, work together to protect and preserve our common home: living, teaching and acting in ways that favour a speedy end to the environmental destruction that offends the Creator and degrades His creatures, and building individual and collective patterns of behaviour that foster a sustainable and integral development for the good of all. We can, and must, be united in a common cause to uphold and defend the dignity of all people. The human person is demeaned by personal and societal sin. In a culture of indifference, walls of estrangement isolate us from others, their struggles and their suffering, which also many of our brothers and sisters in Christ today endure. In a culture of waste, the lives of the most vulnerable in society are often marginalised and discarded. In a culture of hate we see unspeakable acts of violence, often justified by a distorted understanding of religious belief. Our Christian faith leads us to recognise the inestimable worth of every human life, and to honour it in acts of mercy by bringing education, healthcare, food, clean water and shelter and always seeking to resolve conflict and build peace. As disciples of Christ we hold human persons to be sacred, and as apostles of Christ we must be their advocates.[51]

Justin Welby himself represents a growing trend among Anglicans: a deep interest in Catholic spiritual traditions. He himself turns to a Catholic priest for spiritual direction. He has also spoken warmly of Pope Francis's 'deep humility and a consciousness of the complexity of things. He has Ignatian and Franciscan spirituality', suggesting that this shared interest helps overcome divisions.[52]

The commitment to common service and to common spirituality is certainly admirable. But is this too easy an option? Running a soup kitchen together might seem a much simpler option than dialogue over difficult theology. Issues such as the role of women, shared Communion and authority remain unresolved.

As Mark Langham puts it: 'De facto ecumenism is we stand together and that is very much an ecumenical impact – the forces ranged against us. We started ARCIC 3 largely because theology is difficult. It is about drilling down but we have to keep the theology going and we are in danger of falling short. With Francis and Justin, this is a new impulse to action – what's really difficult is doing the theology – and it is the Lord's will that we get back together.'[53]

What does this all mean for Britain's Catholics and Anglicans? On the one hand there is an easy-going relationship at the local level with regular contact, attending services as well as praying together during unity week, and jointly holding processions of witness on Good Friday. But there are also sizeable gaps between the two Churches still, ones that may yet take generations to bridge the divide. The biggest of all remains how Rome sees the role of women, given how popular women clergy are in the Church of England and that it has now ordained women bishops. Pope Francis has mentioned the need to engage women more in decision-making in his Church but this has led to barely any change, bar an announcement that a commission will examine whether the Catholic Church should have women deacons. During a press conference following his visit in October 2016 to Sweden to mark the quincentenary of the Reformation, he referred reporters back to Pope John Paul II's 1994 document stating that women could never join the priesthood. *Pontifex* – the bridge – on this issue he is not.[54] And yet, there is some movement: the issue is at least discussed in the open. John Paul wanted it not to be even mentioned.[55]

For Rome, dealing with the Church of England seems rather akin to dealing with a family relative with whom it once had such a bust-up that they did not speak for years. Over time, loathing, suspicion and estrangement on both sides have given way to renewed contact, even invitations to intimate gatherings. But the past is not entirely forgotten: it is as if the relations are invited round, but not to the extent that they can come and stay overnight and have supper.

Ecumenism does, however, play a significant role in the relationship between the United Kingdom and the Holy See. The British government recognizes this too: its ambassador to the Holy See has frequently hosted a dinner or reception for the Archbishop of Canterbury when he visits Rome, to which he has invited leading cardinals, and despatches are sent to London about any developments in relations between Rome and the Established Church. Those despatches will not be suggesting the dream of unity between Rome and Canterbury; we are a long way from the declaration made fifty years ago by Archbishop Michael Ramsey and Paul VI to aim for complete communion. Indeed, as discussed above, the obstacles have grown in the years since that landmark encounter. Yet the friendship is there, as is a shared, growing commitment to humanity. While Rome has difficulties with women, there is one woman for whom it has the highest regard and who has played a highly significant role in cementing the bonds between the United Kingdom and Rome: the queen. How she has done so, as head of state, Supreme Governor of the Church of England, and Christian believer, follows next.

Notes

1   *Britain and the Holy See – proceedings of the 2012 Rome Colloquium*, Rome: British Embassy to the Holy See, 2012, 39.

2 Interview of Lord (Rowan) Williams (RW) by Catherine Pepinster (CP), July 2015.

3 Ibid.

4 Newman, John Henry (1865), *Apologia Pro Vita Sua*, London: Penguin, para 339.

5 Ibid.

6 *Britain and the Holy See*, ibid, 31, and from Carpenter, Edward (1991), *Geoffrey Fisher*, Canterbury: Canterbury Press, 375.

7 Interview of Mgr Mark Langham (ML) by Catherine Pepinster (CP), October 2014.

8 Interview of RW by CP, ibid.

9 Etchingham, Julie (2016), 'Why unity matters – *The Tablet* Interview with Justin Welby', *The Tablet*, 15 October 2016, 4.

10 *Britain and the Holy See*, ibid, 33.

11 Described by Cardinal Cormac Murphy-O'Connor (CMO'C) in an interview by Catherine Pepinster (CP), February 2015.

12 Carpenter, Humphrey (1996), *Robert Runcie: The Reluctant Archbishop*, London: Hodder and Stoughton, ibid, 238–41.

13 Interview of RW by CP.

14 The Common Declaration (1989), between Pope John Paul II and the Archbishop of Canterbury Dr Robert Runcie, 2 October. Available online: http://www.anglicancommunion.org/media/105825/Common-Declaration-October-1989.pdf?year=1989

15 Interview of Archbishop Sir David Moxon (DM) by Catherine Pepinster (CP), October 2015.

16 Interview of CMO'C by CP.

17 Recalled by a source to Catherine Pepinster during the visit of Justin Welby to Rome, October 2016.

18 Ibid.

19 Interview of RW by CP.

20 Interview of CMO'C by CP.

21 Interview of ML by CP.

22 Kasper, Cardinal Walter (2008), Address at the Lambeth Conference, 30 July. http://www.vatican.va/roman_curia/pontifical_councils/chrstuni/angl-comm-docs/rc_pc_chrstuni_doc_20080730_kasper-lambeth_en.html

23 Koch, Cardinal Kurt (2011), speech at Centro Pro Unione, 15 December. www.prunione.it

24 Interview of ML by CP.

25 John Paul II (1995), *Ut Unum Sint* – On commitment to ecumenism, 25 May, Rome. http://w2.vatican.va/content/john-paul-ii/en/encyclicals/documents/hf_jp-ii_enc_25051995_ut-unum-sint.html

26 Congregation for the Doctrine of the Faith (2000), *Dominus Iesus* – On the unicity and salvific universality of Jesus Christ and his church, 6 August, Rome.

http://www.vatican.va/roman_curia/congregations/cfaith/documents/rc_con_
cfaith_doc_20000806_dominus-iesus_en.html

27 Murphy-O'Connor, ibid, 132.

28 Wilkins, John (1993), 'Basil Hume at 70', *The Tablet*, 27 February, 7.

29 Murphy-O'Connor, ibid, 132.

30 Comment made during interview of RW by CP.

31 Newman, John Henry (1852), 'Second Spring' sermon preached to the
First Provincial Synod of Westminster, 13 July, Oscott College, Birmingham.
https://legacy.fordham.edu/halsall/mod/newman-secondspring.asp

32 Interview of ML by CP, ibid.

33 Interview of RW by CP, ibid.

34 Murphy-O'Connor, ibid, 128.

35 Interview of CMO'C by CP, ibid.

36 Interview of RW by CP, ibid.

37 Common Declaration (2006) between Pope Benedict XVI and The Archbishop
of Canterbury His Grace Rowan Williams, 23 November, Rome. http://w2.
vatican.va/content/benedict-xvi/en/speeches/2006/november/documents/hf_ben-
xvi_spe_20061123_common-decl.html

38 Etchingham, ibid.

39 Interview of Cardinal Vincent Nichols (VN) by Catherine Pepinster (CP),
March 2015.

40 Hill, Christopher (2013), 'Canterbury Pilgrims to Rome: Symbolic Acts and
Common Declarations', *Britain and the Holy See*, ibid, 30.

41 Interview of DM by CP, ibid.

42 Recalled by ML in conversation with CP, ibid.

43 Carpenter (1996), ibid, 234.

44 Quoted by Mark Langham (2013), *Diplomacy and the Holy See*, ibid, 42.

45 Langham (2013), ibid, 42.

46 ARCIC (1999), *The Gift of Authority*. http://www.vatican.va/roman_curia/
pontifical_councils/chrstuni/documents/rc_pc_chrstuni_doc_12051999_gift-of-
autority_en.html

47 Common Declaration (2006), ibid.

48 Kerr, David (2011), 'As new round of Anglican-Catholic talks begin, some
question their purpose', Catholic News Agency, 17 May. http://www.
catholicnewsagency.com/news/as-new-round-of-anglican-catholic-talks-begin-
some-question-the-purpose/

49 Interview of RW by CP, ibid.

50 Pope Benedict XVI (2010), ad limina address to the English bishops, 1 February.
https://w2.vatican.va/content/benedict-xvi/en/speeches/2010/february/documents/
hf_ben-xvi_spe_20100201_bishops-england-wales.html

51 Common Declaration (2016) of His Holiness Pope Francis and His Grace
Justin Welby, Archbishop of Canterbury, 5 October, press.vatican.va/content/
salastampa/en/bollettino/pubblico/2016/10/05/161005g.pdf

52 Moore, Charles (2013), 'Interview with Justin Welby', *The Telegraph*, 12 July www.telegraph.co.uk/news/religion/10176190

53 Interview of ML by CP, ibid.

54 Manson, Jamie (2016), 'It's time to be honest about Pope Francis and women', *National Catholic Reporter,* http://ncronline.org/blogs/grace-margins/its-time-be-honest-about-pope-francis-and-women

55 Kirchgaessner, Stephanie (2016), 'Female priests banned for ever, says Pope', *The Guardian*, 2 November, 19.

8

'The last Christian monarch':

The queen and the papacy

The reigns of the two Elizabeths neatly bookend the relationship between Rome and Britain. One was excommunicated and ruled the nation in an era when some of the most notable of English martyrs – Ss Edmund Campion, Margaret Clitherow and Cuthbert Mayne – were executed for their Catholic faith. The other's long years as monarch have seen relations between the country and Rome become more cordial than they have ever been since the Reformation.

While Elizabeth II may not have the power and influence of her predecessor, this rapprochement has not occurred while history takes place without her. She has played a quiet but highly influential part in reconciling Rome and the UK, while never wavering from her own Anglican faith.

The coolness between Rome and Britain had started to thaw before Elizabeth II's accession: Edward VII visited Leo XIII in 1903 when the pope was effectively a prisoner in the Vatican as the Church and the recently unified kingdom of Italy fought over the papacy's standing. It was regarded as a kindly gesture of solidarity.[1]

The Queen's grandfather, George V, and her grandmother, Queen Mary, visited Pius XI in 1923 while Cardinal Eugenio Pacelli, later Pope Pius XII, attended the Silver Jubilee celebrations of George V as the official papal representative. But while these visits went on under the radar of public opinion, with caution on both sides, the encounters between Elizabeth II and the successors of St Peter have been very public events.

Longevity has played its part in the queen's fruitful relationship with Rome. As the longest-reigning monarch in Europe, she has encountered more popes than any other royal head of state: Pius XII in 1951 (just a year before her accession); John XXIII in 1961; John Paul II in 1980, 1982 (during his pastoral visit to Britain) and 2000; Benedict XVI in 2010 (during the state visit to Britain) and Francis in 2014.

Reading signs and symbols is a way of understanding the relationships of heads of state, be they monarchs or popes, and the clearest indication of

Elizabeth II's relationship with the papacy has been in her dress. The audiences are always formal but as the twentieth century gave way to the twenty-first, certain protocols changed. During her first visits to Rome, the queen wore full-length black gowns, with a sash, insignia, tiara and full-length mantilla. The clothes distinguished her from Catholic queens, who wear white when meeting the pope. There was a different approach in 1982 when she welcomed John Paul II to Buckingham Palace: she wore a simple day dress in blue on that occasion. Back in Rome, eighteen years later, she was again dressed in black, but this time a three-quarter-length day dress, with a black hat and a string of pearls. The state visit in 2010 saw her in a simple grey coat and hat; by 2014, such attire was deemed acceptable for the Anglican queen in Rome.

While the mood has become more relaxed over the years the purpose remains: the queen is welcomed to the Vatican, and visited in Britain, because she is head of state rather than head of the Church of England. These meetings, taking place after centuries of conflict, serve as signposts to improving relations and the bringing down of significant barriers.

As Rowan Williams, the former Archbishop of Canterbury, put it: 'The fact of her breaking the duck – she has done that by meeting so many popes. It is a way of saying whatever was the case in 1535, there is no longer rivalry between the crown and the papacy. Doing what she has done – head of state meeting head of state – shows that we really have moved on from the 16th century.'[2]

To outsiders, such talk may seem outlandish. But in Rome, what happened four or five hundred years ago still reverberates, and England's break with Rome is one of the deepest wounds the papacy ever suffered in Europe.

It is apparent from talking to Catholic officials both in Rome and in Britain that the regard with which the queen is held – and the regard is clearly apparent – is not only to do with the office she has held and for how long, but it is also a respect for her own profound religious faith. Her coins are marked FD – *Fidei Defensor*, Defender of the Faith – the title bestowed on Henry VIII for his opposition to the early Protestant Reformation, before his defection from Rome, and since used by all English monarchs. The queen is undoubtedly seen today as a staunch defender of Christianity, even if the original honour was given to a then Catholic monarch. As well as Defender of the Faith, she is the Supreme Governor of the Church of England, a largely ceremonial role, although she does appoint high-ranking bishops chosen by the Church of England's appointments system and commended by the Prime Minister.

The queen's Christian beliefs were apparent even before her reign. On her twenty-first birthday, 21 April 1947, during a tour of South Africa with her parents, she spoke in a radio broadcast from Cape Town of dedicating her life to the service of the Commonwealth:

If we all go forward together with an unwavering faith, a high courage, and a quiet heart, we shall be able to make of this ancient commonwealth, which we all love so dearly, an even grander thing – more free, more prosperous, more happy and a more powerful influence for good in the world – than it has been in the greatest days of our forefathers . . .

I declare before you all that my whole life, whether it be long or short, shall be devoted to your service and the service of our great imperial family to which we all belong.

But I shall not have strength to carry out this resolution alone unless you join in it with me, as I now invite you to do: I know that your support will be unfailingly given. God help me to make good my vow, and God bless all of you who are willing to share in it.[3]

The speech conveyed learning, a sense of history, a commitment to service and religious faith, and it came from the pen of a Catholic, Dermot Morrah. Biographers of the queen have long assumed that it was written by Sir Alan 'Tommy' Lascelles, King George VI's private secretary, but Morrah was revealed as the author by his grandson, the columnist Tom Utley. Morrah was a gifted writer and intellectual who had been in his time a fellow of All Souls, a *Times* leader-writer and a speechwriter for George VI. After serving the king and queen during the war years, they asked him to take on the crucial task of writing the words that would set the tone for their daughter's future.[4][5][6] The prose, with its sacred vow, may well be explained by Morrah's own faith. Indeed, the queen's biographer, Ben Pimlott, who mistakenly thought Lascelles had written it, described it as 'a nun-like promise'.[7]

Six years later, in June 1953, Elizabeth was crowned in a ceremony that combined formal, public ritual and private, mystical moments. Once more a Catholic – this time the sixteenth Duke of Norfolk, in his role as Earl Marshal – played a notable part. Bernard Fitzalan-Howard went on to also organize the state funeral of Winston Churchill and the investiture of the Prince of Wales.

The Earl Marshal is a senior figure in the Royal Household, taking precedence over all other peers apart from royal dukes, and is responsible for the funeral of the monarch, the accession and coronation of the next one, and other major state ceremonies. It became an hereditary title in 1672 when Henry Howard was appointed to the position. In 1677 he succeeded to the dukedom of Norfolk and the title has descended to successive dukes ever since.[8]

It is a curiosity that the role of Earl Marshal and premier peer should be held by a Catholic layman. This divided inheritance of the Norfolks was described by John Martin Robinson, personal librarian to the 17th Duke of Norfolk, as 'in the middle of things, yet shut out'.[9]

The coronation was a combination of personal drama, almost sacrifice, and a solemn state occasion. It was above all a religious rite with biblical roots and it can be argued that it was almost akin to an ordination: vows were made to serve God and the nation unto death in a life of duty and service.

Nigel Baker, the British ambassador to the Holy See, said that the coronation had a profound impact on how the queen is perceived in Rome: 'While people in Rome are aware of her role as Supreme Governor of the Church of England, it is her sacral role that also matters: they are well aware of the vows she took at the coronation.'[10]

Every aspect of the coronation service in Westminster Abbey emphasized its sacral and indeed sacrificial nature, from the moment it began at the Great West Door. Bishops and archbishops greeted Elizabeth's arrival; the procession moved up the aisle as the choir sang Psalm 122, 'I was glad'; the queen stopped at the Chair of Estate to pray; a bible, paten and chalice carried by the bishops were then placed on the altar.

Readings from the psalms, the epistle of St Peter, and the Gospel of Matthew were then given, followed by the anointing. This part of the ceremony was deemed so sacred a religious ritual that the queen was dressed in a special shift that covered the coronation gown and it was hidden from view by a silk canopy. While the words of the coronation oath, in which Elizabeth pledged to mete out law and justice with mercy, also included upholding Protestantism in the United Kingdom and protecting the Church of England and preserving its bishops and clergy, the religious sentiments expressed elsewhere during the service and its high liturgical practice would all have been very familiar to Rome. The creed was sung, with its commitment to belief in one holy, catholic and apostolic Church. It was then followed by the English translation of the great hymn to the Holy Spirit – known to every Catholic who has been confirmed or ordained – *Veni Creator Spiritus*.[11]

Archbishop of Canterbury Geoffrey Fisher prayed that 'she may so wisely govern, that in her time thy Church may be in safety, and Christian devotion may continue in peace'.[12]

The coronation service, then, set the tone for what was to follow – if not for the entire country, given its growing secularism while retaining an established-Church, but for the queen herself. Her Christian faith has underpinned her years of service. As one official of the Holy See put it: 'In Rome they recognize her faith is strong and they like that. Her constitutional role is seen as important too, that is a key reference point for Rome.'[13]

That Britain's queen is unmistakeably a Christian monarch has been apparent throughout her reign, with her public life punctuated by the Christian calendar: there are always news reports of her attending Christmas service at Sandringham; the distribution of Maundy money in Holy Week; Easter at Windsor; commemoration of the war dead during November, the month of All Souls; and the recording of her Christmas Day message during Advent. She leads the nation in church services at its most notable moments, from the births, marriages and deaths of the members of her family to services of thanksgiving for the end of wars and their anniversaries, and the funerals of notable politicians such as Winston Churchill and Margaret Thatcher.

But it is in her Christmas Day messages that her beliefs are most overtly expressed and increasingly so, almost as if her role as a Christian leader has grown in proportion to the decline in active membership of the Church of which she is head. In her broadcast for Christmas 2000 she said:

To many of us our beliefs are of fundamental importance. For me the teachings of Christ and my own personal accountability before God provide a framework in which I try to lead my life. I, like so many of you, have drawn great comfort in difficult times from Christ's words and example.[14]

Then, in her Christmas 2014 broadcast, she said:

For me, the life of Jesus Christ, the Prince of Peace, whose birth we celebrate today, is an inspiration and an anchor in my life. A role model of reconciliation and forgiveness, he stretched out his hands in love, acceptance and healing. Christ's example has taught me to seek to respect and value all people of whatever faith or none.[15]

Those who know her well quip that she is not a high Anglican, nor even low church, but *short* church: in other words, she has a preference for short sermons. Cardinal Cormac Murphy-O'Connor recalls that he was asked to keep it brief when he was invited to preach at Sandringham, although this preference may also be the view of Prince Philip as much as his wife. She rarely receives Communion: 'apparently it's usually just twice a year, Christmas and Easter,' said one friend.[16] [17]

While the queen's religious faith has remained constant, the make-up of faith in the United Kingdom has changed dramatically during her reign. In 1953, the Christian devotion in the United Kingdom that Archbishop Fisher alluded to in the coronation service meant, to all intents and purposes, Anglicanism. But in the years since, while the Church of England has remained established, other Christian denominations have waxed and waned, not least the Catholic Church, which with its one million Sunday Mass-goers has as many active churchgoing members today in England and Wales as the Church of England. The ecumenical movement, in part inspired by the Second Vatican Council, has encouraged Christians to come together at all levels, from theologians and clerics to local parish councils. Then there is the growth of other religions in Britain, including Islam, Hinduism and Sikhism, caused in part by migration from countries belonging to the Commonwealth, of which the queen is head.[18]

The queen's own view of this multi-faith nation, and her role in it at the head of the Church of England, was made clear during one of the first engagements of her Diamond Jubilee year. On 15 February 2012 she attended an event at Lambeth Palace where she met representatives of Christian Churches as well as those from the Bahai, Buddhist, Hindu, Jain,

Jewish, Muslim, Sikh and Zoroastrian faiths. During her speech she expressed her commitment to the Church of England as a sort of umbrella for others, talking about them having 'the assurance of the protection of the Church of England'. The head of that Church said:

> Here at Lambeth Palace we should remind ourselves of the significant position of the Church of England in our nation's life. The concept of our established Church is occasionally misunderstood and, I believe, commonly under-appreciated. Its role is not to defend Anglicanism to the exclusion of other religions. Instead, the Church has a duty to protect the free practice of all faiths in this country.
>
> It certainly provides an identity and spiritual dimension for its own many adherents. But also, gently and assuredly, the Church of England has created an environment for other faith communities and indeed people of no faith to live freely. Woven into the fabric of this country, the Church has helped to build a better society – more and more in active co-operation for the common good with those of other faiths.[19]

While the queen may have had considerable experience of reading speeches conveying other people's sentiments (the State Opening of Parliament the most obvious frequent example during her reign), it is highly unlikely that she would have been asked as head of the Church of England to express such views if she did not support them herself. Indeed her advisers indicated that day at Lambeth that she was very comfortable with them.

Such views about the place of faith in society and the cultural importance of Christianity certainly resonate with Rome. Just the day before the queen's speech at Lambeth, the then Conservative Party co-chair, Baroness Warsi, spoke at the Vatican in very similar terms, talking of the importance of different faiths to be mutually supportive of one another in a speech which was greatly admired.[20]

The queen's analysis of the role of the Church of England is understandably appealing for a monarch whose role includes embodying unity, but it is a very modern interpretation. For centuries, the Church of England not only had a privileged position in Britain but also retained a monopoly of religion. Roman Catholics had limited rights until the nineteenth century; for example, they were barred from fellowships at Oxford and Cambridge until the University Tests Act of 1871.

And while the improving relationship between Rome and Britain owes much to the role the queen has played in recent years, it is ironic that it is in matters involving the sovereign that discrimination against Catholics lingered for far longer than in other areas of life.

Succession to the British throne is still determined not only by legitimacy and descent but also by religion. Under the Act of Settlement of 1701, brought in to secure the English and Irish thrones, succession is restricted to the descendants of Electress Sophia of Hanover – and only to her Protestant descendants in communion with the Church of England. Sophia's line was the most junior of the House of Stuart, but the Act's purpose was to exclude all Roman Catholics, and all other lines were Roman Catholic. The Act effectively barred anyone who becomes a Roman Catholic, or who marries one, from the line of succession, with the words: '[E]very Person [who] shall professe the Popish Religion or marry a Papist should be excluded [. . .] to inherit [. . .] the Crown [. . .] of this Realm [. . .].'[21]

Two royal marriages in recent times highlighted very different responses to the restrictions. In 1978, Prince Michael of Kent, grandson of George V, and a cousin of the queen, married the Catholic Baroness Marie-Christine von Reibnitz, thereby forfeiting his place in the line of succession. Thirty years later, in 2008, Peter Phillips, son of the Princess Royal and grandson of the queen, married Autumn Kelly, a Canadian raised in the French-speaking, largely Catholic province of Quebec. That she was a Roman Catholic herself jeopardized Phillips' place in the line of succession. But on this occasion, the royal family member did not renounce his right for love. Miss Kelly chose to renounce her religion, and became a member of the Church of England before her marriage.[22] Earlier that year the former Conservative Cabinet minister John Gummer, who had himself converted to Catholicism fifteen years earlier, had tried to overturn the restrictive legislation regarding Catholics marrying into the royal family. On this occasion he complained: 'It is unacceptable that the part of the Christian Church that has more adherents than any other should be discriminated against in this way.'

John Gummer's intervention was unusual, for many Catholics have declined to speak openly about the issue, perhaps having an historic sense that it was important not to seem to be disloyal to the Crown, and that it was wiser to keep heads down. Charles Moore was one such Catholic to maintain support for the Act of Settlement. During his editorship of the *Daily Telegraph* between 1995 and 2003, the paper consistently opposed repeal of the Act, on the grounds that it would pave the way for a split between the monarch and the Church of England and would lead to disestablishment. But other supporters of the status quo hinted in their arguments at the age-old suspicion of Catholics and their divided loyalties, as if being loyal to the pope would compromise their allegiance to the United Kingdom and the Crown. This was exactly what made many Catholics fret about speaking out. In a *Spectator* article in 2003, Adrian Hilton warned that it would be 'intolerable to have, as the sovereign of a Protestant and free country, one who owes any allegiance to the head of any other state'.[23]

But reform was coming. Two years after Peter and Autumn Phillips married, Prime Minister Gordon Brown announced that he was committed to addressing what he called an 'anomaly' that bans Catholics from marrying into the royal family. The route to reform involved unlikely allies to this Catholic cause: Brown, son of a Presbyterian minister, agreed it was an injustice, speaking out ahead of a debate on a private member's bill promoted by Evan Harris, a Liberal Democrat MP who was usually a stern secular opponent of many of the Catholic Church's positions on issues such as assisted dying. Brown's position was diametrically opposite to that of Tony Blair – married to a Catholic and a regular Mass attender while in office – who had declined to overturn the law.[24]

The coalition government, elected in 2010, shared Brown's enthusiasm for change. Under the terms of the Perth Agreement of 2011, it was announced that the rules on both primogeniture and marrying Catholics were being changed. The statement said that all sixteen Commonwealth countries, of which the queen was head, had agreed to change the law and it made it clear that the situation was iniquitous:

> All countries wish to see change in two areas. First, they wish to end the system of male preference primogeniture under which a younger son can displace an elder daughter in the line of succession. Second, they wish to remove the legal provision that anyone who marries a Roman Catholic shall be ineligible to succeed to the Crown. There are no other restrictions in the rules about the religion of the spouse of a person in the line of succession and the Prime Ministers felt that this unique barrier could no longer be justified. The Prime Ministers have agreed that they will each work within their respective administrations to bring forward the necessary measures to enable all the realms to give effect to these changes simultaneously.[25]

While the Perth Agreement, which came into law as the Succession to the Crown Act 2013, restored those members of the royal family to the line of succession who had been forcibly moved upon their marriage to a Catholic, it did not change the requirement under the Act of Settlement that the monarch must be a Protestant. Given that the British sovereign is also in law the head of the Church of England, this seems an intractable problem, unless that role is abolished.

Meanwhile the queen's family ties to Catholicism have become stronger over the years with some of them even treading the path to Rome themselves. Fourteen years after Prince Michael of Kent married a Catholic, his sister-in-law, the Duchess of Kent, became the first royal convert to the Catholic Church in 1994, when she was received by Cardinal Basil Hume, after the queen had sanctioned the conversion. The Duchess's elder son, the Earl of St Andrews, married the Catholic academic Sylvana Tomaselli, while her other son, Lord Nicholas Windsor, was also received into the Catholic Church. But Lord Nicholas Windsor was a very different convert and the queen herself noted the distinction regarding Lord Nicholas' choice; when Benedict XVI visited Holyrood Palace, she asked that he be introduced to the pope because he was a Catholic who was also a 'blood Royal' – in other words, he was born royal rather than having married into the royal family.[26]

There is another, little-known family link between the queen and her family, and the Catholic Church. Through her mother she has Stuart blood, thus linking her to the 'Old Pretender', the son of deposed James II, and sometimes called James III. After a life in exile he died in Rome where Pope Clement XIII gave him a state funeral. His tomb and that of his son, Henry Benedict, Duke of York, who later became a cardinal, was designed by Canova and can still be seen in St Peter's Basilica. In the 1940s, the then Queen Elizabeth, later the Queen Mother, paid for the restoration of the tomb, and in January 2016 her daughter approved a wreath to be placed on the tomb to mark the 250th anniversary of the Old Pretender's death.

Another sign of the royal family's warming relations regarding the Catholic Church is its participation in Catholic services. Thirty years ago, when it was suggested that the Prince and Princess of Wales should not only meet the pope but publicly attend Mass at St Peter's during a trip to Rome, the idea was vetoed by Buckingham Palace just a fortnight before the visit. Twenty years later, Prince Charles attended vespers in Westminster Cathedral in April 2005 to mark the death of that same pope, John Paul II, accompanied by Camilla Parker Bowles. Days later, he was in Rome to represent the queen at the funeral Mass of John Paul, with his own wedding to Mrs Parker Bowles delayed so that he could do so. Then in 2014, Prince William represented the queen when he attended Mass in St John's Cathedral in Valetta to mark the fiftieth anniversary of Malta's independence.

But the queen's own presence at Catholic services is extremely rare, although she did become the first monarch in 400 years to attend a Catholic liturgy when she went to Westminster Cathedral for vespers to mark the Church's centenary in 1995. The choice of vespers suggested attendance at Mass itself by the monarch was not acceptable for some Anglicans who held such store by her coronation promise to uphold the Protestant religion. But just a couple of years earlier, she had set tradition aside to honour a friend: in 1993 she made a little-noticed trip to Brussels to attend the Requiem Mass for King Baudouin of the Belgians, sitting amid other European royals during the obsequys. There was no question of the queen receiving Holy Communion, however; that was still a step too far.[27]

Other changes in the institutions surrounding the queen suggest that there has been a rapprochement between her and the Catholic Church that affects life at home as well as in her immediate relations with the Vatican. In 1998, Lord Camoys, whose family is one of the oldest recusant families in England, was appointed Lord Chamberlain, the senior officer of the Royal Household who oversees those who support and advise the Sovereign. Lord Camoys, who served until 2000, was the first Catholic to hold the post since the Reformation. It was an appointment that took him by surprise, but not the queen. 'She doesn't distinguish in that way. As far as she is concerned, British Catholics are as much her subjects as anyone else,' he said.[28]

Lord Camoys is a Privy Councillor, a member of one of the most ancient organizations of the United Kingdom, originally formed to advise the monarch on important matters of state. The council today has over 500 members, mostly made up of politicians and retired politicians, particularly those who have served in government. Members of the royal family, the archbishops of Canterbury and York, and leading members of the judiciary, are all members. Its monthly meetings are usually only attended by a few of the lifelong members and consist mostly of seeking the queen's formal approval of orders approved by ministers, but it also acts as court of appeal for overseas territories and Crown dependencies, and is concerned with the work of 900 chartered bodies.

More than two dozen of its members are Catholics, including the Secretary-General of the British Commonwealth, Baroness Patricia Scotland, the current Scottish Lord High Advocate, Dame Elish Angiolini, and various retired politicians including Des Browne, Ruth Kelly, Chris Patten and Shirley Williams. According to an early draft of a memoir by the former coalition and Liberal Democrat minister, David Laws, and reported by BBC Newsnight policy editor, Chris Cook, there is a particular order set by Buckingham Palace for ennoblement, reflecting an order of precedence and indeed, discrimination. Mr Laws recalled that when he was admitted as a member due to his appointment as chief secretary to the Treasury he was not surprised to be at the back of the group being admitted, because his was not a senior post. However, he was astonished that also at the back of the group being sworn in on 13 May 2010 was Liam Fox, who, as defence secretary, had a far more senior post in the Cabinet. David Laws said that out of curiosity the two men inquired how the order is drawn up. The official they asked told them that they were at the rear because of their Roman Catholicism.[29] Lord Camoys was taken aback by this account and said he doubted any such order exists.

It certainly sits uneasily alongside other notable gestures made by the queen over the years indicating what matters to her today is continuity, longevity and faith held in common rather than a focus on the divisions between Church and Crown. A personal fondness has also emerged, with her calling first Basil Hume and later Cormac Murphy-O'Connor 'my cardinal'. This respect was most apparent when she appointed Cardinal Hume to the Order of Merit in 1999, an honour in her personal gift, weeks before he died. One reason for it may have been that the queen felt he had dealt sensitively and discreetly with the marriage of Princess Michael of Kent and the Duchess of Kent's conversion to Catholicism. While the cardinal and the queen met infrequently, there was reciprocated warmth. As Hume's biographer, Anthony Howard put it: 'In a sense, no doubt, the presence of the one tended to reassure the other; in a changing world in which the politicians and officials change and move on all the time, a Cardinal Archbishop of twenty years standing becomes almost as much a symbol of continuity as the Crown itself.'[30]

The Order of Merit was offered after Basil Hume had announced that he was terminally ill with cancer, but there is no evidence to suggest the illness was the cause of the queen's offer of the honour.[31] But by the time he received it he was in hospital, and made the trip from there to Buckingham Palace. He spent half an hour with the queen, later telling his confessor that they had talked about 'death, suffering, the after-life – that sort of thing', although in his acceptance letter he had focused on more worldly but vital matters – the relationship between the Crown and Catholics. 'I am happy too', he wrote, 'to think that this honour will strengthen the ties between your Catholic subjects and Your Majesty'.[32]

While these personal encounters indicate that the connections between Britain and Rome have become more intimate over the years – and its importance was evident when the queen met Benedict XVI and spoke of the 'warm hospitality' with which family members had been received in Rome – the head of state's role is about far more than this: it is a crucial aspect of diplomacy and governance.[33]

This is evident in the addresses which are given when the queen and the pope meet, using the occasions to reinforce ties between the UK and the Holy See, and to identify common ground. John Paul II, for example, used his address to the queen when she visited the Vatican in 1980 to speak about Britain's ideals of freedom and democracy, growing connections between the Catholic Church and the Church of England, but also to warn of the importance of spiritual values being vital if peace and development were to thrive.[34]

The reasons for Britain's relationship with Rome were highlighted clearly in both the speech of the queen and of Pope Benedict as he began his visit to Britain at Holyrood Palace in Edinburgh in September 2010. Elizabeth II emphasized the role of the Holy See in peace and development issues and in addressing common problems such as poverty and climate change. And she also made it clear that Rome has played its part in Northern Ireland: 'In this country, we deeply appreciate the involvement of the Holy See in the dramatic improvement in the situation in Northern Ireland,'[35] a sentiment which might not have been uttered thirty years earlier during tensions over interventions by John Paul II.[36]

The importance of religion in national life and the risks it can pose to stability was also referred to by the queen:

Religion has always been a crucial element in national identity and historical self-consciousness. This has made the relationship between the different faiths a fundamental factor in the necessary cooperation within and between nation states. It is, therefore, vital to encourage a greater mutual, and respectful understanding. We know from experience that through committed dialogue, old suspicions can be transcended and a greater mutual trust established.[37]

These encounters between sovereign and pope have always been conducted with the sanction of the British government of the day, and in twenty-first century Britain they go ahead with barely a murmur of controversy.

But in 1980, just days after the queen's visit to Rome and during the planning for the visit of John Paul to Britain, a warning note was sounded by Enoch Powell about the consequences of the papal visit to Britain for the monarchy. Powell, a noted expert on the unwritten British constitution, argued that because the source of authority in the national Church was the same as the source of secular authority – namely, the Crown in Parliament – the visit of the pope had immense consequences. 'It is constitutionally and logically unthinkable for England to contain both the queen and the pope,' he said.

'Before that could happen, the essential character of the one or the other would have to be surrendered. If the queen is on earth "the Supreme Governor of the Church in England" then His Holiness is not in this realm "Christ's vicar on earth". Either the pope's authority is not universal or the Church of England is not the Catholic and Apostolic Church in this land. The assertion that His Holiness personifies and the assertion that Her Majesty personifies are irreconcilable.'

Powell did not take issue with the queen visiting Rome but with rather with the pope's presence on English soil, seeing it as a threat to her position in the country where she is sovereign. And that in turn, he argued, jeopardized Britain, for royal supremacy is a living reality on which the Church of England and the British nation depend.[38]

Powell's thesis is worth considering because it highlights how inextricably woven together Church, state and monarch have been in the United Kingdom, and underlying it, for centuries, was a deep suspicion of Rome. Article 37 of the Thirty-Nine Articles of 1562, outlining the doctrine of the Church of England, states the royal role in the Church of England and makes it clear: 'The Bishop of Rome hath no jurisdiction in this Realm of England.'[39]

But by 1980, the strength of that argument was waning. Cabinet papers for 25 May 1982, discussing the visit of John Paul II, confirmed the view of Mrs Thatcher's government: 'The Queen would receive the Pope as a fellow head of state.'[40]

The mutual suspicion that Britain and Rome once shared has given way today to a mutual regard, with the odd hint here and there on both sides of an historic tension. In the past thirty years the queen has played a key role in developing warmer relations, not least because of her personal faith. That was evident in the letter sent to her by Benedict XVI, two years after his state visit, on the occasion of her Diamond Jubilee in 2012, in which he praised her dedication to duty, 'and a commitment to maintaining the principles of freedom, justice and democracy, in keeping with a noble vision of the role of a Christian monarch'.[41] It was also apparent in the comment made by Pope Francis two days after his election when he spoke to Cardinal Cormac Murphy-O'Connor in the Hall of Benedictions, where all the cardinals had come to greet the new pope. Murphy-O'Connor revealed: 'Just as I was leaving he said, "Don't forget: give the queen my warmest greetings".' The cardinal promptly rang the queen's secretary from the English College where he was staying to pass on the message.[42] Within six months, the queen and the Duke of Edinburgh flew to Rome for a meeting with the Italian president followed by a visit to the Vatican, where they spent an hour with Pope Francis. There were no formal speeches or statements, just an exchange of gifts and private conversation, plus a brief photocall. But the visit – within less than a year of Francis's election, and just a week after he met President Obama at the Vatican – confirmed the importance given to the queen by the papacy, and vice versa.

In the words of former UK Ambassador Nigel Baker, 'You get the sense that given her vows, duty and service, Rome thinks she is the last Christian monarch.'[43] That might put the Spanish Catholic royal family's nose out of joint. But it enforces, once again, that while the papacy and its officials may have long memories, and the split with England has not been forgotten, 400 years on, memories have sometimes given way to realism. In secular Europe, a Christian monarchy matters enormously to the Vatican, particularly when that monarch has such a clearly strong, personal faith. The British monarchy is also an institution which has survived, as historian Peter Hennessy puts it, through the successful juxtaposition of tradition and modernity – something Rome might wish to emulate.

As Elizabeth II enjoyed her ninetieth year, thoughts in Rome, as in the United Kingdom, turned to the inevitable succession. Quite what they will make of the Prince of Wales' desire to alter the British monarch's ancient papal honour of Defender of the Faith to Defender of Faith will doubtless become apparent in the near future. It will require a change to the law of the Royal Titles Act of 1953 which Prince Charles thinks necessary because of the nature of multi-faith Britain.[44]

The prince has regularly made known his interest in religion, from his comments about his devotion to the Book of Common Prayer to his interest in dialogue with Islam. In recent years he has regularly met persecuted Christians from the Middle East and spoken out about their suffering.[45] At the time of writing, various leaders of Christian charities indicated to me that they had noticed in Prince Charles a growing interest in Christianity, as if his mother's great age and the moment when he would take on the mantle of Supreme Governor of the Church of England grew ever closer, were sharpening his focus.[46] His own coronation will indicate how he sees the role of religion in a twenty-first century British monarchy. Will it be a traditional service upholding the Protestant religion? A Christian ecumenical one? A multi-faith event? Or even some sort of secular jamboree? Rome will be among watching closely.

In April 2017, the Prince travelled with his wife, the Duchess of Cornwall, to Rome to meet Pope Francis as a part of a European tour, perceived by the press to be part of the Foreign Office's efforts to enhance relations with the

EU nations in the wake of the Brexit referendum vote. The encounter focused on the shared interest of prince and pontiff in the environment, with Francis giving Charles as a gift a copy of his 'green' encyclical *Laudato Si'*. The document echoes many of the concerns that the Prince of Wales has been expressing about the plight of the planet for forty years.[47] The pair, who were in talks for around an hour, were also understood to have discussed the plight of persecuted Christians in the Middle East. Again, both have been vocal about the issue, the prince complaining at a Lambeth Palace reception that the British were more bothered about Brexit than the plight of Christians.[48] In Rome, where he also met the secretary of state, Cardinal Pietro Parolin, he would have met diplomats highly sympathetic to his way of thinking on that particular issue.

Concern about people caught up on both sides of political and religious divides has also taken Prince Charles to Northern Ireland, a part of the UK which has caused both regular dialogue and conflict between Britain and the papacy. It is this complicated issue to which I will turn next.

Notes

1 Remembered by Pope John XXIII in his memoir, *Journal of a Soul* (1965), trans. D. White, London: Chapman, 181.

2 Interview of Lord (Rowan) Williams (RW) by Catherine Pepinster (CP), July 2015.

3 Speech of HRH Princess Elizabeth, Cape Town, 21 April 1947. http://www.royal.gov.uk/imagesandbroadcasts/historic%20speeches%20and%20broadcasts/21stbirthdayspeech21april1947.aspx

4 Pimlott, Ben (1996), *The Queen*, London: Harper Collins, London, 115, claims Sir Alan Lascelles as the author but family members have since revealed it was Morrah.

5 Utley, Tom (2012), 'Grandad's words made Churchill and the Queen cry', *Daily Mail*, 8 June. Available online: http://www.dailymail.co.uk/debate/article-2156173/Grandads-words-Churchill-Queen-How-sad-Beardy-misquoted-week-.html

6 Notebook (2015), 'The Queen's Speech', *The Tablet*, September 12.

7 Pimlott, ibid, 117.

8 Earl Marshal page, The British Monarchy, www.royal.gov.uk.

9 Obituary of Miles, Duke of Norfolk, John Ezard, *The Guardian*, 26 June 2002, http://www.theguardian.com/news/2002/jun/26/guardianobituaries.johnezard

10 Interview of Nigel Baker (NB) by Catherine Pepinster (CP), October 2015.

11 The Form and Order of Service that is to be performed and the Ceremonies that are to be observed in The Coronation of Her Majesty Queen Elizabeth II in the Abbey Church in Westminster on Tuesday the Second Day of June 1953,

An Anglican Liturgical Library, http://www.oremus.org/liturgy/coronation/cor1953b.html

12 Ibid.

13 Interview with an unnamed Holy See source.

14 HM The Queen (2000), Christmas broadcast. Available online: http://www.royal.gov.uk/ImagesandBroadcasts/TheQueensChristmasBroadcasts/ChristmasBroadcasts/ChristmasBroadcast2000.aspx

15 HM The Queen (2014), Christmas broadcast. Available online: http://www.royal.gov.uk/ImagesandBroadcasts/TheQueensChristmasBroadcasts/ChristmasBroadcasts/ChristmasBroadcast2014.aspx

16 Comments made in off-the-record conversation with the author.

17 Interview of Cardinal Cormac Murphy-O'Connor (CMO'C) by Catherine Pepinster, February 2015.

18 'How many Catholics are there in Britain?' (2010), BBC News Online, 15 September. http://www.bbc.co.uk/news/11297461

19 HM The Queen (2012), Speech at Lambeth Palace, 15 February. Available online: http://www.royal.gov.uk/LatestNewsandDiary/Speechesandarticles/2012/TheQueensspeechatLambethpalace15February2012.aspx

20 See Chapter 4.

21 Act of Settlement, available online: http://www.bailii.org/uk/legis/num_act/1700/1565208.html

22 Norton, Thomas and Hugh Farmer (2007), 'Queen's grandson and Catholic fiancée revive Act of Settlement row', The Tablet, 4 August, 36.

23 Hilton, Adrian (2003), 'The price of liberty', The Spectator, 8 November.

24 Watt, Nicholas and Andrew Sparrow (2009), 'Gordon Brown committed to ending anomaly of Royal ban on Catholics', The Guardian, 27 March. Available online: http://www.theguardian.com/politics/2009/mar/27/gordon-brown-royal-succession

25 The Perth Agreement (2011), available online: https://en.wikipedia.org/wiki/Perth_Agreement#Published_content_of_the_official_announcement.2C_Perth.2C_October_2011

26 Reported to the author by a witness to the meeting.

27 Footage of the funeral of King Baudouin, featuring Queen Elizabeth II, 7 August 1993. https://www.youtube.com/watch?v=1hQC7Jd19Yo

28 Interview of Lord Camoys (LC) by Catherine Pepinster (CP), January 2016.

29 Cook, Chris [Policy editor, BBC Newsnight] (2015), 'How civil servants kept the Privy Council's secrets', 18 September. http://www.bbc.co.uk/news/uk-politics-34281691

30 Howard, Anthony (2005), Basil Hume: The Monk Cardinal, London: Headline, 287.

31 Ibid, 288.

32 Ibid, 290.

33 Speech of HM The Queen (2010) to Pope Benedict XVI at Holyrood Palace, 16 September. Available online: http://www.catholicherald.co.uk/news/2010/09/16/papal-visit-2010-queens-speech-to-pope-benedict-full-text/

34 John Paul II (1980), Speech to HM The Queen. Available online: http:2.vatican.va/content/john-paul-ii/en/speeches/1980/october/documents/hf_jp-ii_spe_19801017_regina-elisabetta.html

35 http://www.catholicherald.co.uk/news/2010/09/16/papal-visit-2010-queens-speech-to-pope-benedict-full-text/

36 See Chapter 9.

37 Ibid.

38 Speech by Enoch Powell to East Grinstead Young Conservatives, 5 December 1980. http://enochpowell.info/Resources/Sept-Dec1980.pdf

39 The Thirty Nine Articles. http://acl.asn.au/the-thirty-nine-articles/

40 Cabinet papers for 23 May 1982, the Margaret Thatcher Foundation Archive.

41 Letter from Benedict XVI to HM The Queen, 23 May 2012. https://w2.vatican.va/content/benedict-xvi/en/messages/pont-messages/2012/documents/hf_ben-xvi_mes_20120523_queen-elizabeth-ii.html

42 Cullen, Miguel (2013), 'Pope sent greetings to the Queen straight after his election, says cardinal', *Catholic Herald*, 12 September. Available online: http://www.catholicherald.co.uk/news/2013/09/12/pope-sent-greeting-to-queen-straight-after-his-election-says-cardinal/

43 Interview of Nigel Baker by Catherine Pepinster, October 2015.

44 Pierce, Andrew (2008), 'Prince Charles to be known as Defender of Faith', *Daily Telegraph*, 13 November. http://www.telegraph.co.uk/news/uknews/theroyalfamily/3454271/Prince-Charles-to-be-known-as-Defender-of-Faith.html

45 Creegan, Clare (2015), 'Prince Charles: Help Middle East Christians before it's too late', *Aid to the Church in Need*, 18 December. w.acnuk.org/news.php/613/uk-prince-charles-help-middle-east-christians-before-its-too-late

46 Confidential conversations between Catherine Pepinster and Christian charity leaders.

47 Lamb, Christopher (2017), 'Be a man of peace, pope urges Prince Charles', *The Tablet*, 4 April. http://www.thetablet.co.uk/news/6942/0/be-a-man-of-peace-pope-urges-prince-charles-

48 Mendick, Robert (2017), 'Prince Charles complains Brexit "obsession" has stifled debate on Christian persecution', 27 January. *Telegraph* Online: http://www.telegraph.co.uk/news/2017/01/27/prince-charles-complains-brexit-obsession-has-stifled-debate/

9

Northern Ireland:

Emissaries and backchannels in search of peace and justice

To most people in mainland Britain, Armagh signifies bandit country, a place where the Irish Republican Army and the British army fought during the Troubles, losing members on both sides. But to the Irish it also signifies something else: the heart of Irish Catholicism, the episcopal see of the Primate of All Ireland. Rome does not always see the United Kingdom as Britain's establishment sees it: Scotland is recognized as a separate place, with its own bishops' conference, and no distinction is made between Ireland and Northern Ireland, which are treated as one ecclesiastical entity.

So in 1979, at the height of the Troubles, when John Paul II made the first ever visit by a pontiff to Ireland, it would have been appropriate for him to honour the primatial see of Armagh. But there was another pressing reason for him to head north: to make his contribution to the peace process. Politics made any plans by the Holy See tricky; while the Irish government and Catholic bishops might have been happy about a cross-border trip, British ministers were more circumspect. They knew that Ulster loyalists such as Ian Paisley would readily express their outrage. Terrorism finally put an end to such a trip: on 27 August, eighteen British soldiers were killed at Warrenpoint. Hours later, Lord Louis Mountbatten, cousin to the queen, was blown up on his boat off the coast of County Sligo. Crossing the border now seemed too risky to the Vatican, which announced any visit north was off. Yet such was the eccentric geography of dioceses that John Paul *did* visit Armagh, albeit the southernmost part of the diocese, just north of Dublin.[1]

That is why on 29 September 1979, just one month after Warrenpoint, Drogheda became the location of one of the most outspoken speeches of John Paul's pontificate when he called for peace in Northern Ireland, directly addressing the terrorists on both sides: 'I wish to speak to all men and women who engage in violence. I appeal to you in language of passionate pleading. On my knees I beg you to turn away from the paths of violence and return to the ways of peace.'

John Paul's speech, widely regarded as having been written for him by Cahal Daly, the Bishop of Down and Connor who was to later be appointed Archbishop of Armagh and a cardinal, was not only frank in its denunciation of violence, but acknowledged too the lingering frustrations of the Catholic minority community of the north: 'Christianity understands and recognizes the noble and just struggle for justice; but Christianity is decisively opposed to fomenting hatred and to promoting or provoking violence or struggle for the sake of "struggle". The command, "Thou shalt not kill", must be binding on the conscience of humanity, if the terrible tragedy and destiny of Cain is not to be repeated.'

While the pope conveyed his understanding of the Catholic community's experience of centuries of prejudice, he was emphatic that the years of terrorism had not offered an answer: 'You may claim to seek justice. I too believe in justice and seek justice. But violence only delays the day of justice. Violence destroys the work of justice. Further violence in Ireland will only drag down to ruin the land you claim to love and the values you claim to cherish.'[2]

John Paul's approach was similar to that adopted by some of the Catholic clergy during the Troubles, who would be regularly outspoken over the years, rejecting violence, but given their understanding of their own community, they would also be frank about the frustrations of Catholics and sympathetic to the nationalist cause. Others, including Cardinal John O'Connor of New York, would even appear to condone the violence of the IRA, using the theology of just war to support it.[3]

John Paul's denunciation of violence was seen by the British government to offer a potential opportunity for progress in Northern Ireland. It turned the attention of the world to the situation there and Humphrey Atkins, the Northern Ireland secretary, advised his Cabinet colleagues that they should build on what the pope had said. In a memorandum to members of the Cabinet's defence and overseas policy committee, he commented that the beneficial effects of the pope's visit in Northern Ireland were 'only slight' but should be exploited. John Paul, in reiterating traditional doctrines – an allusion, presumably, to the pope's rejection of violence at Drogheda – had raised expectations on the mainland, of some kind of settlement, but conversely it had 'reinforced Protestant loyalist prejudice'.[4] Sean Donlon, a former head of the Irish diplomatic service and adviser to the Irish government on Northern Irish matters, believed that an opportunity was missed to pursue a moral call to the men of violence. He recalled: 'The hugely emotional speech put huge pressure on the IRA. But it did not have long-term impact. The follow-up was missing.'[5]

Further troubles in Northern Ireland would soon lead to marked tensions between London and Rome. There had been plenty of difficulties over the years regarding diplomatic relations between the United Kingdom and the

Holy See over Northern Ireland. But these were due to concerns about how Protestants in the United Kingdom might perceive the British government being on good terms with the Vatican if it upgraded relations with Rome to full diplomatic status, rather than problems with the Holy See itself.

This had gone on throughout the 1960s, when the sectarian divide between Catholics and Protestants was widened by the inflammatory remarks of Unionists such as Ian Paisley. Paisley was unbridled in his anti-Catholicism; as his 2014 obituary in *The Guardian* put it, 'he loved to abuse the pope as "old redsocks" and inflame his listeners with rumours of seditious plots being hatched in Romish chapels'.[6]

C.M. James, head of the Western European Department in the Foreign Office, had warned eight years before the Drogheda speech, in a November 1971 minute, of the risks of an ambassadorial upgrade and the implications for British politics:

'Bearing in mind Paisley's ability to detect Papist conspiracies behind every bush, I think it would be better to hold up a decision [about diplomatic status for the Apostolic delegate] ... I think we should try to choose a moment when there is a lull (if this occurs) in the Irish crisis in the coming months to put right what I entirely agree is an anomalous situation).'[7]

The following year – the year of Bloody Sunday – the permanent secretary at the Foreign Office, Sir Thomas Brimelow, warned that the present state of the Irish question made the change from minister to fully fledged UK ambassador and from delegate to papal nuncio 'undesirably controversial'.[8] The issue of an 'upgrade', transforming British representation at the Holy See in Rome from legation to embassy and the Holy See's apostolic delegation to pro-nunciature in London, was not just box-ticking. Without it, the apostolic delegate in London would not be received by a government minister.

There had not been difficulties between the United Kingdom and the Holy See over British sovereignty in Northern Ireland. On the contrary, Rome had been Anglo-friendly, supporting the status quo. But two years after the pope's visit to Ireland, the relationship between Britain and the papacy was to undergo one of its greatest tests – and it was over Northern Ireland. It was nothing to do directly with sovereignty. Instead the focus of attention was the hunger strike of nationalist prisoners in the Maze prison.

The strike had its origins in the so-called 'dirty protest' by convicted members of the IRA against the loss of the special category status of political prisoners, which had been removed in 1978. Two years later, tensions escalated as prisoners began refusing food.

While Irish Catholic priests, north and south of the border, expressed solidarity with Catholics in Northern Ireland, and some voiced support for the hunger strikers, the Irish government had long had difficulties with interventions from Rome regarding the Troubles. Many British people assume that as Ireland is a Catholic country, its relationship with the Catholic Church is a cosy one, particularly given the place that Eamon de

Valera gave to the Church in the new country's constitution. But Ireland has no concordat or international treaty with the Holy See. The Irish government of the time often found Rome less than helpful, as if it did not fully appreciate Ireland's point of view.

During the 1970s and 1980s diplomatic difficulties between Ireland and the Holy See were compounded by the nuncio to Ireland, Archbishop Gaetano Alibrandi, who served for nearly twenty years, and played a part in the appointment of twenty-six bishops. According to Sean Donlon, Alibrandi was probably behind the Irish ambassador to the Holy See being summoned to the Secretariat of State, where he was handed a formal note criticizing Ireland over hunger strikers and was told how his government should deal with them. Despite Ireland's close links with the Catholic Church, Liam Cosgrove, the *taoiseach*, privately complained in forceful terms about this intervention.[9]

The nuncio's own behaviour also deeply concerned the Irish government. Donlon recalls that it became known Alibrandi was in contact with leading IRA men and that not only did he regularly make representations about the conditions in which the hunger strikers were held, but that he had given sanctuary to IRA members on the run in his nunciature. Representations were made to the Holy See about moving Alibrandi from Dublin, but to no avail. Eventually investigations by revenue officers found he had mysterious bank accounts in Ireland that involved inappropriate international financial dealings. These had no connection with the Holy See but were linked to his Sicilian family. At that point, in 1987, he agreed to retire.[10]

According to Donlon: 'We never saw Rome as helpful during the Troubles. It was a big problem. The Holy See took a line on the status quo with Northern Ireland and sovereignty. Meanwhile we had local pastors going in all directions. There were well-known IRA men who went to confession after their deeds and they picked their priests carefully. The priests would say to me that their job was to maintain links with their flocks, while the nuncio and Cardinal Tomas O'Fiaich of Armagh went beyond the bounds of what was appropriate in their approach to the Troubles.'[11]

For the British, it was 1980 when relations between the UK government, the Holy See and Cardinal O'Fiaich became most heated over the hunger strike, leading to the Bobby Sands affair. Protests by Northern Irish prisoners during the late 1970s escalated after the British government withdrew special category status for convicted paramilitary prisoners, with seven prisoners eventually embarking on a hunger strike in 1980. They were demanding political status which would have meant special privileges such as not having to do prison work or wear a prison uniform. On mainland Britain and among Ulster Unionists there was almost unanimous support for resisting the demands of the hunger strikes, but elsewhere, including in the United States and other European nations, the view was that a solution should be found. Among those who felt the British should respond in a more humanitarian way to the men starving themselves to death was the pope.

While dialogue with the Catholic Church over the strike began at the local level, within weeks it had involved John Paul II and Prime Minister Margaret Thatcher.

Letters went back and forth between the Northern Ireland secretary, Humphrey Atkins, and Cardinal Tomas O'Fiaich of Armagh and Bishop Cahal Daly of Ardagh and Clonmacnois. On 13 October, Bishop Daly wrote to Humphrey Atkins what he called a 'cri de coeur' about the hunger strike:

A hunger strike can be expected to produce far-reaching and highly adverse repercussions in considerable sectors of the community. Once a strike of this kind is entered upon, it is extremely difficult to have it called off before it reaches a tragic end. I realise fully the immense difficulties and complexities of the situation. I am concerned only that the situation will become still more difficult and still more complex if a hunger strike is launched . . . I have always felt that more concessions could be made within the context of over-all reform of prisoners' conditions, in line with the widely accepted principles of progressive modern penology.[12]

Another Catholic bishop, Edwin Daly of Derry, had written earlier in the year to urge Humphrey Atkins to agree concessions to the H Block prisoners regarding clothing. But he also warned that the IRA could become the benefactors of a propaganda war should one of the prisoners die:

My own experience would also suggest that support for the IRA is at its lowest ebb ever in the Catholic community. I am hoping that this attitude will persist. That is why I am worried about the Maze situation. The death of a prisoner there would certainly signal a massive IRA propaganda campaign that might attract some more support to them, especially amongst the young.

It was a striking example of how the Catholic clergy, including bishops, could provide useful intelligence about the situation on the ground, thanks to the structures and pastoral work of the Church. But the Thatcher government seemed in no mood to take such lessons on board.[13]

It was in October that John Paul became personally involved, when the British legate to the Holy See, Sir Mark Heath, was summoned to the Vatican and given a personal message from the pope to the Prime Minister. The Pope's letter began by saying: 'I am receiving disturbing information about tensions in the Maze Prison in Northern Ireland where IRA prisoners have begun a hunger strike.'[14]

There will have been several channels for information to reach the pontiff: Rome's own diplomatic channels with its nuncios, or ambassadors, who feed information to the Secretariat of State which in turn briefs the pope. And then there are the bishops themselves in each country who approach the Vatican with their concerns. Ireland's most senior churchman, Cardinal

Tomas O'Fiaich, was himself a Northern Irish Catholic, with a known sympathy for a united Ireland. As the *Irish Times* put it in his obituary: 'He was also unashamedly an Irish nationalist, declaring himself firmly in favour of national unity even at the risk of being accused of thus offering support in some degree to those engaged in murder and violence to achieve that end.'[15]

John Paul's informants had clearly kept him briefed, for his letter went on: 'I am aware that the secretary of state for Northern Ireland, Mr Atkins, has already been asked to examine the problem and to seek possible solutions.

In the spirit of the call for peace and reconciliation which I made at Drogheda during my pastoral visit to Ireland last year, I would express my deep concern about both the tragic consequences which the agitation could have for the prisoners themselves and also the possible grave repercussions upon the whole situation in Northern Ireland. I would ask you to consider personally possible solutions in order to avoid irreversible consequences that could perhaps prove irreparable.'

The legate to the Holy See reported to Number 10 that when he asked the Secretariat of State official, Mgr Silvestrini, what more could be done in addition to the concession on clothing, Mgr Silvestrini was silent. He then said the clergy would continue to urge the prisoners to give up and that the message from the pope was a personal one to the PM.[16]

It certainly seemed to have hit home. Today history views Margaret Thatcher and John Paul, together with Ronald Reagan, as staunch allies, given their fierce anti-communism. But in 1980 there was tension between the pope, urging in effect mercy, and a stubborn prime minister who refused to back down. On 13 November she composed a response to the pope, arguing:

> Their hunger strike is in pursuit of a demand for a political status which would involve their receiving privileges greater than those available to other convicted criminals in Northern Ireland. I have made it clear that the British Government cannot and will not accede to this demand. To do so would be to accept that political motivation in some way excuses such serious crimes; it would encourage the use of violence as a means of obtaining political objectives; and it would be likely to provoke a violent confrontation between the two communities in the North.[17]

Thatcher went on to suggest that the situation in Northern Ireland might be discussed during her visit to Rome later that month, but the appointments diary for that day, 24 November, shows that she was in the Vatican for just half an hour – barely time to scratch the surface of such a complex situation, although earlier she also had thirty minutes with Cardinal Casaroli, secretary of state.[18]

While that meeting might have been brief, it was clear that John Paul II was directly involved in the situation. On 30 November, Ray Harrington, the private secretary to the secretary of state for Northern Ireland, had written to Thatcher's private secretary, Michael Alexander, about the dialogue between the UK and the Church. He intimated that intelligence had picked up that a statement from the Catholic bishops of Northern Ireland, issued the day before, was objected to by the IRA and that the statement 'closely reflects the guidance to the bishops which the Pope has given'. But Harrington indicated that any involvement of the government in these Church affairs had to be undisclosed and 'the statement must now be left to do its work with no public response from us.'[19]

That same day Mrs Thatcher wrote again to John Paul regarding her recent trip to Rome and indicating her approval of the explicit involvement of the Church in trying to end the strike. But she otherwise remained intransigent: 'It would be utterly wrong to take any steps which conceded that political motives can excuse murder or other serious crimes. We are greatly encouraged, however, by the statement that has been made by Cardinal O'Fiaich and his episcopal colleagues. They made an impassioned plea to the hunger strikers to give up a claim that has no moral justification and to desist from a course that can so gravely imperil the life and safety of others.'[20]

She went on to suggest that the proposals from the prison chaplains for concessions would have persuaded people that the prisoners had gained political status, something she abhorred. The to-and-fro dialogue between ministers, the prime minister, the clergy and the pope did nothing to lessen the strike, which persisted, while the government refused to back down on prisoners' clothing and work obligations.

John Paul II's intervention over the hunger strikers was one of the most clear-cut interventions that the papacy ever made in British politics but it emerged from an humanitarian concern about the situation in the Maze Prison. It also illuminates the complicated nature of the Troubles. Mrs Thatcher characteristically saw them as being about criminality; the Catholic churchmen of Northern Ireland, rooted in their community, saw a bigger picture involving lingering prejudice and discrimination. The structures of the Catholic Church gave the clerics various routes to the pope, from their own visits to Rome and through the Church's own diplomatic channels, and some of them may well have used these channels to promote their own views, verging on the political rather than merely pastoral.

There was another avenue for the views of the Irish clerics, too, to be transmitted right into the heart of the papal household. John Paul's private secretary at the time was a priest from Northern Ireland, John Magee. And Magee became the conduit for an even more direct intervention by a pope in the political affairs of the UK than letter-writing to the British prime minister, when John Paul sent him as his personal emissary to visit hunger striker Bobby Sands. Magee was a powerful Vatican figure, and is the only person in papal history to have been private secretary to three popes: Paul VI, the short-lived John Paul I and finally John Paul II, who later made him Master of Ceremonies. Magee subsequently became Bishop of Cloyne in 1987.

Both the British and Irish governments saw this papal intervention as most unhelpful, suggesting sympathy for the hunger strikers. They saw the strikers as threatening the stability of the state, something that needed to be dealt with through the force of the law. Behind the scenes the British government engineered the visit of John Magee to be leaked to the Press Association and Reuters news agencies so that it could not be described by the press as 'secret'. Whether Magee guessed or not at these machinations, he later expressed regret to Northern Ireland secretary Humphrey Atkins that the visit had been leaked because it risked Sands cancelling it. The press were already waiting for him when he landed at Heathrow en route to Belfast.[21]

There were more journalists waiting for him in Belfast and the reports of the time provide a reminder of what a dramatic move this was by the pope at such a tense time. On the very day that Magee arrived for his hour-long talk with Sands, there were thousands of Loyalists on the streets and rioting in Republican areas of the city.

Magee had been met at Aldergrove Airport by Cardinal O'Fiaich but, as the *Glasgow Herald* of 29 April reported, Magee left the prison after seeing Sands by a side entrance and 'his destination was kept secret'.[22] In fact his next appointment was to meet Humphrey Atkins. The Newry-born Fr Magee must have had a sense of the full might of the British state as he drove into the heavily guarded Stormont Castle at lunchtime to see Atkins after his session with Sands.

It turned out that John Paul had entrusted him with a message for the British government as well as a message for Sands. As Atkins later reported to the prime minister, Magee stressed that John Paul had sent him on a mission of peace, goodwill and concern deeply felt for strife anywhere, especially where life was at stake (Sands, aged twenty-seven, had by then been on hunger strike for sixty days).

According to Magee, the visit involved him telling Sands of the pope's condemnation of violence at length and urging the IRA man to end his strike, but Sands replied 'Do not ask me that'. It was clear from Magee's account to Atkins that Sands still wanted some sort of negotiation; and there was a hint that even at that late stage he would consider ending his hunger strike even temporarily if certain conditions were met, including being visited by a Northern Ireland Office civil servant to discuss the situation, with priests and other prisoners present as witnesses.

But Atkins made clear to Magee that there was no chance of any conditions being set by Sands, because the government would not enter into any form of negotiation with the IRA – at least not at that stage, as it became apparent in the years to come that there was the possibility for negotiation after all. But on this occasion, despite papal intervention, there was stalemate.[23]

An indication of the divide between the parties involved comes from the Cabinet papers for 30 April, the day after the meeting, when Atkins reported to his colleagues on the situation with Magee and described this Catholic priest from Newry as an 'Ulsterman', which, while technically correct, has no sense of how that term is understood by nationalists.[24]

Fr Magee, with no progress made, told the secretary of state that he would return to Rome the following day but he planned to visit Bobby Sands's family, and that he had asked Cardinal O'Fiaich, at the pope's suggestion, to meet the families of members of the security forces killed by terrorists as well as pass on the pope's pleas to other hunger strikers. Mr Atkins raised no objections. But he was also firm: there could be no more meetings between the two of them because 'to do so would risk creating the impression that some form of negotiation was going on'. As Sands edged closer to death, Tomas O'Fiaich not only sent a telegram to the prime minister, urging her to back down and agree to prisoner concessions, but also persuaded Cardinal Manning of Los Angeles and Cardinal Cooke of New York to telegram the same message. It was unlikely, given Mrs Thatcher's dislike of being told she was wrong, that these messages would have changed her mind.[25] Instead they seemed to make her even more resolute, writing to Cardinal O'Fiaich in reply that the British government was determined to stand firm, for 'To do otherwise would be to abandon sound principles in the face of the threat of violence'.[26]

Fr Magee left Stormont for Dublin, returning later to Rome. Six days later, on 5 May, Bobby Sands died. Does this mean the pope's intervention in such a tense situation had ended in abject failure? That Sands was not persuaded to end his hunger strike means yes. That the Troubles continued for so many years might suggest failure too. But it is hard now to recall just how tense the situation was in Northern Ireland at that time. People on both sides of the divide predicted at the time that the death of Sands – the leader of the hunger strikers and the MP for Fermanagh and Tyrone – would lead to something akin to war on the streets. Ian Paisley claimed Ulster would be plunged into 'a savage war' if Sands died, according to the *Glasgow Herald* on the day of the Magee visit, while Irish MP Neil Blaney, who had also visited Sands, said that Northern Ireland would suffer unprecedented violence and many people would die as a result of the escalation. There was certainly terrible violence to come: the killing of soldiers and civilians in Armagh, Belfast, Derry, Ballymena, Ballykelly, as well as mainland attacks at Hyde Park, Regent's Park, Harrods, and finally the 'spectacular' – the bombing of the Brighton Tory party conference in September 1984. But there was no civil war as such – and some would argue that John Paul's acknowledgement of the situation in Belfast at the time consoled the nationalist and Catholic community. It showed that people were watching and listening elsewhere in the world to what was happening in Northern Ireland, and so may have pre-empted further violence.

Nor did the Catholic Church let up. Cardinal O'Fiaich regularly urged the prime minister to step back from the brink regarding the hunger strikers. But there was little sympathy between the cardinal and the prime minister. Later that year the cardinal recalled during a visit to the US that in a private meeting with her, Mrs Thatcher had told him that she knew about Northern Ireland because she had read the documents and she wondered if the continuing hunger strike was to demonstrate the men's virility. She could not understand the continuing Irish animosity towards the British, considering that even the Germans were now willing to be friends. According to Cardinal O'Fiaich, he retorted that perhaps the reason the Germans were now friends with the British was because 'the British were no longer occupying their country'.[27]

Mrs Thatcher did have a tendency towards being tone-deaf about the Catholics of Northern Ireland. During the 1980s, David Goodall, a career civil servant and Catholic, was drafted in to help with negotiations regarding Northern Ireland. At one point, he attended a meeting at Chequers in 1984 with the prime minister, Jim Prior and Geoffrey Howe, to discuss the situation. Goodall recalled that at one point Mrs Thatcher suggested that those who did not want to live under British rule should move to the Irish Republic, given that the Irish were used to large-scale population movements. Goodall wrote: 'At this point the silence round the fire became transfused with simple bafflement. After a pause, I asked if she could possibly be thinking of Cromwell. "Cromwell, of course." "Well, Prime Minister, Cromwell's policy was known as 'To Hell and Connaught' and it left a scar on Anglo-Irish relations which still hasn't healed." The idea of a population transfer was not pursued.'[28]

David Goodall continued working on negotiations between the British and Irish governments which eventually led to the Anglo-Irish agreement of 1985. It gave the Irish government an advisory role in Northern Ireland, set out plans for devolution, and confirmed there would be no constitutional change unless the majority of people wanted to join the Republic. While it gave Dublin a role in Northern Ireland for the first time in sixty years, it could not wipe out the bitterness many felt about the Catholic community's experiences over the years.

Tomas O'Fiaich's statement on 21 May 1980, five years before the Anglo-Irish agreement, and following the death that same day of a third IRA hunger striker, Raymond McCreesh, whose brother was one of O'Fiaich's priests, was uncompromising in its criticism of the British. It also gave an insight into how young people might become caught up in the nationalist cause.

Raymond McCreesh was born in a community which has always openly proclaimed that it is Irish, not British. When the Northern Ireland troubles began he was barely twelve, a very impressionable age at which to learn of discrimination. Those who protested peacefully against it were harassed and intimidated. Then followed Burntollet, the Bogside, Bombay Street, and Bloody Sunday in Derry, all before he was 15. These events gave rise to very deep emotions in nationalist areas. Sectarian murders in Co. Armagh made many young Catholics and Protestants easy recruits for paramilitary organisations. I repudiate unequivocally this recourse to arms, but I well remember how easy it was in the mid-seventies for many young men on both sides to become convinced that this was the best way to defend their community.

Raymond McCreesh was captured bearing arms at the age of 19 and sentenced to 14 years' imprisonment. I have no doubt that he would never have seen the inside of a jail but for the abnormal political situation. Who is entitled to pronounce him a murderer or a suicide? I leave his judgment to a just and merciful judge.[29]

In the volatile atmosphere of that summer, O'Fiaich was facing vilification in the media while fellow Catholics on the mainland were deeply disturbed by the cardinal's edging towards political commentary, with one establishment Catholic, Lord Rawlinson of Ewell, who as Sir Peter Rawlinson served as attorney general, including in Northern Ireland from 1970 to 1974, taking to the radio to describe his statement as 'excessive', leaving him 'horrified and ashamed'. 'I do not really see,' he said, 'what Cardinal O'Fiaich's role is in this matter as Primate of All Ireland'.[30] His priests, though, publicly supported him, pointing out in a statement on 12 May that the cardinal had regularly repudiated violence and urging Catholics to have nothing to do with it.

As a fourth hunger striker, Patsy O'Hara, died on 22 May, Bishop Edward Daly of Derry also intervened, his words evoking the impact of the Troubles on the people of Northern Ireland, as they made the divisions in society wider and wider: 'This issue is bringing about divisions, not only in the wider community, but even within families, between brother and brother. While all appeals now seem to fall on deaf ears, I must plead once again for new efforts to find an urgent solution to this dreadful problem. Some kind of acceptable compromise must be found and found soon.'[31]

However much these statements by Church figures might irritate the government, it also recognized that it needed to try to get the Catholic Church on side. After the death of McCreesh, civil servant David Blatherwick, who had been seconded to the Political Affairs Division of the Northern Ireland Office, wrote a memo to Number 10 after being asked how to deal with Cardinal O'Fiaich. Blatherwick, in a covering note delivered with a draft letter to come from the prime minister, acknowledged that 'the feelings of bitterness, despair and frustration which show through the Cardinal's statement' were widely shared in the Catholic community, and in a frank comment untypical of the memos of Sir Humphreys of Whitehall, advised that the government should 'butter up the Cardinal'. The reason for doing so was evident, said Blatherwick, although he had not included it overtly in his draft: 'the influence of the Church is the key to progress.'[32]

The influence of the Catholic Church was also at work on the mainland. Cardinal Basil Hume had been keeping a weather eye on Northern Ireland since his early days as Archbishop of Westminster, writing to the prime minister in March 1979, urging a meeting with the then Archbishop O'Fiaich and Bishop Edward Daly. Hume intervened again soon after the hunger strike deaths, meeting Humphrey Atkins to discuss the situation in Northern Ireland. Hume spoke of the distress of English and Welsh Catholics regarding the suffering of the people of Northern Ireland. While the British government had long believed that Hume was more 'on side' than O'Fiaich, the English cardinal stressed that the Irish and English bishops were as one in their stand against violence in any form, and regretted widespread public misunderstanding about the Irish bishops' stance on this issue.

It was an opportunity for Mr Atkins to be conciliatory, emphasizing that the government was equally concerned about the loss of life, injury and damage inflicted on all sections of the community in Northern Ireland, as well as on the security forces. His remarks to the cardinal about Mrs Thatcher's public comments in Belfast – that the violence and discontent had its roots deep in the past but could never be used to justify violence today – was standard policy yet at the same time much more conciliatory than the way in which Mrs Thatcher had spoken in private to Tomas O'Fiaich, reflecting both the personalities of those involved but also the way in which Basil Hume had succeeded in building the trust of the British establishment.[33]

It took until October to end the strike, and the British government effectively backed down. It agreed to concessions – including the prisoners wearing their own clothes, free association and no work – that were wanted all along. On this occasion a key Church player was Fr Denis Faul, the Roman Catholic chaplain to the Maze, who had long been a conduit to the IRA for both the Irish government and Cardinal O'Fiaich. Faul and O'Fiaich went back a long way, to the days when O'Fiaich taught the younger man at the Maynooth seminary. He was trusted by the Republicans, having gathered information about British ill-treatment of prisoners that helped bring a prosecution of the British government for the use of torture by the European Court of Human Rights.

However, on this occasion, Fr Faul's focus was not the IRA but the relatives of the hunger strikers, and his intervention persuaded them to act independently of the Provisional IRA leadership and get the men to end their strike. After that, some outraged fellow Maze inmates refused to attend Mass said by him.[34]

The conclusion of the strike and the granting of concessions were welcomed by churchmen in Ireland and England and Wales, with Cardinal O'Fiaich describing the prisoners' right to wear their own clothes at all times as 'a fuller recognition of human dignity'. In London the International Justice and Peace Commission for the Bishops' Conference of England and Wales grounded its response in the pope's deploring of violence in Northern Ireland. It was now two years since John Paul II's intervention at Drogheda. His words might not have taken immediate effect among the men of violence, but they had certainly encouraged churchmen in their efforts to seek peace while at the same time seeking to stand by their Catholic community.[35]

In many ways, maintaining that support was simpler for Tomas O'Fiaich than it was for Basil Hume. For O'Fiaich, as for the vast majority of Catholics of Northern Ireland, their nationalism and Catholicism were intertwined, as they were for the Irish of the Republic. As the historian Eamon Duffy comments, English Catholics do not have that same interlocking of patriotism and faith.[36]

For the English, being Catholic and being a British citizen while observing the situation in Northern Ireland could be complicated. On the one hand, there was loyalty to one's country, but on the other, there was an instinctive sympathy for one's fellow believers and many were deeply troubled by what the rest of the world saw as a repressive policy being pursued in Northern Ireland towards the majority population.

For Basil Hume, the situation was made yet more delicate by Ireland having its own hierarchy and any intervention on his part might lead to conflict with the bishops there. This was made more difficult for Hume because of the character of O'Fiaich who served as Primate of All Ireland for thirteen of Hume's twenty-three years in Westminster and was plainspoken in his criticism of the British. In the circumstances Hume, instinctively a subtler commentator, became forthright in the opposite direction, condemning the Maze hunger strike as something he saw as more overtly political.[37]

But where Hume and O'Fiaich overlapped in their thinking was their deep concern with what O'Fiaich had termed 'the fuller dignity of the human person', a concern steeped in Catholic teaching about human dignity and one of the major themes of John Paul II's pontificate.[38] In a 1968 letter to the theologian Henri de Lubac, the then Karol Wojtyła had written: 'The evil of our times consists in the first place in a kind of degradation, indeed in a pulverization, of the fundamental uniqueness of each human person.'[39]

It was this concern with human dignity, and an associated love of justice, that led Cardinal Hume to become immersed in a campaign that caused him to confront the British state over Northern Ireland: that of the Guildford Four.

The Guildford Four – Gerard Conlon, Paul Hill, Paddy Armstrong and Carole Richardson – were found guilty in 1975 and sentenced to life imprisonment for planting bombs in two Guildford pubs, which caused the death of five people and injured many more. By the late 1970s growing numbers of people both in mainland Britain and in Northern Ireland were saying that there had been a miscarriage of justice; among those at the early start of the campaign was Fr Denis Faul. The interest of Faul and other priests caused Hume to also investigate and meet the Four.

Hume's interest was also inspired by his concern for another prisoner: Giuseppe Conlon, the father of Gerard. Together with Anne and Patrick Maguire, Gerard's uncle and aunt, their two sons and two others, Giuseppe had been found guilty of running a bomb-making factory at the Maguires' North London home. The Maguire Seven were accused of supplying bombs for the Guildford atrocity.

Giuseppe's health, already poor, deteriorated markedly in prison. The Catholic chaplain at Wormwood Scrubs, the biggest prison in Hume's diocese, suggested to Giuseppe that he write to the cardinal. Gerard Conlon, in his account *Proved Innocent*, recalled that he was called in from playing football at the Scrubs (where he too was incarcerated) to meet the cardinal, who was dressed in a black cape. 'My first impression was, here is Batman come to see me . . . and the caped figure just put his arms round me and said, "I'm Cardinal Hume. Will you take me to see your father?"[40]

After his initial conversation with Giuseppe, Hume, who put great store by his intuitive feelings about people, was convinced of his innocence. But at this stage Hume was not the political sophisticate he later turned out to be. His campaign began with a letter to Merlyn Rees, the Labour home secretary, urging an act of clemency on the grounds of Conlon senior's health. He made little progress, however, not least because Labour was defeated at the general election a month later. Hume's next move was to raise the issue during a meeting he requested with the new prime minister, Margaret Thatcher, for whom he had done a favour by helping overcome the doubts of the Catholic politician Hugh Rossi over accepting a role in the Northern Ireland office.[41]

Mrs Thatcher suggested the cardinal call on the new Conservative home secretary, William Whitelaw. But it turned out not to be a friendly one-to-one. Whitelaw was surrounded by a team of civil servants. Hume got no further than he had with Merlyn Rees: there was talk of keeping the case under review but nothing more than that. Cardinal Hume's public affairs adviser, Charles Wookey, recalls that the meeting gave the cardinal a valuable lesson: 'He was ill-prepared on the detail. This meant he learnt about the need for back office support but he also knew that he had to be canny and not become part of a particular lobby group.'[42]

Giuseppe Conlon died in hospital in January 1980 while still serving his sentence, although Whitelaw had allowed him out of prison for a few days. He wrote to the cardinal after Giuseppe's death explaining that he thought it would not have been right to have sent him back to prison after hospital.

In 1984, Cardinal Hume wrote again to the prime minister following a Yorkshire Television documentary on the Maguires, urging that evidence be re-examined. His letter indicates how he saw the role of a Catholic cardinal tiptoeing through the quagmire of British politics. 'I am understandably reluctant', he told Mrs Thatcher, 'to cause fresh controversy in the present state of Anglo-Irish relations. That, however, can never be the only consideration. Justice remains an absolute priority.'[43]

Little came of this latest intervention and within a few months the public mood was to harden following the attempted assassination of the prime minister and her Cabinet by the IRA during the Conservative Party's Brighton conference. Perhaps with concern for how Catholics might be perceived at such a time, but no doubt with instinctive compassion for the victims and intended victims of the atrocity, a series of letters from senior Catholic clerics arrived at Number 10. Mrs Thatcher wrote back in turn to Cardinals Hume and Gray of St Andrews and Edinburgh, as well as Archbishop Worlock of Liverpool and Bishop Murphy-O'Connor of Arundel and Brighton in whose diocese the attack had occurred. Cormac Murphy-O'Connor later recalled that the morning after the bomb, he had driven over to Brighton with the Anglican Bishop of Chichester and gone to the hotel where the Thatchers had been transferred from the bombed Grand. When the prime minister heard they were there, she asked them to her room where she said; 'Bishops, will you pray with me?'[44] [45]

It was two years later that the campaign for the Guildford Four took a decisive turn. Robert McKee, who had interviewed Anne Maguire on her release from prison in 1985, and had already begun researching the Maguire and Guildford Four cases, published his book *Trial and Error*. The book explored in detail the shortcomings of evidence and the police's intimidatory tactics. It not only brought McKee and Cardinal Hume together but also led to a group of influential people, nicknamed the 'Cardinal's Deputation', to push for the cases to be reopened. Those who joined were Roy Jenkins and Merlyn Rees, both former Labour home secretaries who changed their minds on the cases, together with two former law lords, Lords Scarman and Devlin.

A series of meetings were held, with Home Secretary Douglas Hurd refusing to reopen the case. The discreet members of the Deputation upped the ante. Letters putting forward their case were released to the press. Lords Scarman and Devlin produced a tightly argued legal paper on 'Justice and the Guildford Four' that was reproduced in full in *The Times*. Then on 16 January 1989, Douglas Hurd announced that he would refer the Guildford Four case back to the Court of Appeal. In October that year, two days before the hearing, the Director of Public Prosecutions announced that the convictions could not be sustained on the basis of new evidence. Basil Hume's approach was similar in the case of the Birmingham Six, applying pressure through lobbying and backing new evidence. They too were freed on appeal in March 1991.[46]

Throughout the Troubles the Catholic Church came in for criticism on all sides, from those who believed it condoned violence to those who felt it should have stood in greater solidarity with its people. Since they ended, its response has been critiqued further by academics. The sociologist John D. Brewer has identified the difference between what hierarchies achieved and what individual, sometimes maverick priests managed to do. It was clear that certain individuals such as Fr Denis Faul and Fr Alec Reid were able to gain and maintain the trust of people engaged in the republican cause. And as Brewer maintains, the role of religion in helping end the Troubles was sometimes belittled by politicians who failed to see the opportunities offered by 'backchannel' negotiations, such as when Sinn Fein's Gerry Adams and the Social and Democratic Labour Party's leader John Hume met in Clonard Monastery, the Redemptorists' home on the Falls Road, where Fr Alec Reid was based. (In 1988 a photograph of Fr Alec, kneeling in prayer beside the body of one of two lynched British soldiers, was beamed around the world. Years later it emerged that at the time he had in his coat a document from Sinn Fein that he was carrying to the SDLP about how to resolve the crisis).[47] [48]

The work of individual priests is also praised by historian Maggie Scull who has studied the hunger strike of Bobby Sands, making the comment that: 'During Sands' strike, many lower-class Irish clergymen who cared less about British political sensitivities than the hierarchy, sympathised with the hunger strikers' cause.'[49]

It is hard to see, however, that Cardinal Tomas O'Fiaich cared more about the British establishment than he did about the hunger strikers, while his counterpart in Westminster, Basil Hume, although frequently more nuanced in his dealings with government than O'Fiaich, was also prepared to put himself on the line in his campaign to free the Guildford Four, Maguire Seven and Birmingham Six. Scull argues that the Archbishop of Westminster's responses were personal rather than theological or philosophical. It is certainly true that Hume's initial involvement in the miscarriages of justice cases was a personal response to the plight of Giuseppe Conlon but it was also steeped in his belief that the Church must be a witness to the good and that action must be ground in coherent principles. As he said in his 1985 lecture to the Thomas More Society, the philosophy on which the law was based was about giving 'witness to the principles which true law should not transgress'.[50]

If the Catholic Church did help in Northern Ireland and in associated miscarriages of justice during the Troubles, it is in part down to one of the most effective aspects of its organization: the priests based at the local level, either in parishes or in prisons. Their connectedness with the people enables them to not only understand themselves what is happening on the ground, as happened with Reid and Faul, and also Fr George Ennis, the chaplain to Giuseppe Conlon at Wormwood Scrubs, but to transmit that knowledge to the hierarchy.

John Brewer's more controversial critique of the Catholic Church in Northern Ireland comes with his analysis of how the structures supported by the Church, such as segregated schooling, have continued to negatively impact on Northern Irish society, and he quotes Fr Des Wilson as saying: 'It always seemed to me that what the Churches were looking for was peace without change.'[51] In fact the greatest challenges to the Church and the greatest calls for change have come in Northern Ireland since the 1998 Good Friday Agreement and the ceasefire and are less to do with sectarianism than changing mores.

One of the increasingly neuralgic issues for Northern Ireland is abortion. The Abortion Act of 1967 does not apply to Northern Ireland, which means that performing a termination there is an offence. However, causing the death of a child in good faith in order to preserve the life of the mother is permitted under the Criminal Justice Act (Northern Ireland) 1945. This means that aborting a foetus on the grounds only of abnormality is unacceptable. These tough restrictions mean that the number of abortions carried out in Northern Ireland is the lowest in the United Kingdom, with just sixteen taking place in 2014.[52] But Northern Irish women also go abroad for them; 837 travelled to other parts of the UK for this operation that same year.[53]

The Catholic Church in Northern Ireland has remained profoundly opposed to abortion, given that it is a central tenet of Catholic teaching which sees it as gravely contrary to the moral law. Although it is the strongest critic of abortion among the Churches in Northern Ireland, its belief in the sanctity of life is shared by Protestant denominations which accept abortion only in cases of extreme risk to the mother. Major political parties, including the SDLP, Sinn Fein and the Democratic Unionist Party remain opposed to abortion too, and since devolution the Stormont Assembly has resisted any attempt to change the law.

The challenges now emerging to the Catholic Church's position and its forceful opposition to abortion are coming from increasingly vocal campaign and interest groups, such as Amnesty International and Marie Stopes. In November 2015, the Belfast High Court ruled that it was incompatible with the human rights of women to not allow abortion in the case of rape, incest and fatal foetal abnormality but for the legal landscape to change, legislators would have to act. The Catholic Church, which had been recognized by the court as an interested party during the case, thus giving it the right to be heard, protested against the High Court judgment. Tim Bartlett, secretary of the Catholic Council for Social Affairs, said after the case that: 'In the Church, we work with women whose babies have life-limiting conditions, and these children can live for minutes, hours, days, weeks and in some cases years. The child is still technically, clinically and in every sense alive as a human person, and is entitled to have their life protected.'

The Catholic Church's position, explained Mr Bartlett, was that 'the right to life of an innocent person is always inviolable, and that is a fundamental moral principle on which society and human rights should stand. That right begins from the moment of conception, and science affirms that.'

This was also the situation in the case of rape. Although rape was 'the most heinous of crimes, the answer is not to take the life of an innocent third party. The challenge is to give that person every possible support and care.'[54]

Despite the growing protests, in February 2016 the assembly voted for the status quo. Both the SDLP and the DUP ensured neither amendment to abortion law was passed: 59–40 voted against legalizing abortion when there is a fatal foetal abnormality, and 64–30 voted against any law change in the case of rape, confirming that abortion is a key issue on which Catholic and Protestant politicians agree.

Indeed, the sectarian divisions in Northern Ireland are not what they once were in domestic politics. Historically, there has been a correlation between Church membership and voting patterns in Northern Ireland. And with Northern Ireland's Catholics reaching 45 per cent of the population, according to the 2011 census, and with them projected to be in the majority by 2037, one would expect parties like the SDLP and Sinn Fein to be in the ascendant. But voting patterns show that at the same time as the census, the vote for unionist parties was rising, indicating they are attracting Catholic voters. This did not surprise the commentator and former British ambassador to the Holy See, Francis Campbell, who wrote in *The Tablet* that:

> The Northern Ireland conflict was never as binary as some suggested. It was always more about equality, civil rights and respect than sovereignty. During the Troubles, as with any conflict, identities simply became more polarised. It is therefore to be expected that as part of the normalisation, identities will become less rigid and more diffuse and this will cause shifts in society.[55]

There is also a possibility that Catholic voters are changing as their links to the Church change and even loosen. It is sex abuse that has caused the greatest challenge to the Catholic Church's position and relationship with the laity in Northern Ireland. After a history of fidelity to the Church in Ireland, the faithful have been distressed and angered by a series of scandals about the sexual abuse of children by clergy. Subsequent attempts by the hierarchy in Ireland and officials in Rome to hide scandal have also caused once loyal Catholics to become deeply sceptical about its power and about those in high office. Some of the very men who were once seen as standing shoulder to shoulder with Catholics of Northern Ireland during the Troubles have become pariahs.

Among them are John Paul II's former private secretary, the man who acted as the pope's intermediary between Rome and Bobby Sands. John Magee's career ended in ignominy when, as Bishop of Cloyne, he was disgraced after an inquiry into abuse revealed cover-ups in his diocese and that he had falsely told the government that the diocese was reporting all abuse allegations to the civil authorities.[56]

Cardinal Cahal Daly, who succeeded Tomas O'Fiaich as Archbishop of Armagh and Primate of All Ireland, was once a key player in efforts to bring about peace during the Troubles and spoke out fiercely against IRA violence. He was later booed on the live Irish TV programme *The Late Late Show* over his response to questions about how the Church covered up the activities of abusive priests. Then there were revelations about Daly's successor, Cardinal Sean Brady, and his involvement in a case in the 1970s. Fr Brendan Smyth was a serial child abuser who assaulted young people during his time as a priest in Belfast, Dublin and America. His first conviction was for the abuse of four siblings in the Falls Road in Belfast but he fled to the Republic. In 2010 it became widely known that as a young priest, Sean Brady had witnessed two young teenage boys being made to sign oaths of silence about Smyth during a Church inquiry into his wrongdoing. Five years later, in June 2015, Cardinal Brady gave evidence to Northern Ireland's historical institutional abuse inquiry about the Smyth case and admitted the focus of attention at the time was the Church's reputation and covering up the scandal. 'There was a shroud of secrecy and confidentiality with a view to not destroying the good name of the Church,' he said.

The structure of the Church once enabled its priests and bishops to retain strong links with the people – links which helped them lobby for prisoners, admonish men of violence, and act as intermediaries with government. But that same structure gave clerics the opportunity to exploit their power. Priests and bishops who were trusted because of their role in the Troubles were able to use that trust to hide the truth and exploit the most vulnerable in society.[57]

The abuse scandals of Ireland and Northern Ireland led to discussions in Rome in 2010 during an unprecedented summit. Twenty-four of Ireland's bishops, including those whose dioceses are in the north, met Pope Benedict XVI and Curial officials for two days to discuss the abuse scandal. The gathering was prompted by the Murphy Report, commissioned by the Irish government into abuse in the diocese of Dublin, which had revealed the focus of the Church had been on protecting its reputation, the avoidance of scandal, and secrecy. It was a familiar response to scandal seen across the world where abuse by priests had taken place. By the time of the exposures of scandal in the twenty-first century, senior churchmen from the pope down spoke of regret for past wrongdoing. But the damage – not only to the actual victims – but to the reputation of the Church and to trust between priests and people was considerable, especially in places such as Northern Ireland where the Church's power over individuals' lives had been so profound and now lay broken.

The abuse scandal reinforces the anomaly of Northern Ireland in Church–state affairs: the Vatican responded to the Murphy Report by bringing to Rome all its bishops, whether their dioceses covered part of the United Kingdom or the Republic of Ireland, even though the Murphy Report focused on what went on in the republic. This led to a spat with the Irish government when Rome insisted that requests for information must come through diplomatic channels because the Holy See is a sovereign state. So even though the abuse scandals came about because of close contact between the faithful and their priests due to their pastoral roles, the Church insisted that this was an issue of governance rather than spirituality.[58] [59]

At other times, the Church has seen even its diplomatic work as inextricably linked to theology. Mark Pellew, the former British ambassador to the Holy See, recalls that when he presented his credentials in 1998, John Paul expressed his hope that progress in ecumenical relations would help facilitate an agreement in Northern Ireland – although successive politicians of course did not see it so much as a theological but a political matter.[60]

The similar intertwining of theology and politics came again with the Good Friday Agreement in April 1998, when John Paul welcomed it in his Easter address. Pellew recalled: 'We knew that it would be welcomed by the pope in his Easter address. My only concern was to ensure that the pope's welcome would not be too effusive. Otherwise the Paisleyites would have scented a Catholic plot and raised all sorts of further difficulties.'[61]

Since then Rome has continued to closely monitor the peace process. Just how important it was was emphasized in 2010 during Pope Benedict's visit to Britain when he mentioned it during his opening remarks on his arrival at Holyrood Palace. In the years since John Paul II made his devastating speech demanding an end to violence, Northern Ireland has found some semblance of peace and the Church played its own significant role in that. Today it is the relationship between the Church and its people that is damaged and in need of repair.

A test of the Church's capacity for repairing the damage will come in 2018 when Ireland hosts the World Meeting of Families and Pope Francis will attend. His visit was first announced in November 2016 and the invitation followed diplomatic form: the government stepped in to invite the pope after the Irish bishops had already asked him to attend.[62]

The then *taoiseach*, Enda Kenny, invited the pope in person during a visit to the Holy See where the pair conversed about climate change, unemployment and Church–state relations; these had sunk to an all-time low in 2011 after Kenny had denounced the Vatican in a speech made following publication of the Cloyne Report into child sexual abuse. Then, he had accused the Church of 'trying to frustrate an inquiry in a sovereign democratic republic' and said the report had excavated 'the dysfunction, disconnection, elitism, the narcissism that dominate the culture of the Vatican'.[63]

Kenny's remarks from the floor of the Irish parliament were unprecedented in a once unquestioningly loyal Catholic country. 'The rape and torture of children were downplayed or "managed" to uphold the primacy of the institution, its power, standing and reputation,' he had said then.

Later the Irish government withdrew its ambassador to the Holy See as a mark of disapproval for the way child sex abuse had been dealt with. But behind the scenes, diplomacy had continued to restore relations, helped undoubtedly by the election of Pope Francis, to whom Kenny paid fulsome tribute that day in Rome. But he also indicated that he had urged the pope to speak about the scandal during his visit to the World Meeting of Families – a global gathering that the Catholic Church holds every four years. It will not be without controversy. Four months after his meeting with Kenny, the pope wrote to Cardinal Kevin Farrell, head of the Vatican office for Laity, Family and Life, and indicated that he wanted the gathering to discuss his apostolic letter, *Amoris Laetitia*, which has led to outright criticism of the pope by conservative hierarchs, especially over his approach to Holy Communion for the divorced and remarried.[64] Two months earlier, the Irish bishops visited Rome for their ad limina visit where they also discussed with the pope issues that affect the Catholic Church in Ireland, especially the child abuse scandals and the position of women. Then there is the issue of same-sex marriage, voted for by the Irish people in a referendum, but opposed vehemently by the Vatican.[65]

With the territory of the Irish bishops' conference covering the whole of Ireland, including the north, there is also the possibility of the pope travelling to Northern Ireland. If he does, it will be a measure of how much that region has changed in the past thirty years: as noted earlier in this chapter, due to security risks John Paul II did not go there during his visit to Ireland in 1979. The late Deputy First Minister of Northern Ireland, Martin McGuinness, indicated that the pope would cross the border, while First Minister Arlene Foster, the leader of the DUP, said it would be a matter for the Foreign Office whether he would come or not, and carefully noted that she would meet him in his capacity as head of state.[66] That brief response signalled the complexity of the forthcoming visit and of diplomatic relations for the Holy See: a visit to a pastoral gathering requires an invitation to come from the government of a host nation. But in Ireland's case, a geographical territory regarded as an ecclesiastical single entity by the Church cuts across a political reality and the traumatic history of division, not just between two nations but between Christians. Then there are the difficulties surrounding Brexit and the future of the border between north and south. If the visit to the north does go ahead, it will be one of the biggest tests of the Holy See's diplomacy in some time – and a moment when the pope in his role as *pontifex*, the bridge-builder, will need all his peacemaking skills.

That bridge-building will not just be between Church and state, north and south, Catholic and Protestant, but between once devout Catholics and the institution of the Church. The relationship of trust has deteriorated. A similar development has taken place in Scotland, where so many Irish Catholics migrated in the nineteenth and twentieth centuries. Today the divides between Protestant and Catholic are no longer so deep and so damaging as they once were, and the blatant discrimination against Catholics by wider Scottish society have dissipated. Instead a crisis over sexual misdemeanours – on this occasion involving a cardinal – is the crisis whose fallout has scarred the Church. It is the subject of the next chapter.

Notes

1   'How an outbreak of ragwort brought John Paul II to a field in Drogheda' (2015), *The Journal*, October 10. http://www.thejournal.ie/drogheda-the-pope-grant-family-2378465-Oct2015/

2   Homily of His Holiness John Paul II, 29 September 1979. https://w2.vatican.va/content/john-paul-ii/en/homilies/1979/documents/hf_jp-ii_hom_19790929_irlanda-dublino-drogheda.html

3   FitzGerald, Garret (1991), *All in a Life: Garret FitzGerald – An Autobiography*, Dublin: Gill and MacMillan, 579.

4   Atkins, Humphrey (1979), memo to the Defence and Overseas Policy Committee, 12 October, the Margaret Thatcher Foundation Archive. http://www.margaretthatcher.org/document/116722

5   Interview of Sean Donlon (SD) by Catherine Pepinster (CP), January 2016.

6   *The Guardian* (2014), Obituary of Ian Paisley, 12 September. Available online: http://www.theguardian.com/politics/2014/sep/12/the-rev-ian-paisley

7   *Britain and the Holy See – proceedings of the 2012 Rome Colloquium*, Rome: British Embassy to the Holy See, 2012, 65.

8   Ibid.

9   Donlan, Sean (2012), 'Garret FitzGerald and Irish Foreign Policy', The Dr Garret FitzGerald Memorial Lecture, National University of Ireland, Dublin.

10 Interview of SD by CP.

11 Ibid.

12 Letter from Bishop Cahal Daly to Humphrey Atkins, 13 October 1980, Public Records Office, CAIN website: http://cain.ulst.ac.uk/proni/1980/proni_NIO-12-189_1980-10-13.pdf

13 Letter from Edward Daly, Bishop of Derry to Humphrey Atkins, 5 January 1980, Public Records Office, CAIN website: http://cain.ulst.ac.uk/proni/1980/proni_NIO-12-175_1980-01-05.pdf

14 John Paul II (1980), personal message to Margaret Thatcher, 30 October, the Margaret Thatcher Foundation Archive. Available online: http://www.margaretthatcher.org/document/120465

15 Obituary of Tomas O'Fiaich (1990), *The Irish Times*, 9 May. Available online: www.cregganhistory.co.uk/ofiaichcentre/obituaries.htm

16 Recorded with the message from John Paul II to Margaret Thatcher, ibid.

17 Margaret Thatcher (1980), Letter to John Paul II, 13 November, the Margaret Thatcher Foundation Archive. Available online: http://www.margaretthatcher.org/document/119884

18 Margaret Thatcher engagement diary (1980), meetings with Cardinal Casaroli and John Paul II. Available online: http://www.margaretthatcher.org/document/113644

19 Ray Harrington, private secretary, Northern Ireland Office (1980), letter to Michael Alexander, private secretary, 10 Downing Street, 30 November, National Archives. Available online: http://discovery.nationalarchives.gov.uk/details/r/C11555972#imageViewerLink

20 Thatcher, Margaret (1980), letter to John Paul II regarding the hunger strike in the Maze prison, 29 November, Thatcher Foundation Archive. Available online: http://www.margaretthatcher.org/document/119900

21 Gaffin, Neville (1981), memo regarding organized press leak, 28 April 1981, the Margaret Thatcher Foundation Archive. Available online: http://www.margaretthatcher.org/document/125157

22 Parkhouse, Geoffrey and Gordon Petrie (1981), 'Pope's envoy pleads in vain with Bobby Sands', the *Glasgow Herald*, 29 April. Available online via news.google.com/newspapers

23 Atkins, Humphrey (1981), record of conversation with Fr Magee, Stormont Castle 29 April, the Margaret Thatcher Foundation Archive. Available online: http://www.margaretthatcher.org/document/125159

24 Minutes of full Cabinet (1981), discussion of Northern Ireland, 30 April, the Margaret Thatcher Foundation Archive. Available online: http://www.margaretthatcher.org/document/127206

25 O'Fiaich, Tomas, Timothy Manning and Terence Cooke (1981), telegrams to Margaret Thatcher, the Margaret Thatcher Foundation Archive. Available online: http://fc95d419f4478b3b6e5f-3f71d0fe2b653c4f00f32175760e96e7.r87.cf1.rackcdn.com/938F48B3C63846898ABF0760F15103E1.pdf

26 Thatcher, Margaret (1981), message to Tomas O'Fiaich, 28 April, the Margaret Thatcher Foundation Archive. Available online: http://www.margaretthatcher.org/document/125158

27 'Declassified documents reveal Church's role during Troubles' (2012), *The Universe*, 4 January. Available online: www.thecatholicuniverse.com/declassified documents reveal Church's role during Troubles – 1826.

28 Moore, Charles (2015), *Margaret Thatcher, The Authorised Biography: Volume Two – Everything She Wants*, quoting a David Goodall unpublished manuscript, London: Allen Lane, 306.

29 Statement of Tomas O'Fiaich (1981), *The Tablet*, 30 May, 25.

30 Ibid.

31 Ibid.

32 'Secret hunger strike documents released' (2012), BBC Northern Ireland, 4 July. http://www.bbc.co.uk/news/uk-northern-ireland-18694742

33 'The Cardinal meets Mr Atkins' (1981), *The Tablet*, 13 June, 19.

34 McHardy, Anne (2006), 'Obituary of Fr Denis Faul', *The Guardian*, 22 June. Available online: http://www.theguardian.com/news/2006/jun/22/guardianobituaries.mainsection1

35 'Maze hunger strike ends' (1981), *The Tablet*, 10 October, 27.

36 Interview of Eamon Duffy (ED) by Catherine Pepinster (CP), December 2015.

37 Howard, ibid, 325.

38 For a full account of John Paul II's theology, see Weigel, George (1999), *Witness to Hope: The Biography of John Paul II*, London: Harper.

39 de Lubac, Henri (1993), trs. Anne Elizabeth Englund, *At The Service of The Church*, San Francisco: Communio Books, 172.

40 Stanford, Peter (1993), *Cardinal Hume and the Changing Face of English Catholicism*, London: Geoffrey Chapman, 113.

41 Hume, Cardinal Basil (1979), Letter to Margaret Thatcher, 8 May, the Margaret Thatcher Foundation Archive. Available online: http://www.margaretthatcher.org/document/117974

42 Interview of Charles Wookey (CW) by Catherine Pepinster (CP), October 2015.

43 Howard, ibid, 182.

44 Margaret Thatcher (1984) letters to and from senior Catholic clergy, October, the Margaret Thatcher Foundation Archive.

45 Murphy-O'Connor, ibid, 118.

46 For fuller accounts of Hume's involvement, see Stanford, ibid, and Howard, ibid.

47 For further exposition of Brewer's arguments, see Brewer, John D. with Gareth I. Higgins and Francis Teeney (2011), *Religion, Civil Society and Peace in Northern Ireland*, Oxford: Oxford University Press.

48 Obituary of Fr Alec Reid, *Daily Telegraph*, 22 November 2013. http://www.telegraph.co.uk/news/obituaries/10468267/Father-Alec-Reid-Obituary.html

49 See Scull, Maggie (2016), 'The Catholic Church and the Hunger Strikes of Terence MacSwiney and Bobby Sands', *Irish Political Studies,* Vol. 31. Available online: https://kcl.academia.edu/MaggieScull

50 Stanford, ibid, 117.

51 Brewer, ibid, 203.

52 Northern Ireland Termination of Pregnancy Statistics 2014/15: Department of Health, Social Services and Public Safety.

53 Abortion statistics, England and Wales: 2014, Department of Health, 2015.

54 Harriet Sherwood, *The Guardian*, 7 January 2016. http://www.theguardian.com/world/2016/jan/07/abortion-law-catholic-church-northern-ireland-opposing-high-court-ruling

55 Campbell, Francis (2016), 'The Northern Ireland conflict was never as binary as some suggested', *The Tablet*, 21 May 2016, 5.

56 BBC (2011), Cloyne Report: a detailed guide, 13 July http://www.bbc.co.uk/news/uk-northern-ireland-14143822

57 Black, Rebecca (2015), 'Cardinal Brady apologises to Fr Brendan Smyth's victims', *Belfast Telegraph*, 26 June 2015. http://www.belfasttelegraph.co.uk/

news/northern-ireland/cardinal-brady-apologises-to-fr-brendan-smyths-victims-after-revelations-two-teenage-boys-were-asked-if-they-enjoyed-abuse-they-suffered-31331361.html

58 Poggioli, Sylvia (2010), 'Pope rebukes Irish bishops over abuse scandal', National Public Radio, 16 February 2010. http://www.npr.org/templates/story/story.php?storyId=123778485

59 'Vatican: Wikileaks document a matter of "extreme gravity"', Breaking News. ie, 11 December 2010. http://www.breakingnews.ie/ireland/vatican-wikileaks-documents-a-matter-of-extreme-gravity-485314.html

60 *Diplomacy and the Holy See*, ibid, 68.

61 Ibid.

62 McDonald, Henry (2016), 'Pope Francis to visit Ireland in 2018', *The Guardian*, 28 November. https://www.theguardian.com/world/2016/nov/28/pope-francis-to-visit-ireland-in-2018

63 Kenny, Enda (2011), Speech on the Cloyne Report, 20 July, transcript available via https://www.rte.ie/news/2011/0720/303965-cloyne1/

64 Pope's letter for Dublin World Meeting of Families (2017), Vatican Radio, presented 30 March. http://en.radiovaticana.va/news/2017/03/30/popes_letter_for_dublin_world_meeting_of_families_presented/1302212

65 Pope Francis meets with Irish bishops on ad limina visit to Rome (2017), Vatican Radio, 20 January. http://en.radiovaticana.va/news/2017/01/20/pope_francis_meets_with_irish_bishops_in_rome/1287138

66 Moriarty, Gerry (2016), 'Arlene Foster would meet Pope Francis if he visits the North', *Irish Times*, 28 November. http://www.irishtimes.com/news/ireland/irish-news/arlene-foster-would-meet-pope-francis-if-he-visits-the-north-1.2885603

10

Tricolours, saltires and papal flags:

The papacy and Scotland

The sixteenth of September 2010 was one of the greatest days in the Catholic history of Scotland. A thousand pipers arrived in Edinburgh from across the country, hundreds of Catholic children lined the streets, and dozens of people dressed as Scottish historical figures walked through the centre of the capital city of Edinburgh as part of the St Ninian's Day Parade. It was an event that marked the arrival of Pope Benedict XVI in Scotland at the start of his state visit to the UK and his meeting with the queen at Holyrood Palace.

This Scottish leg of the papal visit was the culmination of months of planning by Rome, the Foreign Office and Scottish politicians. The parade was the brainchild of Cardinal Keith O'Brien, the Archbishop of Edinburgh and St Andrews, and Scotland's premier Catholic cleric.

Having got what he, Jim Murphy, the Scottish Labour politician who had worked on the visit in the early days of its planning, and the then Scottish National Party leader, Alex Salmond, had wanted – a key role for Scotland in the papal visit – O'Brien dreamt up the St Ninian's Day parade. True, it had existed centuries before, but it had long been forgotten. O'Brien decided to resurrect it to both mark the pope's arrival in Scotland and reinforce a sense of strong Scottish Catholicism. The idea was a triumph, and thousands turned out to salute the pope and wave their saltires.

Catholicism in Scotland has certainly always been distinctive, a faith that is rather different from its quieter English cousin. The Catholic Church was outlawed in both countries following their two different Reformations, and both have been profoundly influenced by the migration of the Irish working class. While the English Reformation of the mid-sixteenth century had its origins in the sexual obsession of Henry VIII, as well as a certain growing interest among English intellectuals in the ideas of Martin Luther, the Scottish

Reformation's origins were strongly intellectual, lying in burgeoning Protestant thought in continental Europe. John Knox's encounter with John Calvin in Geneva in particular helped shape Scottish reformed theology and the reformed Church, the Kirk.

By 1560, the Scottish Reformation Parliament outlawed the Mass and rejected papal authority. Liturgical practices were dependent on having clear scriptural authority and all feasts, including Christmas and Easter, were banned. Only baptism and Holy Communion were retained as sacraments. Communion was given to those sitting; kneeling was said to be a sign of accepting the Real Presence, a Catholic doctrine. Church and state were separate jurisdictions. As the official guide to Benedict XVI's visit to Scotland put it: 'The appeal of Protestantism in 1560 can be overestimated but its triumph is indisputable.'[1]

Restoration of Catholicism seemed increasingly unlikely following the deposition of the Catholic Mary, Queen of Scots in 1567, and the union with England when her son, James VI of Scotland, became James I of England. Opposition to full union with England in 1705 first fed Jacobitism: then opposition to the Protestant Hanoverian kings led to the desire for the thrones of England, Scotland, France and Ireland to be held by a Catholic, Stuart monarch. The Jacobites backed first the deposed James II and VII, then his son James, the Old Pretender, begetter of the 1715 rebellion and later his grandson Charles Edward Stuart, the Young Pretender and leader of the 1745 rebellion. But there was also concern among supporters of the union that the Jacobites would drive Scotland back into poverty, for the country had enjoyed economic prosperity since unity. The opposition was led by many of the Presbyterian clergy of the west, central and south-east Lowlands, effectively the economic heart of Scotland, who were bitterly opposed to the claim of the Young Pretender. Their appeal to the Scots was anti-papist at its core, as Scots historian Tom Devine has described:

> A fundamental obstacle for the Stuarts was their Catholicism. They were not prepared to sacrifice their faith for political ambition and so inevitably paid the price . . . [Presbyterian clergy] stoked up fears that the return of the House of Stuart would bring in its train an autocratic papist regime that would threaten both the 'liberty' and 'true religion' of Presbyterian Scots. Whig propaganda relentlessly identified Charles as a foreigner who had come from Italy (the home of popery) and every attempt was made to exploit the anti-Catholic passions of the people in order to encourage opposition to him.[2]

The last hurrah for the Jacobites came with their rebellion in 1745, forty years after the union. The Young Pretender led his supporters south, first to Carlisle and then as far as Derby. There they were met by English forces, which forced the Scots to retreat back to Scotland where they were defeated at Culloden. Opponents of the rebellion identified the Young Pretender and his followers with the antichrist and the pope, so much so that their response was concerned with religion as much as anything. As Devine says: 'The response to the rebellion took the form not only of military and judicial repression but also an attempt to transform Highland society and culture through legislation designed to encourage economic improvement, the expansion of Presbyterianism and the removal of cultural differences with the rest of Britain.'[3]

There was also the role played by the realpolitik of the papacy, which, after the death of James 'III' refused to recognize the claim of the Young Pretender and instead focused on rapprochement with the Protestant House of Hanover. This decision also caused a division between Scottish Catholics and Rome authorities that disapproved of the Scots College continuing to refer to Charles Edward Stuart in the style of a king, despite Rome's acceptance of the Hanoverians.

While the Jacobite rebellion was suppressed, Catholicism grew in Scotland, particularly due to steady Irish migration as Scottish towns industrialized. The Catholic population was strong in the west – the area closest to Ireland – but it led to the creation of the Scottish Reformation Society and Scottish Protestant Association and the journals *The Scottish Protestant* and *The Bulwark* as defenders of the Protestant religion and as opponents of popery. By 1851, the number of Irish-born Scots had risen to around 204,000, as they escaped across the Irish Sea from famine and in order to find work. The 1829 Catholic Emancipation Act and the 1878 restoration of the Scottish hierarchy consolidated the place of the Catholic Church in Scotland. By then, the Catholic population had increased to around 300,000 and included Italians and Lithuanians as well as the Irish. Areas such as Aberdeenshire, Banffshire and Inverness had remained Catholic since the Reformation, but the Industrial Revolution had led to a growth in numbers in the west around Glasgow; by 1900, around 100,000 Catholics were living there.

Parish churches, halls and schools helped create a strong Catholic network, providing a migrant community with a sense of identity and a structure to their new lives. The sense that the Church would look after its own was further consolidated by efforts to help the poorest Catholics through organizations such as the St Vincent De Paul Society. Devine calls these efforts 'a new social Catholicism . . . which created almost an alternative community in Scotland'.[4]

The difficulty, though, was that separation and distinctiveness can exacerbate divisions and lead to tribalism. This danger can be seen in what began as a benign intention of the Marist Brother Walfrid in Glasgow's East End to not only feed and clothe the poor but to provide a means for young Catholic men to play sport with their own kind, rather than mix with Protestants. The result was Celtic Football Club, whose rivalry with the Protestant Glasgow Rangers led to regular bouts of violence, particularly at the time of matches between the two clubs, known collectively as the 'Old

Firm'. Match days would also see the Union flag flying at Rangers' ground while the Irish tricolour would be displayed at Celtic. In recent times efforts have been made to counter sectarianism linked to football with the anti-sectarian organization, Nil by Mouth, being formed following the sectarian murder of a Celtic fan in 1996. By 2003, the Criminal Justice (Scotland) Act set out situations where a criminal offence was caused by religious prejudice, and in the following years substantial numbers of incidents motivated by religious hatred were reported to police, with Catholics bearing the brunt of attacks.[5]

While tribalism and sectarianism remained a problem for decades, other developments encouraged the integration of Catholics in Scottish society. The most significant efforts of the Church to enhance the lives of Catholics were, as in England, through education. The 1872 Education Act made schooling mandatory but the Catholic schools proved a substantial financial burden on people who were not well off at all. Christmas bazaars, fetes, raffles, the weekly church collection: all these funded a schooling system that served more than 20,000 children by 1876. Despite the voluntary funding efforts, the Catholic system could not compete with the state-run one's resources, leaving Catholic young people unable to compete in the jobs market and social mobility a pipe dream.

It was the 1918 Education (Scotland) Act that made the most significant difference to the Catholics of Scotland and paved the way for Catholics to play a substantial role in Scottish society. Poor Catholics no longer had to fund their own schools while also contributing to the Presbyterian system. Instead, Catholic schools were funded and thrived within the state system. But the bishops struck a hard bargain: priests had full access to the schools under the Act; religious education was to be maintained and only those deemed acceptable to the Church in terms of religious faith and character were to be appointed as teachers.

It was the start of growing prosperity among Catholics and even the formation of a substantial Catholic professional class in Scotland, as well as greater political engagement. Although Irish Catholic migrants had backed the Liberal Party, with its support for Irish Home Rule, the electoral reforms of 1918 drew more working-class voters to the Labour Party. Political activism increased throughout the twentieth century, and substantial numbers of Scottish Labour MPs were Catholics. This intertwining of the fortunes of Catholics and the Scottish Labour Party continued for many years until the emergence of a strong relationship between influential Catholics and the Scottish National Party (SNP), of which more later.

But in the earlier part of the twentieth century, the consequences of Catholics' growing fortunes led to further attacks on them and their faith. During the Depression of the 1920s and 30s, Catholics were blamed for taking the jobs of Protestants, there was sectarian violence against Catholics and their churches, and even incidences where children were stoned. The opposition was often focused on the pope: in 1922, the Church of Scotland published *The Menace of the Irish Race to our Scottish Nationality*, which blamed the Irish for being part of a papist conspiracy to subvert Presbyterian values, and accused them of being the source of drunkenness and criminality. Complaints also continued about state funding of Catholic schools as 'Rome on the rates'.[6]

Paranoia about rival religious factions was put to one side during the war years due to the threat from a common enemy. Both the Catholic and Protestant communities contributed side by side to the war effort from 1939–45, and there was also a subsequent growth in religious ecumenism and a decline in discrimination at work. New businesses in foreign ownership tended to have more faith-blind hiring policies compared to the old 'smokestack' industries. Catholics became more integrated and the old prejudices declined.

One of the most symbolic acts of improving relations between the different religious traditions came with the ecumenical landmark of the then Archbishop of Glasgow, Thomas Winning, being invited in 1975 to address the General Assembly of the Church of Scotland. It broke the silence between the two Churches that had lasted 400 years.

Winning addressed the General Assembly just a year after being appointed Archbishop of Glasgow. The son of a devout Catholic family from Lanarkshire, Winning's route to episcopal office was typical of many high-flyers in the hierarchy who come from a humble background. After a solid education in Catholic schools and a time as an altar boy, Winning trained for the priesthood at Blairs College, Aberdeen and St Peter's Seminary, Bearsden. He was then selected to attend the Scots College in Rome, and after just a year as a newly ordained curate in Lanarkshire, returned to Rome to study for a doctorate in canon law. Then there were four years back in Scotland, before his appointment in 1961 as spiritual director of the Scots College – in effect looking after the well-being of the students. Being in Rome as student and teacher steeps a man in the ways of the Vatican, and for Winning it was a particularly useful time to be there: it coincided with the Second Vatican Council and enabled him to encounter bishops as they debated the future of the Catholic Church. Within five years of his return to Scotland in 1966, he joined the episcopacy, as an auxiliary bishop to Archbishop Scanlan of Glasgow whom he replaced three years later in 1974.

Glasgow was a sizeable diocese in the early 1970s with more than 300,000 Catholics, including 300 priests. It did not take Winning long to become the outspoken hierarch who was to appear frequently on Scotland's public platforms over the years. He was installed as archbishop on 3 September 1974 and just three days later he was quoted in the *Scottish Catholic Observer* as saying:

We live in a world where man has acquired a new arrogance, a false independence: he senses a victory over the forces of nature and had pushed the true God into the background of his life and fashioned new Gods to worship . . . How are we to penetrate this darkness? That is the task of the Church today. It has never had to tread quite the same depth of darkness. But it has to pierce it.[7]

For him, the darkness consisted not only of what he perceived to be a lessening of sexual morality but also of poverty, and Winning was a staunch champion of the deprived of his archdiocese. In 1976 he abandoned plans to restore St Andrew's Cathedral in Glasgow and instead spent the £1.6 million budget on a campaign against poverty in Glasgow, describing it as Britain's most deprived city.

The softer side of Winning emerged with his approach to ecumenism, a likely legacy of his time in Rome during Vatican II rather than growing up in sectarian Scotland. Although a devoted supporter of Celtic, he never attended an Old Firm game against Rangers, disapproving of the sectarianism on display. During the homily given at his installation, he called for 'a rejection of bigotry and discrimination based on religion'. He followed this with his address to the Church of Scotland a year later, an event so significant in Scotland that it was broadcast on television. Dressed in a simple black suit rather than his episcopal purple and without his usual pectoral cross, he told the General Assembly that the Catholic Church was 'fully committed to working with you and the other Christian Churches towards unity'. The Moderator for 1975, the Revd James Matheson from Skye, told him: 'You have won our hearts!'[8]

For all his ecumenical enthusiasm, Winning was above all a Catholic Scot, and his commitment to the Church and his drive proved crucial in 1982 when he became part of the British contingent that campaigned hard to keep the pastoral visit of Pope John Paul II to the UK on track when it came so close to being cancelled because of the Falklands War. As noted in Chapter 2, he and Archbishop Derek Worlock of Liverpool were part of a team that travelled to Rome to persuade John Paul to come to the UK, despite the conflict between the nation and Argentina over the Falkland Islands and the protests against his British visit by Latin American bishops.[9]

The planning of the visit had not been plain sailing. The Scottish events were added on as an afterthought because Cardinal Basil Hume, after inviting the pope, forgot to brief the Scottish bishops about it. Sectarian tensions had risen in Glasgow in 1981 following Republican marches in support of the H block hunger strikers in Northern Ireland, and counter-marches by the Scottish Loyalists, formed by a breakaway group of the Grand Orange Lodge of Scotland. Ian Paisley, then the chairman of the British Council of Protestant Christian Churches, also declared that he would tour Scotland during the papal visit to protest against it. The Free Church of Scotland declared the visit a propaganda exercise to encourage a Scottish Catholic revival while the Revd David Cassells, a relative of Paisley and chairman of the militant loyalist Scottish Constitutional Defence Committee, warned that 1,500 men would stand at the gates of Bellahouston Park in Glasgow during the pope's planned celebration of Mass there and threatened violent action if they were stopped.[10]

When the papal visit looked increasingly in jeopardy, Derek Worlock and Thomas Winning decided to act, rather than accept any defeatism from their respective cardinals. But first Winning went into overdrive, getting every Catholic lay organization in Scotland to telegram the pope urging him to not cancel his visit, and then organizing a telegram from the Scottish bishops saying much the same thing. It was then that Derek Worlock phoned him and asked him to join him in his mission to Rome, something to which Basil Hume had given his blessing.

Winning spent his time on the flight out to Rome composing his arguments regarding the visit, including the thought that cancellation would be used by Protestant critics to prove that the Catholic Church wasted the pennies of the poor and would prove that Rome led the way while Scottish Catholics merely obeyed, regardless of what was decided. Yet during lunch with John Paul the next day, he also used Protestant interest in the visit to argue for it not being cancelled, offering the pope a telegram from the Moderator of the Church of Scotland for that year – a new Moderator is appointed annually— Professor John McIntyre, who described the pope as a prophetic figure for the Scots.

The conversations over lunch continued and, according to Winning's biographer, Stephen McGinty, it was the Glaswegian's suggestion that the pope make a visit to Argentina as well which helped provide a solution to the difficulty over him visiting Britain while it was at war with that Catholic nation. Worlock and Winning then urged their respective cardinals, Hume and Gray, to also come out to Rome on Friday 21 May and press the importance of the papal visit to the UK. Over lunch, the British and the Argentinian cardinals both secured their visits, while that night, British troops landed in San Carlos. The cardinals of the two countries then celebrated Mass with John Paul the following day in St Peter's Basilica. According to McGinty, Winning later revealed at the Mass that: 'The irrationality of the war came home to me as I looked around St Peter's at the young men [seminarians] from South America and Britain. It was just possible that their blood brothers were killing one another in the Falklands at that moment.'[11] A week later, Winning made his way south to Gatwick Airport to be part of the entourage that greeted Pope John Paul on his arrival in Britain. It is said that when he saw Winning, the pope told him, 'This is England – I'm not in Scotland yet,' a humorous remark yet one that illustrates how the Holy See makes a clear distinction between the two nations.[12] The recognition of Scotland's nationhood was also apparent on 1 June when the papal plane touched down near Edinburgh and John Paul II emerged to an 8,000-strong throng who cheered as he kneeled and kissed the grass of Scotland.

The days of anti-Catholic bigotry seemed behind the Scots when John Paul II greeted the young people of the country at Murrayfield. The atmosphere was as exhilarating as any rugby international when 50,000 cheered 'We want the pope', and John Paul could only stand with his hands reaching out to the crowd. This was a Church which was at ease with itself, its young members confident of their place in the nation.

Similarly arresting was the moment of historic ecumenism when John Paul encountered the Moderator of the Church of Scotland, and they shook hands in the courtyard of the Assembly Hall beneath a statue of John Knox. Although a small gathering of 200 Protestant protesters stood nearby, led by Ian Paisley and with banners saying 'We don't want you', it was clear that the Scottish Protestant Establishment *did* want to meet the pope. John McIntyre told him that they shared 'One Lord, one faith, one baptism', and while Scotland was a country shaped by religious conflict, this was a day of reconciliation.

Glasgow, too, was to share in the papal excitement, with the city's Bellahouston Park crammed with people for the papal Mass to be celebrated there. In his homily, John Paul did not shy away from the traumas of the Reformation, but he urged Scottish Catholics to look forward to the future: 'You belong in the present and your generation must not be content simply to rest on the laurels won by your grandparents and great-grandparents . . . But we find it harder to follow Christ today than appears to have been the case. Witnessing to him in modern life means a daily contest, not so quickly and decisively resolved as the martyrs of the past.'[13] The faith that had once been rejected by Scotland, that had struggled against adversity to first survive and then thrive there, was confirmed by the visit as a notable part of Scottish culture and spirituality. And the pope, who had been labelled for so long as an enemy of Protestant Scotland, was now a welcome guest of the nation – a nation that he and the Holy See confirmed as distinctive and separate from England.

For Thomas Winning, witnessing to Christ in Scotland meant being outspoken and relentless in his efforts to counter what he saw as the decadence of modern life, highlighted for him by abortion. It also meant being committed to those less fortunate than others, something that the Scottish Church had done within the Catholic community via its schools and other charitable endeavours. The papal visit of 1982 confirmed that Catholics had become integrated into Scottish society, which was welcomed, yet something had been lost. The unity that Catholics had forged in adversity had broken down, and Thomas Winning wanted to restore that sense of community. In the mid-1980s he tried to reform the archdiocese of Glasgow by encouraging more lay participation, based on the ideas of the Second Vatican Council, with varying degrees of success. The response to these protracted efforts to reform the archdiocese – it went on for a decade – was but a murmur compared to the uproar that beset Winning publicly over his attitudes to abortion and homosexuality, particularly after being created cardinal in 1994, when he succeeded Cardinal Gray as Scotland's prince of the Church. By 1997, the year of the election that would see Tony Blair become Labour prime minister and the thirtieth anniversary of the Abortion Act, Winning was known as a vociferous opponent of abortion, but he was about to find another way of fighting for the pro-life cause rather than just speaking out.

A speech planned for a rally to be held in Glasgow by the Society for the Protection of Unborn Children was deliberately leaked to the press in advance and immediately caused the impact that Winning had wanted. The cardinal decided to counter the argument that being pro-life meant that you believed women did not have a right to choose, by helping women facing an unwanted pregnancy to choose life by offering them practical and financial help. As the *Sunday Telegraph*, which had been given the leaked speech, put it: ' "We'll pay you not to abort," says cardinal.'. The headline had immediate impact with donations being offered to Winning for his project. The words he offered in the speech were not ones of condemnation. Instead he said, over and over again: 'We will help you.' Winning had no plans, no money and no office for his project but within a fortnight donations amounted to £250,000 and the requests for help began coming in. Winning's initiative had won the support of the people, and of his fellow bishops. Rome was also impressed. But his overtly critical position on abortion did not fully win over the Scots; despite a pre-election pastoral letter that told Catholic voters that abortion took precedence over any other issue when considering which candidate to vote for, pro-life parliamentary candidates got nowhere and Labour in Scotland trounced its opponents. Episcopal direction of voters – the undue influence of the papists, as the Church's critics would have it – was a fantasy.[14]

There had always been a strong connection between Catholicism in Scotland and politics. Irish Catholic migrants to Scotland had first tended to vote for the Liberal Party, believing it would deliver Home Rule, but after partition they favoured the Labour Party. By the 1990s Thomas Winning was becoming disillusioned with Labour, as the party became increasingly in favour of gay and abortion rights. His antipathy became particularly pronounced once Tony Blair became the party's leader. Winning's spat with Blair began with the cardinal's consternation in finding that a stall belonging to the pro-life Labour for Life organization had been banned from the Scottish Labour Party Conference. After attempts at behind the scenes negotiations to get it accepted, Winning went public with a highly personal attack on Blair, published in the *Daily Mail*, in which he denounced the ban on the stall as restricting free speech. 'The embers of totalitarianism are not far from the surface of New Labour. Its capacity for intimidation can be gauged by Mr Blair's shirking from uttering a word about blatantly undemocratic behaviour within his own party, lest he provoke wrath and find his leadership crippled,' he wrote.[15] Blair was furious, writing to Winning that an attack in the *Mail* did nothing to help engender trust, but the Scottish Labour Party did eventually allow Labour for Life space for a stall at the conference, with supportive MPs, including John Reid and George Galloway, paying for it.

The conflict with Blair did not stop there. Winning, a member of the Vatican's Pontifical Council for the Family, did his research into Blair's voting record on abortion, finding that he voted in favour of it on many occasions and voted against the Alton Bill to restrict it. He raised abortion at a private meeting with Blair at Westminster a year before the general election but Blair prevaricated, saying he was personally against it but could not impose his personal view on women. A further public attack on Blair came with a BBC Everyman documentary on religion and politics in which Winning again criticized the Labour leader for his record on abortion, describing him as inconsistent and his claim to have Christian values as being a sham. The attacks were made again at a Scottish press conference, and neither man gave way. The gap between the Labour leader and the leader of Scottish Catholics seemed to yawn as wide as ever. The cosy days when Labour candidates could expect Catholics to vote for them were over – and canny Scottish Nationalist politicians such as Alex Salmond were already aware of an opportunity. It would take some years to bear fruit.

Before that astute cultivation became obvious, though, another major moral issue was to cause upheaval in Scottish Catholicism. In the late 1980s, homosexuality and attitudes towards it became caught up in party politics when the Thatcher government introduced what became known as Section 28 to the Local Government Act to prevent local councils from promoting homosexuality or endorsing it as an accepted family relationship. Although Section 28 did not create any criminal offence, it did cause some groups for gay people to be closed down because they were thought to be in breach of the Act. By the time the new Scottish Parliament was established during the early years of the Blair government, there was pressure for Section 28 to be repealed, and members of the new parliament were keen to do so in Scotland. Not everyone in Scotland was supportive, however, in particular the evangelical businessman, Brian Souter, who took on the new Executive over repeal. It was at this point that Cardinal Winning intervened in the most spectacular way. In January 2000, he gave an interview to his later biographer, Stephen McGinty, in which he said that: 'The truth of Section 28 is that it is sodomy. For anyone to deny that this is not a perversion is nonsense. The Universal Catechism calls it an act of grave depravity. It is condemned by all the world's religions.'[16] Winning went further during a visit to Malta, when he addressed the Catholic Families movement, claiming that there was a 'militant and homosexual lobby' threatening family values all over Europe.[17]

The approach taken by Winning in Scotland was in sharp contrast to that adopted by Basil Hume in England, who chose his words very carefully when speaking on this issue. When the Congregation for the Doctrine of the Faith issued a document on homosexuality that upset many gay Catholics, Basil Hume published his own document in response that was far more measured in tone.[18] Winning did no such thing and was far more inclined to accept the language of the Curia that described homosexuality as an intrinsic moral evil and objectively disordered. The approach taken in London led to compromise: after lobbying from the Catholic Church and the Church of England, Education Secretary David Blunkett agreed that on repeal of

Section 28, children would be taught the importance of traditional marriage. In Scotland, however, with Winning at loggerheads with not only Westminster MPs (including George Galloway) who had once been close allies of the cardinal, but also with the Scottish Executive, there was little hint of pragmatism winning the day. First Minister Donald Dewar refused to accept similar wording to that agreed with David Blunkett, conceding only that children be taught the value of stable family life.

The end of the twentieth century and the start of the twenty-first produced mixed messages about the relationship between Scotland and the Catholic Church. After the excitement of the papal visit in 1982, there had been a new acceptance of the Catholic Church; relations between it and the Protestant denominations had warmed considerably, and Scottish Catholics were putting the days of prejudice and discrimination behind them. This new era of friendship between Church and state was symbolized in 2000 when Cardinal Winning travelled to Rome to mark the 400th anniversary of the Scots College and, at a special audience, introduced Scotland's first minister, Henry McLeish, John Reid, the first Catholic secretary of state for Scotland, and the Rt Revd Andrew McLellan, the Moderator of the Church of Scotland that year, to John Paul II. Once such a visit would have caused uproar but by the dawn of the new millennium it was a welcome sign of the warm relations between Rome and Scotland.

But in sharp contrast, all was not well in Scotland. Church attendance was declining, with younger people falling away. The Church's attitude to homosexuality, highlighted by Winning's intransigence and intemperate remarks, alienated people, and not only gay activists but also homosexual Catholics and those with homosexual family members. The issue would not go away, either. Instead it would come back to haunt the Church and create the greatest scandal in its history.

The sudden death of Cardinal Winning from a heart attack in 2001 left two vacancies in Scotland: one for the Archbishop of Glasgow and the second for a member of the College of Cardinals. There is no set rule regarding the choice of cardinal in Scotland. But with Winning, the red hat had been given to Glasgow and before him, it had been given to Cardinal Gordon Gray of St Andrews and Edinburgh, the nation's other archdiocese. Within two years of Winning's death, the red hat passed not to his successor in Glasgow, Mario Conti, but went back east to St Andrews and Edinburgh and to Keith O'Brien.

O'Brien was Northern Irish by birth, his family moving to Scotland when his father served with the Royal Navy at Faslane. After gaining a chemistry degree at Edinburgh University, he had trained for the priesthood, worked as a maths and science teacher, and then served as a parish priest. He later became a spiritual director of St Andrew's College, a now closed Scottish seminary, and also served as rector of Blairs College. He was chosen to be the Archbishop of St Andrews and Edinburgh in 1985, becoming cardinal in succession to Thomas Winning in 2003.

To those who did not know O'Brien well, he was a friendly man who had none of the airs and graces that some cardinals accumulate once they have been chosen as princes of the Church and become members of the College of Cardinals that elects the pope. Indeed, that is how he seemed to me. I recall lunching with him once at his favourite Edinburgh hotel where he greeted staff by name, chatting about Scotland's chances in the Six Nations rugby match that weekend at Murrayfield Stadium. When he offered me a lift after lunch to my next appointment, I assumed that meant a chauffeur would drive me there in the cardinal's limousine. Instead he drove me himself in his humble estate car.

Like Cardinal Winning, O'Brien was outspoken in support of various causes. He was a keen backer of the Scottish Catholic aid organization, Sciaf, and regularly travelled with them, moved by the poverty he saw overseas. He was critical of the UK's nuclear programme and described the retention of Trident as immoral. The cardinal's thinking was that the use of nuclear weapons was wrong and that retaining them, which meant the option of using them, was therefore unacceptable.[19]

But, like his predecessor, it was homosexuality that caused Keith O'Brien to be most outspoken in his public pronouncements, opposing homosexuality and gay adoption and going so far as to call gay marriage a 'subversion' – a comment that brought to mind Winning's description of homosexuality as a perversion. O'Brien's similarly pugilistic tone on issues of personal morality came as a surprise, however, for before he gained his red hat, he had been a more liberal voice in the Catholic Church. But just before his departure for the consistory in Rome, where he would be installed as a member of the College of Cardinals, he had spoken of the need for the Church to discuss issues such as birth control, women priests and celibacy. He was then forced to make a public pledge to be faithful to the Church's teaching at his own cathedral of St Mary's in Edinburgh. The stage was set for O'Brien to adopt what was known in Scotland as 'the Winning Way'.

By the time of Benedict XVI's visit to Scotland in 2010, Keith O'Brien was an established public figure in Scotland. There is no ecclesiastical or bureaucratic office of leader of the Catholic Church in Scotland, but like Winning, O'Brien readily accepted the role, and it gave the Catholic Church a certain prominence in public life. The parade for St Ninian's Day, which O'Brien was so key in organizing, confirmed that prominence and also established that the Church could use such events as a bridge to the wider Scottish community. Those on the streets that day were by no means all Catholic; their waving of saltires as well as papal flags was a confirmation of Scottishness as much as Catholicism and the importance of the papacy.

It turned out to be O'Brien's swansong. For within two years, Keith O'Brien, the genial Scottish cardinal, was summoned to Rome to discuss allegations of sexual impropriety. Unbeknownst to many people, O'Brien had been living a double life for some time. While his public pronouncements verged on the homophobic, in private, he used the power of his office to force his attentions on priests. The cardinal, who, like all other Catholic priests, had taken a vow of celibacy, was not averse to physical relations. And they were homosexual relations – the very thing he denounced so loudly.

By October 2012, O'Brien's double life began to unravel, when a priest made a complaint to the Congregation for Bishops – the Vatican department responsible for episcopal matters – about O'Brien's sexual misconduct. The cardinal was summoned to Rome and it was then agreed that he would announce his resignation in November but it would take effect in March 2013 when he reached his seventy-fifth birthday, the official retirement age for bishops. None of this was imparted to the people of Scotland.[20]

Then, rumours started to circulate about the complaint made to the Congregation in Rome, and among those who discussed the allegation were three serving priests and one who had left the ministry. They shared their memories of inappropriate sexual advances made to them by O'Brien decades ago when they were young – just as the original complainant had said. The four included one man who said that O'Brien made inappropriate sexual advances to him after night prayers when he was training for the priesthood at St Andrew's College, Drygrange. Another claimed inappropriate contact took place when the cardinal visited his parish; a third reported 'unwanted behaviour' after late-night drinking, and the fourth spoke of the cardinal using night prayers as an excuse for inappropriate contact. Their concerns were not just about unwanted sexual attention but focused on the power that Keith O'Brien had over them as a spiritual director and a bishop. He could decide what happened to them, where they served as priests – indeed their entire futures. They took their complaints in early February to the papal nuncio, Archbishop Antonio Mennini, and called for O'Brien to go.

Within a day or so, Pope Benedict shocked the world with his resignation. The nuncio's response to the O'Brien scandal was one of concern but also to indicate that the cardinal should still go to Rome to vote in the forthcoming conclave to elect Benedict's successor because then it would be easier for O'Brien to retire in prayer and seclusion like the pope. In other words, O'Brien could be quickly and quietly forgotten. Unimpressed, the complainants' next stop was the press.

O'Brien nearly got away with going quietly. By Saturday 23 February, the cardinal was staying in a church house in a quiet town outside Edinburgh where he planned to move when he retired a few weeks later after serving nearly twenty-eight years as archbishop. But his time was up. That day, *The Observer* newspaper was in contact with the Scottish Catholic Media Office requesting a response to the allegations from the four men. O'Brien's first response was to bluster, contesting the allegations and threatening legal action. He demanded the story should not be published. By 9.30 that evening, *The Observer* decided on the classic journalistic response: publish and be damned. It put the story on its website and in its print edition the next day.[21]

By Monday, O'Brien announced that the Vatican had accepted his resignation. After a lifetime spent reaching the very top of the Catholic Church, he was brought down by his human foibles and quit within thirty-six hours of their being exposed to the world and being ridiculed as a hypocrite.

The episode could not have come at a more awkward time for the Church. The conclave was just a couple of weeks away. With Cardinal Cormac Murphy-O'Connor of England and Wales too old to vote in the conclave, and his successor Archbishop Vincent Nichols not yet a member of the College of Cardinals, British interests would have been represented by Cardinal O'Brien in the vote to find a successor to Benedict, the pope whom O'Brien had honoured with such pomp and ceremony at the start of his UK visit three years earlier. But O'Brien and the Vatican realized the impossibility of his position, the circus that would surround him in Rome and which might threaten to overshadow the conclave. He announced he would not attend, leaving only Cardinal Sean O'Brady of Armagh, the Irish seat that covers Northern Ireland, to fly the UK flag at the conclave. Within four days of O'Brien's resignation, *The Times* carried details of the 2012 allegation made against O'Brien by a separate complainant.

The shock that the Church in Scotland underwent following O'Brien's spectacular fall from grace was immense. He had been archbishop for nearly twenty-eight years, a cardinal for ten, and was well liked by the laity. Priests were different: some suffered from his advances, others had noticed how some were favourites and others were left out in the cold. They in particular felt profoundly let down although the laity, too, expressed their distress in the most effective way: by no longer going to Mass or cutting their offerings to the church collection.

Fr Jock Dalrymple, an Edinburgh parish priest, described the reaction to Cardinal O'Brien's downfall: 'O'Brien had no idea of right and wrong. He was a narcissistic sociopath. Certain people had a hold over him and could do what they wanted. There was a gay subculture. The damage including financial damage is huge. So some people have left and the funds are down. Other Catholics have been resilient and they keep coming but anecdotal evidence suggests that for many Catholics in Scotland it has been a shattering blow.'[22]

O'Brien's counterpart in Glasgow, Archbishop Philip Tartaglia, admitted in a homily in his own cathedral, that: 'the most stinging charge which has been leveled against us in this matter is hypocrisy and for obvious reasons. I think there is little doubt that the credibility and moral authority of the Catholic Church in Scotland has been dealt a serious blow and we will need to come to terms with that.'[23]

The difficulty for many Scottish Catholics was understanding what had happened. The Congregation for Bishops in Rome, the nuncio, the Scottish bishops and the Scottish Catholic Media Office all seemed unwilling to speak on the record or explain further what had gone on and what was to be done about it, although Archbishop Tartaglia, who took over the diocese of St Andrews and Edinburgh as apostolic administrator, repeatedly apologized and said the Church had been compromised. It was certainly a difficult time for the Scottish Church and its leadership; five out of eight dioceses either had no bishop, or one past the age of seventy-five, while another had a bishop due to retire on the grounds of ill-health.

By May, Rome ordered Keith O'Brien to go into exile for a period of prayer and penance while one of Pope Francis's earliest actions after his election was to send a message to Scotland, speaking of the recent challenges and cross recently borne by Scottish Catholics, and urging forgiveness.[24] Nearly a year later, the new pope also ordered an investigation into sexual misconduct in the archdiocese of St Andrews and Edinburgh. The gravity of the situation was evident in the choice of Bishop Charles Scicluna to conduct the enquiry. Scicluna has a reputation for forensically investigating sexual abuse cases and examined many of these during his time as a promoter of justice at the Congregation for the Doctrine of the Faith.

There were other issues that remained outstanding, including the extent to which the hierarchy – and even Rome – knew about O'Brien's proclivities and what they did about the situation, and whether O'Brien had ever wavered in his acceptance of the promotions offered to him by the Church. After all, he was well aware of the damage that sexual secrets could do to both the individual and the Church: he had been with Cardinal Winning years earlier when they two of them had sat and listened to Roddy Wright, Bishop of Argyll and the Isles, following public revelations about his sex life, as he told them he should never have accepted the post of bishop, given that he had already fathered a child when the role was offered. O'Brien had witnessed the damage done by Wright when his double life was exposed. There was also the issue of sexual abuse in the Church and the extent to which it remained covered up. Within months of Cardinal O'Brien's resignation, his former archiepiscopal counterpart in Glasgow, archbishop emeritus Mario Conti, alleged that O'Brien had blocked an independent examination of clerical sex abuse files held by Scottish dioceses during his time as president of the Bishops' Conference of Scotland. The files dated back sixty years. O'Brien, however, could not be blamed for every flaw in the Scottish Catholic Church. Calls have been made for it to have a rigorous enquiry into abuse but the Church was slow in reporting any structure for the inquiry, let alone any findings.

There was also the issue of timing of the revelations about O'Brien. Just the day before his exposure, he appeared to go back on his word regarding fidelity to Church teaching when he gave an interview to BBC Scotland and said the Church should reconsider its teaching on mandatory celibacy. Did someone think it was time to pull the plug on O'Brien?

The consequences of the O'Brien scandal for the Catholic Church in Scotland and particularly in Edinburgh and St Andrews are far more wide-reaching. There has been a further decline in churchgoing. There have been divisions among priests, who now realize that their suspicions about progress through favouritism of Cardinal O'Brien have been confirmed. The days when the Catholic Church had an outspoken, in-at-the-deep-end leader are gone. Indeed there is no real prince of the Church in Scotland any more. O'Brien is in exile in Northumberland and still technically has cardinal status, even if Rome removed the rights and privileges of his office, including voting in a conclave. But nobody else has them in Scotland either.

O'Brien's successor as archbishop, Leo Cushley, is very different from the disgraced cardinal and from Thomas Winning, as is the current Archbishop of Glasgow, Philip Tartaglia. Both have to deal with falling Mass attendance and neither plays the noisy role of their predecessors in the media. They tend to opt for carefully crafted homilies rather than soundbites. Leo Cushley came to Edinburgh from the Holy See after serving for most of his priestly career as a diplomat. He has the urbane manner of the sophisticated negotiator about him, and indeed there is the hint of the rather proper Romanized cleric about him. But his problems in Edinburgh are far removed from diplomatic telegrams and the Holy See's role on the global stage. Now he has to worry about closing and merging parishes, winning back the confidence of disillusioned Catholics and rebuilding the morale of a shattered priesthood in the wake of the O'Brien scandal.

The major test of the relationship between the Catholic Church and the state is now education. The Church secured a deal with the state that has existed for more than 100 years and out of 377 state-funded Scottish faith schools, 373 are Catholic. Now secularists are calling for religious leaders to be removed from local authority education committees, saying their involvement is undemocratic and discriminatory. It is a claim that the Church utterly rejects.

'These represent hundreds of thousands of Scottish citizens,' explained Archbishop Cushley in an interview. 'I don't know how many tens of people the secularists represent. But 95 per cent of Catholic children go to Catholic schools.'[25]

It is all part of the rough and tumble of Scottish politics, in which the Church has played its part ever since Irish migration caused Catholic Church membership to increase speedily in Scotland. For years the Labour Party and the Catholic Church enjoyed a relationship based on the Labour premise that the Church could deliver thousands of votes from a mostly working-class membership. The death of Labour leader John Smith in 1994 not only led to the emergence of Tony Blair as leader, and all the attendant increasing tensions between Labour and the Church over personal morality issues such as gay marriage and abortion, but also the growing connection between Scottish Church leaders and the SNP.

Not that Smith's death first intimated any sort of alliance between the two. The SNP had long been considered a Protestant party by the Catholic Church and during the Monklands by-election, caused by Smith's death, there was little sign of any sympathy for Catholics during the SNP campaign.

The constituency had been the focus of sectarian disputes for some time, with claims that Catholic councillors there had provided jobs and housing for their own in Catholic Coatbridge to the detriment of Protestants in nearby Airdrie. The SNP were accused of highlighting Labour candidate Helen Liddell's Catholic name and she was accused of being a 'Fenian bitch' during election appearances. She eventually won the seat, albeit with a much reduced Labour majority and during her victory speech, accused the SNP of playing 'the Orange card', something that the SNP leader of the time, Alex Salmond, denied.[26]

Within weeks of the by-election, the then Archbishop Winning (just months away from gaining his red hat), met both Liddell and Salmond. The meetings proved to be a turning point. While Winning chastized Liddell for Labour's attitude to the Church, he was won over by Alex Salmond. Salmond had already spotted that Catholic voters were worth tapping and that the SNP needed to lose its Protestant image. He took the opportunity of a speech at Stirling University, some months after meeting Winning, to call for the repeal of the Act of Settlement as outdated and prejudiced legislation. Salmond and Winning enjoyed a friendship that lasted for seven years until the cardinal's death. Salmond described the cardinal as a 'fearless fighter for the poor and dispossessed'.

The relationship between the SNP and Catholic leaders was further cemented by the friendship between Winning's successor as cardinal, Keith O'Brien, and Salmond, who endorsed Catholic schools and was cautious as first minister in his backing of bio-medical advances. It was cemented by their efforts during the run-up to the 2010 papal visit to ensure Scotland played its part and would not be left on the sidelines. Salmond's efforts to have Pope Benedict XVI address the Scottish Parliament were rebuffed by Lord Patten, the government's chief architect of the visit, but Salmond played a key role in helping Cardinal O'Brien organize the St Ninian's Day parade that became the most significant demonstration of Scottish nationalism-cum-Catholicism the nation had ever seen. It was Salmond's idea, for example, to create a St Ninian's tartan and present the pope with a scarf made of it.

Just how embroiled Catholic leaders had become with Salmond was evident on his departure as leader of the SNP following the Scottish independence referendum in September 2014, when Scots voted to keep the Union. The Scottish bishops wrote an unprecedented letter to Salmond, extolling his virtues as leader and making plain the extent to which the SNP had supported the Catholic Church.

The president of the Bishops' Conference of Scotland, Archbishop Philip Tartaglia, normally so careful about what he writes and publishes, wrote to Mr Salmond praising his 'long and outstanding career in politics, and your distinguished service as First Minister of Scotland'.

He added: 'With good reason, you have been described as one of the most able and influential political leaders that Scotland and the United Kingdom has ever produced. The bishops are especially grateful for your recognition of the important place of religion and faith in Scotland, for your support of Catholic education as making its own distinctive contribution to the good of Scotland as a whole, and for your sensitivity to the issues around religious freedom which are emerging in our country as they are elsewhere.'[27]

Salmond's courtship clearly worked. A year later, Labour's stronghold of Scotland was wiped out in the general election, when the SNP took fifty-six of the country's fifty-nine Westminster seats. The role of Catholic voters was vital in the dramatic political turnaround, for a YouGov poll before the election showed that Catholics were going to desert Labour, the party they had supported for generations. The poll showed that 48 per cent of Catholics polled in Scotland planned to vote for the SNP while 38 per cent were going to vote for Labour. At the time of the election, historian Tom Devine confirmed that the Scottish Nationalists had been courting Catholics for years. 'The old fear about sectarianism had gone and integration had taken place,' the historian said. 'So when Catholics became mainstream, they behaved like other mainstream Scots and reacted the same way as people in other areas of the "Labour empire" to the general reasons for the decline of Labour.'[28]

The decades since the 1982 visit of John Paul II have been turbulent ones for Scottish Catholicism. The Polish pontiff's visit was undoubtedly a time of new confidence and exuberance for a once downtrodden minority who have since found their way into mainstream Scottish society and politics. While Benedict XVI's subsequent visit consolidated that confidence and also highlighted the extent to which differences between other Christian denominations have lessened over the years, it provided no happy ending. The scandal involving Cardinal Keith O'Brien was a shattering blow to the Catholic Church. Keith O'Brien lost his role, his status and respect. The Church lost its credibility and any claim it might make to the higher moral ground in Scotland. It also revealed the extent to which the Catholic Church was out of touch with contemporary Scots on issues such as homosexuality.

Since O'Brien's fall from grace, the Church has had to regroup and consider the challenges ahead, some of them caused by O'Brien, some not. Declining Mass attendance means the Church has to work harder to retain those parishioners that are left and persuade others to come back. It has an opportunity for renewal because Scotland is no longer the monoculture it once was: now there are devout Catholic Poles, Filipinos, Indians and Africans in the pews as well as those of Irish descent.

The popularity of Pope Francis is a reminder that the message of the Church about alleviating poverty and assisting those suffering in society is an attractive one. While the independence referendum was lost, it has led to further powers being given to the Scottish Assembly and renewed the sense of Scotland being a very separate place from England. The Holy See is one of the few international organizations that has recognized that, and where Scotland has separate representation. As Archbishop Leo Cushley puts it:

'Seeing Scotland as a separate entity is not a recent innovation for the Holy See.'[29] Yet this ancient connection between the Scots and the papacy has a markedly contemporary, twenty-first-century resonance. The way in which the papacy adeptly renews itself is the subject to which I will turn my attention next.

Notes

1   Macfarlance, Leslie J. (ed.), *Scotland and the Holy See*, booklet published to mark the visit of Benedict XVI, 19.

2   Devine, T.M. (2012), *The Scottish Nation: A Modern History*, London: Penguin, 48.

3   Devine, ibid, 233.

4   Devine, ibid, 493.

5   Carrell, Severin (2006), 'Catholics bear the brunt of sectarian abuse', *The Guardian*, 28 November. http://www.theguardian.com/uk/2006/nov/28/religion.catholicism

6   http://www.educationscotland.gov.uk/higherscottishhistory/migrationandempire/experienceofimmigrants/irish.asp

7   Archbishop Thomas Winning, from the *Scottish Catholic Observer* of 6 September 1974, quoted in McGinty, Stephen (2003), *This Turbulent Priest: The Life of Cardinal Winning*, London: HarperCollins.

8   Obituary of Cardinal Thomas Winning, *Daily Telegraph*, 18 June 2001. http://www.telegraph.co.uk/news/obituaries/1312145/Cardinal-Thomas-Winning.html

9   See Chapter 2 for full details of this attempt to secure the visit.

10 McGinty, ibid, 225.

11 McGinty, ibid, 237.

12 *Daily Telegraph* obituary of John Paul II, ibid.

13 The *Glasgow Herald*, 3 June 1982.

14 For a full account of Winning and abortion, see McGinty, ibid, 361–70.

15 Winning, Cardinal Thomas (1995), 'The Labour for Life ban is about more than abortion', *Daily Mail*, 20 February.

16 Quoted by McGinty, ibid, 402.

17 Kemp, Arnold and Alex Bell (2000), 'Scots fight to stay in closet', *The Observer*, 23 January. http://www.theguardian.com/politics/2000/jan/23/scotlanddevolution.devolution

18 See Chapter 6.

19 McManus, John (2009), 'Cardinal attacks Trident renewal', BBC Online, 29 June. http://news.bbc.co.uk/1/hi/uk/8124266.stm

20 Morton, Brian (2013), 'Rome confronted O'Brien with allegation months ago', *The Tablet*, 9 March.

21 Deveney, Catherine (2013), 'UK's top cardinal accused of "inappropriate acts" by priests', *The Observer*, 23 February. http://www.theguardian.com/world/2013/feb/23/cardinal-keith-o-brien-accused-inappropriate

22 Interview of Fr Jock Dalrymple by Catherine Pepinster, March 2015.

23 Morton, ibid.

24 Lamb, Christopher (2013), 'Pope calls for "mutual pardon" to help renew Scottish Church', *The Tablet*, 23 June, 28.

25 Pepinster, Catherine (2013), 'Master of tactics and pastor of tact', *The Tablet*, 2 November, 8.

26 Stuart, Mark (2005), *John Smith: A Life*, London: Politicos, 392.

27 Frymann Rouch, Abigail (2014), 'Scotland's Catholic bishops salute "outstanding" Alex Salmond', *The Tablet* Online, 22 September. http://www.thetablet.co.uk/news/1162/0/scotland-s-catholic-bishops-salute-outstanding-alex-salmond

28 Wilkinson, Paul and Christopher Lamb (2015), 'Catholics desert Labour in Scotland, poll reveals', *The Tablet* Online, 15 May. http://www.thetablet.co.uk/news/2075/0/catholics-desert-labour-in-scotland-tablet-poll-reveals-

29 Interview of Leo Cushley by Catherine Pepinster, March 2015.

11

What makes for the 'x' factor?:

The pope as modern leader

The *Daily Mail* has long been one of Britain's most successful newspapers but today it is a global player, thanks to the impact of its website. That in turn feeds the paper, with its executives closely monitoring the number of 'hits' that its online stories receive – in other words measuring the popularity of items with its readers, and using that information to assess what should be included in its content. You would expect that for a tabloid, the biggest number of hits would be gained by celebrities, from film stars to pop idols to possibly members of the royal family. But a religious leader?

In November 2013, Pope Francis became one of the *Mail*'s biggest stars when he proved to have as many hits as a movie star, thanks to a deeply moving photo of him hugging a heavily disfigured man whom he met in St Peter's Square. So vast was the audience for this image that the *Mail*'s newsdesk sent a reporter to track down the man, which she duly did. But what the image – and its number of hits, plus the interest of hardened news executives – showed, was that the pope today is indeed a celebrity, and that his charisma is one of the major sources of his power as a leader.[1]

Charisma forms a major part of the power of a leader, according to classic sociological theory. In his essay on the nature of leadership, 'The Three Types of Legitimate Rule', the German sociologist Max Weber identified three kinds of authority: legal, traditional and charismatic.[2]

The papacy's authority has its foundations in the Gospel account of Jesus giving the keys of the kingdom to Peter: 'You are the rock upon which I will build my kingdom and the gates of hell will not prevail against it.'[3] It is also sanctioned, as Weber would describe it, by tradition and heritage.

Its legality can be seen in the recognition it is given by governments and global organizations, including the UN, and the right it still has to remain within its Vatican City State boundaries, derived from the power it once had in the papal states. The Catholic Church is governed by canon law with final jurisdiction in Rome and the pope has the final word on the appointment of bishops.

These forms of leadership were denied in England by the Reformation, after which the Church in England did not recognize that the pope and general councils of the Church decided doctrine. Several Acts of Parliament that passed between 1532 and 1534 made this break officially recognized in English law, including the 1534 Act of Supremacy which declared Henry VIII the Supreme Head of the Church of England. After being renounced by Mary, it was reasserted by Elizabeth I who took the title Supreme Governor, the one used still today by British monarchs. Final authority over doctrine and legal disputes now rested with the monarch.

Apart from the three-year reign of the Catholic James II (1685–88), Catholicism was illegal in Britain for 232 years. Although the hierarchy of the Church was restored in 1850, the authority of the Church is not its dominant characteristic in this country. Instead it is – particularly in the twenty-first century – the personal charisma of the man holding papal office that above all else gives the papacy if not power a certain influence amongst an increasingly secular British public.

A charismatic leader, Weber stipulated, has 'a certain quality of individual personality by which he is set apart and treated as endowed with supernatural, superhuman, or at least specifically exceptional powers or qualities.'[4] Such a leader, in other words, has exceptional personal qualities and demonstrates insights and accomplishments. These in turn inspire loyalty and obedience.

Expanding on Weber's analysis, the political scientist Ann Ruth Willner, author of *The Spellbinder: Charismatic Political Leadership*, has set out the key characteristics that constitute a charismatic ruler. These include: the importance of image; an individual from a lower social economic background (i.e. not from the established ruling elite); an inexhaustible vitality; great composure under stress; and a determination and stubbornness combined with a revolutionary agenda. Willner has also argued that the projected image, however distant from reality, is absolutely fundamental to a leader's charismatic authority.[5]

Willner's analysis uncannily matches both John Paul II and Francis. John Paul's story is well known: a man once forced to be a manual labourer, who, after a run of elderly popes, was elected in his fifties, demonstrated great vigour and travelled the world. He determinedly changed the papacy, turning it into a globetrotting phenomenon, while also using his skills to push the Catholic Church towards a more conservative position and take on the communist bloc. John Paul's superstar status was confirmed by his funeral, garnering huge crowds in Rome and televized around the world.

Pope Francis, meanwhile, comes from a migrant Italian family which settled in Argentina. He has captured the imagination of Catholics and non-Catholics alike with his mix of modesty and charm. Ever since the day he was elected he has determinedly pursued his efforts to reform the papacy, creating a committee of cardinals to help him change the culture of the

Vatican and update its management, as well as focusing on the Church's teaching on marriage and the family. (The actual impact of his efforts may be limited within the Church but to the outside world he still signifies change.)

It is not so clear, going by Willner's analysis, that Pope Benedict XVI meets the same criteria. The son of a policeman, the then Joseph Ratzinger grew up in Bavaria at a time when Germany was dominated by the Nazi Party, and joined the Hitler Youth (albeit an enforced membership). By the time he was elected he was already seventy-eight, and in many ways pursued a similar, conservative approach to his predecessor, John Paul II. Benedict's greatest impact on people during his papacy was through the books he wrote on Jesus of Nazareth, more popular volumes than his academic works, and his finely crafted encyclicals, particularly his astute treatise on the economy, *Caritas in Veritate*. Eventually his papacy became mired in controversy over child abuse, mismanagement of the Vatican and its finances, and feuding between officials. Nothing became him so much as the manner of his departure – he stood down in February 2013, the first pope to do so for 700 years. There had been little to suggest charismatic authority; instead Pope Benedict seemed a throwback to a different age.

And yet, when Pope Benedict visited the UK in September 2010, the British responded to him in ways that were highly unexpected. Controversy over the visit grew in the weeks leading up to it, with opponents – mostly aggressive secularists – setting up the 'Protest the Pope' group to form protests at major papal events. But from the moment that Benedict landed in Scotland, crowds turned out in their thousands to line the streets wherever he went. On the Saturday of his visit, when the popemobile travelled through central London, the police estimated a million people were on the streets, while a vast crowd attended a prayer vigil in Hyde Park. Pope Benedict led the crowds in mostly silent prayer. There was constant TV coverage of the events of the visit, with the BBC, Sky and ITV using their top presenters, including Huw Edwards, Anna Botting and Julie Etchingham.

What had so captured the imagination of the people of Britain for this event? Does it suggest that the notion of charismatic authority being so crucial for modern religious leaders is wrong?

A useful distinction between different forms of leadership is offered by the philosopher Sidney Hook. He argues that leaders can be categorized as 'eventful' or 'event-making', with eventful leaders influencing the course of later developments by his actions. Hook's example was the Dutch boy who stuck his finger in the dyke and saved his country. It was eventful, but anyone could have done it. But the *event-making* leader is transformational, making changes that only he or she could effect. They alter the course of history, raising new questions and new issues. Transformational change can be a matter of degree; in the history of the Catholic Church, John XXIII was truly transformational, ushering the Church into the modern age with the Second Vatican Council. Pope Francis's creation of a nine-cardinal group of advisers to help him reform the Vatican, and his call for a humbler, poorer Church may yet make him transformational.

John Paul, though, was arguably more of an eventful figure, being the leader who responded to world events, speaking up against the tyranny of communism as it began to crumble. Benedict, too, was eventful, responding to the problems of the moment such as his frequent commentaries about ecology, while also seeming to stem the tide of change in the Church with his reversals such as allowing more frequent use of the Old Rite form of Mass.[6]

But whether eventful or transformational, a pope retains authority through his moral leadership and can depend on morally influencing his followers. Weber's theory gives some indication why a pontiff of limited charisma but of considerable intellectual ability, such as Pope Benedict, can still be a draw in even as secular a country as Britain.

It seems to me that the papacy also highlights that the other qualities of leadership discussed by Weber – the legal and traditional aspects of authority – remain of key importance for the papacy in so far as devout Catholics respond to it. In a world where leadership becomes more fluid and flatter, and where people are usually less deferential, the Catholic form of leadership retains more conventional characteristics: papal leadership remains a form that mobilizes and orientates followers. The difficulty, of course, is that the pope is pope for people in the West where ideas about leadership have changed, but is also leader for people in the developing world who respond to more conventional leaders, focused more on authority.

But back to that visit of Benedict to Britain in 2010 – and to the current papacy of Pope Francis. For younger Catholics and a 'broader Church' of people, the role that the media plays in enforcing papal leadership is key to its fortunes. The papacy starts with a major advantage, as Cardinal Vincent Nichols pointed out: 'Catholicism works for the TV age; it's a very visual religion, things like the ostrich fans and the trappings of the papacy were always eye-catching. The single biggest difference in how we see the papacy in modern times is television. The symbolic nature and manner of the papacy is very effective on television. It seems bound up with gesture and ritual and they understand that in Britain. It gives people here a certain affinity with it.'[7]

Successful use of the media can transform the least promising person and make them charismatic. The pope has become a powerful leader on the world stage in the twentieth and twenty-first centuries to a significant degree because of the media. We saw this with Pope Benedict, who was the first pope of the Twitter age to embrace tweeting (or at least his office did), while the Vatican also promoted him through YouTube. Different notions of the pope were also communicated through websites, with strongly traditionalist sites saluting Benedict's efforts to restore the Old Rite.

These uses of social media as well as more conventional forms such as newspapers and TV have continued in the papacy of Francis. While John Paul II sought to dominate the Church through his travels and lessened his role as Bishop of Rome, Francis has emphasized this latter role, thus stressing the importance of other bishops, but has also travelled widely. Benedict also made major visits abroad, so that all three popes satisfied the media's perennial appetite for a wide variety of images. They in turn served the papacy's need for the pope to be seen at the helm of a universal Church, a global power, with devoted members across the planet.

Like Benedict, Pope Francis has made use of YouTube and Twitter, while the Pope App has also been used to major effect during his papacy. However, social media remains a one-way form of communication for the Vatican: there is nothing interactive about their systems. The Catholic Church, in that sense, retains its authoritarianism: the messages go out, but it does not invite replies.

Yet there is something else very modern about the papacy today: it understands the power of the gesture. This was shown to remarkable effect with Pope Francis's decision to take a dozen refugees home to Rome with him when he visited the island of Lesbos in April 2016, a decision that stunned the media and dominated headlines around the world.[8]

His emphasis on his role as Bishop of Rome also confirms his clear commitment to the values of Vatican II. So while he fulfils the papacy's aim of global influence, he also pleases those Catholics who wish to see a downplaying of the role of Pope as the centralizing figure in the Church and prefer a Vatican II model of ecclesiology.

Cardinal Cormac Murphy-O'Connor sees this as the most important aspect of Francis's papacy: 'The important thing is how Francis is changing things. He is much more collegial than previous people. This is crucial and helps him survive. Collegiality, synodality and subsidiarity are the important issues. John Paul II hit the pause button and Benedict XVI inherited a difficult job. But Francis is going ahead with these three things.'[9]

However, Murphy-O'Connor does acknowledge that Francis has a particular power in the media age: 'Clearly personality has a lot to do with it. Switch on TV and now you see him and people see him as a celebrity.'[10]

While Murphy-O'Connor argues that Francis's focus on collegiality means that the bishops remain important for the local Church, this has not meant that his significance as *the* Catholic leader has lessened. But the consequences of him being such a dominant figure arguably diminish the importance of the bishops. Traditionally, the Catholic Church's clerical structure has four levels – parish priest, bishop, cardinal and pope – but for most people in the UK today they are aware of three figures through personal encounter and the media: their parish priest; the cardinal as a national figure; and the pope.

Cardinal Vincent Nichols acknowledges that the parish priest and the pope are key to so many people's lives, and that the modern age has given the papacy the opportunity to present itself effectively to a global audience. But not surprisingly, he believes the local bishop retains his influence: 'My father said that two people matter in the life of a Catholic – the parish priest and the pope. The pope is the touchstone of unity and the guarantor of faith. We are a universal Church; you are a Catholic wherever you are. People understand the background – that the priest belongs to the diocese and the bishop is the father of the diocese, but it is the pope who is the key figure of stability.'[11]

This stability helps explain a pope's standing in the Catholic community but his popularity across society is more vulnerable, particularly as his leadership intentions become more frustrated. Weber argued that once charismatic leadership has become 'routinized', there is a danger that it is succeeded by 'a bureaucracy controlled by a rationally established authority or by a combination of traditional and bureaucratic authority'.[12]

Early upheavals in Rome caused by Pope Francis's avowed intention to reform Vatican bureaucracy and the tone of the Church suggested a revival or at least a re-ordering of charismatic leadership, countering its routinization. But as Francis has struggled to combat vested interests, so his popularity has declined. In 2015 he was the sixth most popular world leader, according to YouGov's annual poll; in 2016 he dropped to thirteenth. The decline, said YouGov, was due to a possible public perception of failure. 'After the promise of Catholic reform which set the pope apart from his predecessors, the findings may demonstrate a dimming of excitement as the Argentinian becomes institutionalized.'[13]

For all that, Francis remains a counter-cultural figure. Charismatic leaders are often marked by egotism and even narcissism, but Francis's public persona is of a much humbler, man-of-the-people individual. These characteristics can provide a particular form of power and influence, allowing for the kind of transformation that theologians call 'metanoia'. The word is often wrongly translated to mean 'repentance', but the Greek meaning is more accurately described as a 'change in thinking and living', or a 'shift in mind'. Francis's biographers, Paul Vallely[14] and Austen Ivereigh,[15] have both described Francis being transformed by his experiences in Argentina, leading to a change in the way he communicates and behaves. Now at the helm of the Catholic Church, Francis's own personal metanoia is a starting point for an institutional metanoia he desires in the Church. This is evident in what he has been attempting to do in reform of the Vatican but also in reforming the Church's approach to sin, with a renewed emphasis on mercy, rather than failure. In other words, Francis is urging a *cultural* shift in the Catholic Church, rather than some revolutionary upset in traditional teaching. It has nevertheless riled more conservative Catholics, such as the influential writer Ross Douthat, who frequently critiques Francis in the *New York Times*. But responses to Francis in the British media suggest he is having a notable impact on public perceptions about the papacy, albeit with some fall-off in popularity as his pontificate continues.

For all the vagaries of popularity among Catholics and the wider public, Pope Francis's standing is high among world leaders. According to the Holy See's Secretariat of State, more than 200 world leaders met him during the first three years of his pontificate. They recognize his influence and no doubt hope some of the appeal rubs off on them through association.

What a religious leader like Pope Francis has is what political scientists would call 'soft power' – in other words, the ability to attract and persuade – rather than 'hard power' – the ability to coerce – upon which nations have relied in recent centuries. Then, the aim was to use military and economic might to enforce their ambitions. But in an age when power is also dependent on the attractiveness of culture and ideals, a pope can be a template for political leaders.

Joseph Nye, a former US assistant secretary of defense, created the term soft power, by which he meant 'the ability to get what you want through attraction rather than coercion or payments'. He went on:

> When you can get others to admire your ideals and to want what you want, you do not have to spend as much on sticks and carrots to move them in your direction. Seduction is always more effective than coercion, and many values like democracy, human rights and individual opportunities are deeply seductive . . . But attraction can turn to repulsion if we act in an arrogant manner and destroy the real message of our deeper values.[16]

The Catholic Church, and in particular the popes of the last thirty years, have shown just how effective attraction can be, and how the 'sticks and carrots' approach of traditional teaching – 'if you do X, you will have sinned and won't get to heaven' – has been rejected by the contemporary West. The more pastoral approach of Vatican II, with its emphasis on one's relationship with Jesus and with the rest of humanity, has proved appealing. And yet the declining power of sticks and carrots has also, some would argue, led to a decline in church attendance with people no longer as fearful that non-attendance at Mass would be a mortal sin.

In its use of these attributes of soft power, the popes have attempted to attract believers through their own attractiveness and that of the teaching. Popes John Paul II and Francis were particularly effective in using their own charisma. The lapsation of Catholics in the West and even the decisions made by those Catholics still practising, though, suggest that at the same time the message of values and authority for some people has been lost.

A clear case in point is the Church's attitude to divorce and remarried Catholics and their barring from Holy Communion. The debates during the Synod on marriage and the family of October 2014 exposed the conflict that has developed within the Church over it maintaining – officially, at least, if not necessarily at every parish level – that the divorced and remarried are barred from the Eucharist, and the lack of reception for that teaching. A survey conducted by *The Tablet* indicated that a third of the divorced and remarried who have not had their first marriage annulled do receive Communion, even if they had not sought the permission of their priest. They and many others perceived the Church's ban as lacking in mercy and compassion.[17]

The Synod also highlighted the tension between older styles of the papacy to that prophesied during the Second Vatican Council. History shows the popes to have been strongly authoritarian religious leaders although their impact before a mass communication age was more limited. But the Second Vatican Council offered a new model of the papacy, one that would be more collegial in effect. The calling of Synods was one of Paul VI's chief attempts at collegiality.

Effective collegiality is what the council describes in its Dogmatic Constitution on the Church when it says: 'The order of bishops which succeeds to the college of the apostles and gives this apostolic body continued existence is also the subject of supreme and full power over the universal Church, provided we understand this body together with its head the Roman Pontiff and never without this head.'[18]

The Vatican II document says that since early Christianity the collegial character of the body of bishops has been evident in the union of all bishops with one another and with the pope in 'unity, charity and peace'. It also was evident in the ancient Church practice of the Church's bishops meeting in council to settle 'all questions of major importance', it says.

Effective collegiality refers to the sense of unity with the pope and the world's bishops that ought to pervade the ministry of each bishop individually and the common actions of groups of bishops. Even though they do not act with the full authority held by the entire college of bishops gathered in council under the pope, bishops acting as individuals or in groups always 'are related with and united to one another', the document says.

Collegiality has always proved more attractive to liberal Catholics than traditionalists but the irony of the October Synod was the way in which Pope Francis was left having to accept major changes to the draft document of the gathering, because traditionalist hierarchs objected strongly to its pastoral approach to homosexuals and the divorced.

Nye's analysis of soft power highlights other aspects of Rome's influence that may not be always considered in assessments of the papacy. For example he points out the clout offered by strong cultural attractiveness of a nation: it is evident that the Vatican City State is as powerful a global cultural magnet as any European country through the 'offer' it makes via its art and heritage.

Nye also speaks of soft power as being 'a positive force for solving global problems', a strength which the Catholic Church has particularly developed in recent years, evidenced through its network of diplomats, the work of its Secretariat of State, and its aid programmes. Its Caritas organisation is the second biggest aid agency in the world after the Red Cross. Governments across the globe, including the United Kingdom, have increasingly acknowledged its reach. In Africa alone, for example, Caritas has 13,000 people employed in its subsidiaries, supported by 427,000 volunteers and reaching 77 million beneficiaries on the ground, in areas from human trafficking to humanitarian emergency, food production to health care.[19]

Nigel Baker, the former UK ambassador to the Holy See points out: 'It is the Caritas strength at grass roots level that make them an invaluable partner for countries like the UK, as we seek to find allies in our efforts to deliver development and humanitarian aid efficiently and cost effectively to those that really need it, from Syria to the Democratic Republic of Congo.'[20]

Similarly, Andrew Mitchell, former secretary of state for international development, recalls that the Catholic Church was one of the most influential partners of governments in achieving progress in health and education in the developing world, something it achieved through its longstanding grassroots networks combined with a Vatican machine that worked with governments at the global level.[21]

Can this be said to be morality as soft power? The Catholic Church works through Caritas and other agencies as a way of articulating its teaching on the need to put one's neighbour before oneself and serve God. Pope Francis's call for the Church to be first and foremost a Church of the poor has clearly resonated since he came to office in 2013. Its teaching on other morality issues have similarly resonated where it advocated an end to capital punishment and both Benedict XVI and Francis have earned plaudits for speaking out on climate change. But while these attract the interest of young populations in modern democracies, its teaching on, for example, homosexuality and contraception, has not.

The Church and its popes are a prime example of what Nye calls 'a global conscience', and as he confirms, the power of such a nonstate actor has become increasingly important during the information age. While that age has seen the number and types of organizations that exercise soft power escalate significantly, the Church's size, its budget, its bureaucracy and its formidable leader figure have helped it continue to exert its influence. It was early in understanding communications – it began Vatican Radio in the 1930s – and it quickly embraced social media.[22]

The historian Eamon Duffy is not convinced that the trends of the modern papacy – the use of media and the constant travelling – are beneficial in the long term for the Church and the world, however.

I do not think globetrotting is a good idea. It infantilizes people, although popes can make an impact that is for the good. When John Paul II went to Cuba, they let people out of the jails. He was also a major historical figure. The BBC put me under contract to cover his funeral seven to eight years before he died. There was a document called 'The Pope Plan' that was revised every few months. First it was going to be presented by David Dimbleby but as the years wore on, it became Huw Edwards. The BBC was gazumped by an American network for one of the most advantageous location positions. That's how much he mattered. But I still think we need to answer the question: how do popes escape becoming these kinds of superstar?[23]

However powerful a religious figure is, as Nye warns, 'intolerant religious organizations can repel as well as attract', and it is evident that the Catholic Church has done this at times. The most obvious example, at least for many young people in the West, is its position on homosexuality. That may well be the price it is prepared to pay for not compromising on issues. Yet it was evident at the 2014 Synod that many bishops and the pope are concerned about its image as an institution with a hardness of heart that is failing to attract people to Christ.

As Nye says: 'Effective public diplomacy is a two-way street that involves listening as well as talking. Soft power rests on some shared values ... soft power means getting others to want the same outcomes as you want and that requires understanding how they are hearing your messages, and fine-tuning it accordingly. It is crucial to understand the target audience.'[24]

In an increasingly complex modern world, the papacy has to find a way to stay true to its core beliefs and both reach out to people disaffected or even non-believers, as well as maintain the loyalty of more traditional Catholics. It has to ask itself hard questions abut whether it is engaged in effective listening, as well as effective communication of its own position and beliefs. The synods of October 2014 and 2015 suggest it has not solved this particular dilemma, although Pope Francis's document arising from the Synods, Amoris Laetitia,[25] was a more successful attempt at trying to bridge divides, in that it reiterated traditional Catholic teaching while taking a more compassionate approach on issues such as divorce and remarriage. Pope Francis articulated, for example, the importance of understanding people's situations, and ways in which the Church could sustain them. In this sense, he is true to the meaning of his title of pontiff, originating in the Latin word pontifex, or bridge. But can the pope in the modern era be a bridge in societies that are increasingly fragmented, a role that has been identified as a vital one for religions by political science?[26]

The conflict between integrity and pragmatism – of being true to core beliefs and yet finding ways to compromise – is particularly difficult today. The era of globalization has brought the world closer together in that it is easier and simpler to communicate. But it has merely served to show the diversity of beliefs, attitudes, prejudices and commitments. Few societies are as diverse as Britain, in terms of class, ethnic mix and beliefs. If the papacy can find a way to successfully solve how it puts its message across to the British, then it will be some way to solving it across the globe. The United Kingdom is, in other words, an ideal laboratory. I shall next examine the evidence at the governmental level as to how the papacy – and the Catholic Church at national level – has played its part in society. It reveals moments of pragmatism, moments of conflict, and times of deeply entrenched refusals to compromise.

Notes

1   Roberts, Hannah (2013), '"What will happen to them when I am gone?"
    Heartbreak of devoted aunt who cares for disfigured man blessed by the Pope
    and his sister blighted by the same disease', *Daily Mail*, 19 November.
    Available online: http://www.dailymail.co.uk/news/article-2509966/Disfigured-
    man-Vinicio-Riva-relives-moment-Pope-Francis.html

2   Weber, Max (1922), 'The three types of legitimate rule', published in Weber,
    Max and Sam Whimster (2004), *The Essential Weber: A Reader*, Abingdon:
    Routledge Taylor & Francis, 133.

3   Matthew 16:18.

4   Weber, ibid.

5   Willner, Ann Ruth (1968), *Charismatic Political Leadership: A Theory*,
    Princeton, NJ: Princeton University Press.

6   Hook, Sidney (1960), *The Hero in History*, Boston, MA: Beacon Press.

7   Interview of Cardinal Vincent Nichols (VN) by Catherine Pepinster (CP),
    March 2015.

8   Boyle, Darren (2016) '"Welcome to your new home!" Extraordinary scenes as
    Pope Francis visits a Lesbos migrant camp where he stuns crowds by rescuing
    12 Syrian refugees and flying them to Rome to start a new life', *Daily Mail*,
    16 April. http://www.dailymail.co.uk/news/article-3543076/Pope-Francis-visits-
    refugee-camp-Lesbos-plans-TEN-migrants-Rome-leaves.html

9   Interview of Cardinal Cormac Murphy-O'Connor (CMOC) by Catherine
    Pepinster (CP), February 2015.

10 Interview of CMOC by CP, ibid.

11 Interview of VN by CP, ibid.

12 Weber, ibid.

13 YouGov (2016), World's most admired. https://yougov.co.uk/news/2016/05/07/
    wma-2016/

14 Vallely, Paul (2015), *Pope Francis: Untying the Knots – The Struggle for the
    Soul of Catholicism*, London: Bloomsbury.

15 Ivereigh, Austen (2015), *The Great Reformer: Francis and the Making of a
    Radical Pope*, London: Allen & Unwin.

16 Nye Jr, Joseph S. (2004), *Soft Power: The Means to Success in World Politics*,
    New York: Public Affairs.

17 'Communion ban routinely ignored, *Tablet* survey finds' (2014), *The Tablet*,
    18 October, 29.

18 *Lumen Gentium*, the Dogmatic Constitution on the Church, para 27.
    Available online: http://www.vatican.va/archive/hist_councils/ii_vatican_
    council/documents/vat-ii_const_19641121_lumen-gentium_en.html

19 Nye, ibid, 78.

20 Baker, Nigel (2014), blog post, 7 October. http://blogs.fco.gov.uk/nigelbaker/

21 Interview of Andrew Mitchell by Catherine Pepinster, February 2015.

22 Nye, ibid, 90.

23 Interview of Eamon Duffy by Catherine Pepinster, December 2015.

24 Nye, ibid, 111.

25 *Amoris Laetitia*, post-synodal apostolic exhortation on love in the family (2015). https://w2.vatican.va/content/dam/francesco/pdf/apost_exhortations/documents/papa-francesco_esortazione-ap_20160319_amoris-laetitia_en.pdf

26 The role of religious institutions is identified by Fox, Jonathan (2013), *An Introduction to Religion and Politics*, Abingdon: Routledge.

12

The grit in the oyster:

Church, state and domestic politics

Today, the place of religion in Britain is characterized by a complex combination of convention, indifference, dramatic intervention, hostility, enthusiasm and respect. When Grave Davie wrote her seminal work, *Religion in Britain since 1945*, more than twenty years ago, she charted the marked decline of religious practice in the country, while noting religious belief remained high: a conclusion which she described so memorably as 'believing without belonging'.[1] The picture has now changed markedly. Today, almost 60 per cent of the UK population says it is Christian, according to the 2011 Census.[2] These figures are buoyed up by Scotland and Northern Ireland. In England and Wales, 48 per cent of the population says they have no religion, and Anglicanism has suffered the greatest fall in number, with just 19 per cent defining themselves as members of the Church of England, compared to 44 per cent in 1983. Although the migrants that we hear about most are Muslim, migration of Catholics from Eastern Europe, South America, Asia and Africa have helped steady the numbers of Catholics, replacing the lapsed. An estimated 3.8 million in England and Wales identify as Catholics, with more than six million saying they were brought up as Catholics.[3] Research from Linda Woodhead, professor in the sociology of religion at the University of Lancaster, indicates that the Church of England has seen the steepest decline in attendance, and, contrary to the census returns, suggests that there has been an increase in those who have no belief.[4] This was confirmed by an analysis of the British Attitudes Survey data, conducted by the Benedict XVI Centre for Religion and Society.[5]

Yet British culture remains nominally Christian. Christmas remains the biggest celebration of all, although Easter, while still the reason for two Bank Holidays, has been replaced in popularity by Halloween. With its focus on Americanized trick or treating, it has little connection with its origin as All Hallows Eve, the day before the Catholic feast of All Saints Day. Indeed these nominally Christian festivals are all largely secular occasions now, dominated by consumer spending, alcohol and chocolate.

The media remains in many ways entranced by religion, particularly if it involves scandal, fear and rows. But painstaking, moment-by-moment reporting of theological debate and general policy-making of bodies such as the Church of England synod has largely disappeared from the main news channels and newspapers. Religious affairs correspondents are a rare breed.

Church attendance is in long-term decline if all the Christian denominations are banded together. Yet within the picture of decline are pockets of stability and even growth. The Pentecostal churches are thriving; the Catholic Church appears to at least be stable, although this may well be down to its congregations being propped up by migrants, including Poles and Latin Americans. (Not that this is an unusual trait among Catholics in Britain; since the nineteenth century it has been a Church of migrants). But there are loud voices deeply hostile to religion, seeking to undo its impact on morality and society – witness the rows over church schools and same-sex marriage which frequently feature the British Humanist Association and the National Secular Society.

Amid all these different tides and eddies is the continuing relationship between Church and state, one that involves both co-operation and conflict. Medhurst and Moyser noted nearly thirty years ago in *Church and Politics in a Secular Age* that there is a latent religious presence at the heart of English society and politics.[6] Religion, or at least a particular form of Christianity, remains integral to 'official Britain', evident through the place of the queen as head of the Church of England, the prime minister's role in the appointment of the Archbishop of Canterbury and the place of bishops in the House of Lords.

The Church's role – by which I mean not only the Church of England but other denominations too – is a notably different one from the part it plays in society in the United States, where a clear separation between Church and state has existed since the creation of the nation. In the US, the principle of separation is supposed to indicate that the religious sphere is essentially private and different from the public one. Clearly it still has a ceremonial role, where God is called upon to aid America by each and every president at his inauguration, and the United States is said by every citizen saying the pledge to be 'one nation, under God'.

While no such separation exists in Britain, there are similarities. In his classic account of civil religion in America, Robert N. Bellah highlights that 'a set of beliefs, symbols and rituals' is the way that public religion is expressed and that this indicates the ultimate sovereignty of the nation rests with God, which somehow offers the criterion by which right and wrong can be judged.[7]

One can see this too in Britain, where prayers are said in Parliament, religious oaths are still used in the courts, where the queen, who in turn pledges herself to God, is the person who officially appoints the prime minister, once the will of the people is evident.

While God hovers over the nation, manifest through these rituals and ceremonies, the Church has a very different role. Sometimes it has played the irritant, sometimes the conscience of the nation. It is, one might say, the grit in the oyster. This was particularly true during the Thatcher years of the 1980s, when both the Catholic Church and the Church of England clashed with the government of the day. The confrontation between bishops and the first female prime minister caused a lasting shift in the relationship between politics and religion.

Until the 1980s, the Church of England had been seen essentially as part of the Establishment – as indeed it is, given that it is the Established Church. The historian Arthur Marwick saw secular Anglicanism as the prevailing ethos which had guaranteed the 'stability and unity of British society' throughout the tumultuous postwar decades.[8]

During Mrs Thatcher's premiership, however, both the Conservative Party and the Church of England changed. The days of Butskellism were long over. Consensus politics were gone. While Thatcher has long been credited with changing British politics, both in terms of how it is conducted and through her impact on the Tories and Labour, today she can also be seen to have changed the churches too; the way they deal with politicians, and the relationship between Church and state. Marwick contends that secular Anglicanism – a tolerant faith, with a desire for consensus and distaste for the extreme – was effectively silenced during Thatcherism.

But according to Eliza Filby, author of God and Mrs Thatcher, the Church of England emerged at this time not so much silenced but as one of the chief defenders of consensus and community, the very essence of secular Anglicanism. Its bishops protested at the conflict-filled politics of Thatcher, defending welfarism and speaking out in the House of Lords. The Faith in the City report, which was published in the autumn of 1985, is the clearest example of this confrontation between Church and prime minister. Its damning analysis of economic and spiritual poverty in Britain's inner cities concluded that they were caused by the government's policies. Critiques such as these by the Churches had their foundation in evidence garnered at the grassroots via the parishes – a connection with the people that is always the Church's great asset, regardless of whether it is the Church of England or the Catholic Church.[9]

Yet this was not a question of the god-fearing left versus the godless right. Many of those on the right reasserted the link between Protestant values and capitalism and also spoke in moral terms about the failings of socialism. Their emphasis was on individual rather than collective responsibility. Margaret Thatcher herself placed her premiership in a moral context, quoting Francis of Assisi on the steps of Number 10 when she won her first general election in 1979. The idea that she sought to bring peace and harmony seems curious, given that she so clearly did the opposite.

Eliza Filby's account highlights two stages in the conflict between Church and state during the Thatcher years. The first was the early days of her government when she rolled back the state at a time when the Anglican bishops still favoured heavy emphasis on state efforts to alleviate poverty, with employment programmes used to alleviate the impact of unemployment. The second stage took place after 1987, as concerns grew that Britain was becoming a more affluent, selfish society. The Conservatives attempted to counter this with talk of the moral virtues of capitalism that enabled the well-off to be philanthropic. The Church in turn attacked consumerist culture, selfishness, and the amoral nature of the market. As Mrs Thatcher put it: 'The church keeps saying we must relieve poverty and when we do, they say we're making everybody materialistic.'[10]

The nadir in the relationship between the Conservative government and the churches was 1982, the year of the Falklands War and the formation of the team that would produce *Faith in the City*.

The Falklands War proved tricky for both the Church of England and the Catholic Church. The visit that year of Pope John Paul II was supposed to cement friendship between the two Churches but as discussed in earlier chapters, the trip was overshadowed by the outbreak of conflict between Britain and Catholic Argentina. Catholic bishops who had spent months planning the visit were desperate for it to go ahead although it was much more limited in scope, and the pope did not meet the prime minister. The Church of England was anxious about cancellation too, and fully embraced the pastoral visit when it occurred with an encounter between John Paul II and the Archbishop of Canterbury, Robert Runcie, at Canterbury Cathedral.[11]

But the real tensions between the Church of England and the Tories came with the service of thanksgiving at St Paul's Cathedral on 26 July, following the British victory in the Falklands. Runcie, decorated with the Military Cross during the Second World War, described war as a sign of human failure, denounced the arms trade, and led the congregation in praying for both the British and the Argentinian casualties. His sermon made use of the pope's comments in Britain to highlight the Christian sense of failure regarding the conflict: '[John Paul II's] speech in Coventry was particularly memorable when he said "war should belong to the tragic past, to history. It should find no place on humanity's agenda for the future".' But it was Runcie's conciliatory words toward the Argentinians, recognizing their common sense of sorrow, that so enraged those on the right: 'In our prayers we shall quite rightly remember those who are bereaved in our own country and the relations of the young Argentinian soldiers who were killed. Common sorrow could do something to re-unite those who were engaged in this struggle.'[12]

The prime minister's husband, Denis, famously told people on the terrace of the House of Commons later that day: 'The boss is livid'.[13]

Runcie had expressed no more than standard Christian beliefs in reconciliation, forgiveness and penitence, but his comments brought into the open the views of Tories that Anglicanism had become 'wet' and liberal. This was further confirmed by the report which was begun that year and was published in 1985: *Faith in the City: A Call to Action by Church and Nation.*

It was written after its contributors visited thirty towns and cities, holding public meetings, listening to local people, clergy and community leaders. The result was a report that described 'the shabby streets, neglected houses, sordid demolition sites of the inner city . . . obscured by the busy shopping precincts of mass consumption'.[14]

While the bishops saw Christianity as having a valid voice, critiquing society, Mrs Thatcher saw religion as playing a restricted, personal role in people's lives. 'Christianity is about spiritual redemption, not social reform,' she said in a 1988 speech to the Church of Scotland Assembly.[15] In many ways, though, her politics gave the Churches renewed enthusiasm for exactly what she felt was none of their business: reform of society.

The belief that Christianity should play a significant part in the political realm grew through the latter half of the twentieth century. It was highlighted by Ronald Preston in his 1983 Scott Holland lectures when he said with regard to politics: 'Christians are liable to become nervous at this point and to wish to be non-political. This is not possible. To be non-political in the sense of doing nothing is tacitly to support things as they are and to do so irresponsibly without thinking about it.'[16]

Preston, a professor of social and pastoral theology at the University of Manchester and a canon at Manchester Cathedral, went on: 'The Christian life . . . is one of responsibility according to one's circumstances; and it should lessen our propensity to sit down under present social injustices because we have got used to them or are not adversely affected ourselves. Politics needs more of this dimension as a better basis for hope and as a safeguard against fanaticism or despair.'[17]

Preston reflected the views of many clergy at the time as they witnessed the impact of unemployment and poverty and wanted to do something about it. Perhaps typical of this was Alan Billings, the Sheffield vicar who became a Labour councillor at the time when the city council was at loggerheads with the government, particularly during the miners' strike.

During the Thatcher era, political theology was growing in influence within the Anglican tradition while in the Catholic Church, Catholic Social Teaching, which owed its origins to the nineteenth-century Church's response to industrialization, provided a coherent framework for critiques of society. It sought to find a balance between the needs of society, especially its weakest and poorest members, and respect for individual freedom, including the ownership of private property. If it had a mission statement, it would probably be Matthew 25, 40: 'Whatever you have done for the least of my brothers, you have done for me.'[18]

Since the nineteenth century, the nonconformist and Catholic Churches had developed strong voices in speaking up for the poor. This was particularly evident in the Catholic Church when Cardinal Manning, for example, loudly represented the waves of Irish migrants who helped build industrial Britain. Many considered that the Church of England maintained its strongest connections with rural Britain and the more affluent.

With the postwar settlement had come more inclination towards liberal and socialist thinking in the Church of England through the influence of Archbishop William Temple and the political theorist and Christian socialist R.H. Tawney. But the changing social mores of the 1960s also led to a steep decline in churchgoing, lessening the Church of England's claim to be the nation's moral voice or conscience. In the Catholic Church, continuing migration, its stronger emphasis on the need for Sunday churchgoing, as well a fillip to its congregations for some years from the Second Vatican Council, led to higher numbers of attendance for the next couple of decades and to that extent greater influence on churchgoers. Not that the Church of England accepted this Roman Catholic growth: when Clifford Longley, religious affairs editor of *The Times* wrote to the Archbishop of Canterbury in 1983, telling him that weekly Catholic church attenders outnumbered Anglicans, Runcie retorted: 'The ebb and flow of belief and unbelief is not readily translated into statistical bedrock.'[19]

At the same time as Mass attendance increased, so one would have expected Catholicism's influence to grow at the heart of government during the 1980s. For this was the era when the Catholic Church, through Cardinal Basil Hume and the arrival of Roman Catholics in the political elites of Westminster and Whitehall, changed its status from outsider to insider. Yet it was not always easy to have Catholic theology accepted by those with influence. As the historian Peter Hennessy said: 'The one time when Catholics did not fit was during the Thatcher era. The Thatcher government had few of the ideas prevalent in Catholic Social Teaching.'[20]

There was a marked difference between Catholic and Anglican bishops in their public forays into politics. The Anglicans spoke out far less on issues about personal morality – abortion, contraception, homosexuality (at least until the issue of gay clergy emerged to cause deep conflict in the Anglican Communion in the twenty-first century) – whereas Catholic bishops continued to intervene in those areas, particularly on abortion.

Cardinal Hume made regular contact with government ministers over issues relating to Northern Ireland, particularly in the case of the Guildford Four but another cause dear to his heart, homelessness, was dealt with in a much more personal way than via publishing a report, as the Church of England had done regarding poverty.[21]

From early on in his time at Westminster, Basil Hume was deeply disturbed by seeing people sleeping rough in the piazza of Westminster Cathedral, not far from the front door of his home at Archbishop's House. The eventual result was the creation of shelters such as The Passage and the Cardinal Hume Centre, but not before Hume had opened the cathedral's hall to people sleeping outside in the cold.[22]

His former public affairs assistant, Charles Wookey, recalled that: 'He just couldn't bear it. He'd come in and say "I can't live here with people sleeping outside". So we had to open the hall.'[23]

To some of his prosperous neighbours living in the mansion flats of Victoria's Ambrosden Avenue, Hume's practical action was an outrage – until he got them on-side, saying he thought rough sleeping an outrage and enlisting their help to find better accommodation. 'He charmed them,' said Wookey.[24]

During his time at Westminster, Basil Hume would frequently intervene in the public square, be it through letters to ministers or to newspapers such as *The Times*, or in interviews on programmes such as BBC Radio 4's Today.

His approach was often to convene groups of informed Catholics, as he did on nuclear issues in those Cold War days when he set up a committee whose members included Sir Michael Quinlan, at the time a rising young mandarin who was later to be appointed permanent secretary at the Ministry of Defence, and the academic John Finnis, a specialist in jurisprudence. Hume's approach to nuclear weapons had been deeply influenced by John Paul II's comments to the United Nations special session on disarmament in June 1982 when he said that the doctrine of deterrence could be seen as morally acceptable, provided it was not an end in itself but rather a stage on the path to general disarmament. Just where Hume stood had also become a more pressing issue after Cardinal Thomas Winning of Glasgow had spoken out earlier that year in opposition to the country having nuclear weapons. Wookey recalled that his boss tried to be as well informed as possible – even though his advisers eventually said that Hume should say nothing, but not before he had written in *The Times* in November 1983 on 'Towards a nuclear morality'.[25]

Hume's preparations for his interventions in public life were always to try and consider a pressing issue from a theological perspective. 'He used to say a speech needed "*spiritualità*",' said Wookey.[26]

The late twentieth century was an era of exciting theological development through the emergence of liberation theology, and the idea of a preferential option for the poor. Liberation theology was in many ways frowned upon by John Paul II as a result of his deep suspicion of communism and leftwing politics due to his own experience in Poland. But it was rooted in conventional Catholic teaching through the centuries. This rich seam of Catholic Social Teaching, encouraging solidarity with the poor, was reflected in Hume's concerns about the homeless. The Anglicans' *Faith in the City*, meanwhile, reflected similar values, and despite one Cabinet minister dismissing it as 'pure Marxist theology', it owed more to Methodism than Marx, and to a tradition in Anglican thought that could be traced back to William Temple.[27] But Charles Wookey felt that Hume had a rather different approach to Anglican bishops, wishing not to get involved in the cut and thrust of everyday party politics. 'Anglican bishops did sometimes allow themselves to be part of the Opposition,' he said.[28]

One of the evident differences between the Church of England and its critiques of government, and that of the Catholic Church in the late twentieth and early twenty-first centuries, is down to the kind of individuals who have been appointed bishops and how they relate to politicians. Over the years Anglicans such as David Sheppard, Robert Runcie, John Habgood and now Justin Welby have been at ease among the privately educated, Oxbridge graduates who still make up the Establishment, because that was their background too. By sitting in the House of Lords, they have the power to shape public policy through taking part in debates and voting.

The *Catholic* bishops of England and Wales, by contrast, tend not to have been educated in Britain's leading private schools, but typically attend seminaries straight from school, working for degrees as they train for the priesthood. There are occasional exceptions – Archbishop Bernard Longley of Birmingham studied at New College, Oxford, before moving to St John's Seminary at Wonersh, and Bishop John Arnold of Salford read law at Cambridge – but neither Basil Hume, Cormac Murphy-O'Connor nor Vincent Nichols attended university in the UK. They have not had that specific British experience and once anointed bishops, they do not share in that other British experience: sitting in the House of Lords.

Twenty years ago, however, there was a distinct possibility that Catholic bishops might have joined their Anglican *confrères* in the upper chamber. The impetus for giving a Catholic bishop a peerage has its roots in the exceptional regard in which British society held Cardinal Basil Hume, who was offered a peerage by three different prime ministers – James Callaghan, Margaret Thatcher and Tony Blair. According to Cardinal Cormac Murphy-O'Connor, Hume was opposed to this for some considerable time but had a change of heart not long before he died in 1999.[29]

Evidence of Hume's rethink came when he called senior Catholic public figures and several bishops together for a meeting at Archbishop's House in March that year. He intimated to the then Bishop of Arundel and Brighton – his successor as Archbishop of Westminster, Cormac Murphy-O'Connor – that he did not want a life peerage just for himself as a reward for becoming a national figure. Instead he thought it possible that the five Catholic archbishops of England and Wales – Westminster, Southwark, Liverpool, Birmingham and Cardiff – should all sit in the Lords with the Anglicans.

The meeting that Hume had convened but did not attend due to his own failing health revealed great sympathy for the idea of these peerages from the gathered Catholic laity, including Lord Hunt of Tanworth (former Cabinet secretary and Hume's own brother-in-law); former *Times* editor William Rees-Mogg, and former Conservative Cabinet ministers Lord St John of Fawsley and John Gummer. The bishops were not all so keen however, highlighting in their conflicted thinking a key issue for Catholics in contemporary Britain: whether to be insiders or outsiders.

Perhaps that notion of being outsiders owes much to the hostility with which Roman Catholicism was treated for so many centuries, post-

Reformation. It may also be linked to the extent to which in the UK it is a Church of migrants and its clergy should speak up for the poor and dispossessed. Those who felt that the Catholic bishops should be in the Lords felt it was a question of bolstering the Christian voice. As Cormac Murphy-O'Connor put it: 'There was a bit of working-class Catholicism in this, a sort of gut feeling that "we don't want to be part of that lot". Other bishops were . . . feeling that we could have more effect on public policy and law-making if we were on the inside rather than the outside. They were all for rolling up their sleeves and entering the messy world of Parliament.'[30]

With the bishops split and Hume in decline physically, the idea faded away. Instead, the esteem accorded to Hume was given concrete form by the queen, who awarded him in the last months of his life the Order of Merit, which is in her personal gift.[31]

Ten years later, Prime Minister Gordon Brown revived the idea of a Catholic bishop in the House of Lords when he asked Cardinal Cormac Murphy-O'Connor to enter Parliament. Brown's idea was that three key religious leaders – the Chief Rabbi, Jonathan Sacks, the Muslim leader Zaki Bedawi, and Murphy-O'Connor – would all enter the Lords at the same time.

Murphy-O'Connor decided to sound out Rome on the idea, given that canon law states that clerics should not play any formal part in government or hold political office. Pope Benedict, when Murphy-O'Connor explained that peers do not make laws but debate them, seemed open to the idea, but the Secretariat of State was less keen. Its officials could imagine what happened in the United Kingdom could be used to set a precedent elsewhere. Priests, bishops and cardinals might pop up in third-world governments, perhaps corrupt ones, bringing the Church into disrepute. Those who should give voice to the voiceless could become part of an instrument of oppression.

Rome's answer to the Mother of Parliaments was therefore unequivocal: no. Even if centuries of English post-Reformation habits were put aside and Catholics were brought in from the cold, Rome would not allow it. Cardinal Murphy-O'Connor had been keen to go to the Lords. 'I'd even worked out my maiden speech. It would have begun, "As my predecessor, Cardinal Pole, said . . .",' he joked, in a reference to the last Catholic Archbishop of Canterbury, appointed by England's last Catholic queen, Mary Tudor. 'But Rome was worried. It does not want us being politicians, even though they were assured the House of Lords is not that kind of house,' he said.[32]

Would he have been a thorn in the side of government? Bishops certainly can be. Tensions between Margaret Thatcher and the Church of England were clearly documented through voting records. Partington's *The Contribution of the Church of England Bishops*, shows that between 1979–1990, 61 per cent of the bishops' votes cast were against the government compared to 27 per cent in favour. 172 speeches were against; 49 in favour.[33]

But Catholic bishops have found other ways to express their concern about government policy, as was evident during one of the most dramatic eras in urban politics in Britain. It was also the time of one of the most successful ecumenical partnerships between a Catholic bishop and his Anglican counterpart: that of Derek Worlock and David Sheppard, of Liverpool.

Riots had spread throughout urban Britain in 1981 at a time when people other than the poor had fled city centres. Even people who had once worked and lived in these areas – the local bobby and the GP – left at the end of their working day. When Dixon of Dock Green and Dr Finlay went, just Father Brown was left. The vicars and parish priests reported back to their bishops. In Liverpool, Worlock and Sheppard responded in practical, pastoral and political or prophetic ways. They set up a law centre in strife-torn Toxteth and spoke up for the rioters, pointing out the burdens of life in a deprived nation where industry no longer offered mass employment. Worlock wrote to his correspondent Frank Judd that he was 'almost the only non-political voice which can be raised at the moment and people appear to be listening'.[34]

Worlock's engagement had a two-fold cause. On the one hand it was pragmatic: he already knew that there were working-class parishes where only 5 per cent of the male parishioners went to Mass on Sunday, blaming their non-attendance on disillusionment with the Church for failing to speak up about unemployment. Then there was Catholic Social Teaching, the doctrine of the Church outlined in various papal encyclicals since the days of the Industrial Revolution, which outlined the importance of solidarity. As Clifford Longley put it in his biography of Worlock: 'If the cost of seeming to be indifferent was high, the rewards of solidarity were enticing.'[35]

Michael Heseltine, one of the cannier politicians of the past fifty years, was appointed minister for Merseyside by Margaret Thatcher in the wake of the riots and he quickly identified that working with the Churches would be fruitful. He and the civil servants of the Merseyside Task Forces understood that the Churches had local expertise and knowledge, together with a respect that politicians had lost.

As Heseltine put it in a letter to Worlock, the views of the Church leaders 'were among the most disinterested which I heard, while being based on well-founded information and a clear view of the problems and the needs of the area'.[36]

Some years later there was another effort at partnership between Worlock and Sheppard, this time during the miners' strike, showing how Churches and their leaders could be seen as symbols of unity and reconciliation during a time of national strife. Together with Howard Williams, moderator of the Free Churches, they were appointed to head the TUC's Miners' Hardship Fund in November 1984, which had been organized to provide food and help for families and children during the dispute. A letter was sent to Worlock at the time from a parishioner saying he had sold his newly privatized British Telecom shares and donated the proceeds to the fund, a gesture that could be seen to symbolize solidarity in the face of Thatcherite policies.

While these incidents highlight the capacity for conflict between Church and state, at the same time the Church of England is intertwined with the Establishment and also sees itself as the nation's Church and as the nation's religion, in a way that the Catholic Church does not. This was apparent in the *Faith in the City* report. Its authors noted 'the British people are by a great majority a believing people' and that there existed a 'strong substratum of religion in British society'. They concluded that the thoughts and resolutions in the report were in line with the 'basic Christian principles of justice and compassion' which were shared by 'the great majority of the people of Britain'. The commission directly connected this to the role and purpose of Anglicanism, proclaiming that because the Church of England was: 'in the position of being the national Church, it has a particular duty to act as the conscience of the nation.'[37] Here the Church of England was managing to embrace a nation that was secular, yet at the same time had latent belief. Before sociologist Grace Davie coined the term, it had spotted that the British were 'believing without belonging'. In fact, the Church of England in this instance was rather like Mrs Thatcher, says Eliza Filby, with both having the 'idea of a diffusive Christianity amongst a non-churchgoing public'.[38]

That is not the case for Catholics whose Church, after centuries of illegality in Britain, plays a very different role, with the insider–outsider tension cited by Cormac Murphy-O'Connor. So while its laity has made great strides in joining the Establishment, the Church prides itself on playing a significant role both as the guardian of the underprivileged through its charitable work – organizations for the homeless such as those established by Cardinal Hume in central London and Anchor House in the East End spring to mind – and as a body willing to take on the government to protect its own interests.

It is in the field of education that the Catholic Church is most prepared to fight its corner. From the nineteenth century onwards, Catholic schools have always been the Church's most precious asset, but particularly after bishops secured the agreement in 1944 that it could have its own schools with the Government funding 50 per cent and Catholics, through church collections, putting in the rest. Today Catholic school premises are owned by the Catholic Church, which funds 10 per cent of maintenance costs. Day-to-day-funding of the schools is provided by the state.

The matter of who attended Catholic schools was down to selection processes until recent times, when governments banned interviews. Critical politicians claimed the interview system enhanced the prospects of more middle-class children. They also disliked any attempt at selecting children on the basis of how much of a contribution their parents made to the parish, be it cleaning the pews or running Communion preparation classes, as too easily manipulated by the more knowing.

It was long apparent that the Church's critics, including journalists and politicians, were shaped by their experience of living in London where many

Catholic schools were heavily oversubscribed. Elsewhere in the country Catholic schools willingly took in non-Catholic pupils to fill their rolls. Indeed, in some parts of England, Catholic schools now educate more Muslims than Catholics, as Catholic migrants have grown prosperous, leaving their schools behind, particularly in the northern inner cities.[39]

The Church prizes its own independence, regarding its schools very highly and this has led it into conflict with government of varying political stripes. In 1988, the Thatcher administration brought in the Education Reform Act, aimed at bringing schools out of the hands of local education authorities – frequently at that time, Labour-run, staunchly anti-Thatcher city councils – as well as the Inner London Education Authority. But the policy also affected any church school with more than 300 pupils. It meant schools founded and often in their early days funded by the Catholic Church would become grant-maintained schools. Among the concerns that the Catholic Church particularly had about the implications of the Act was that schools that 'opted out' of local authority control would be opting out of the collective efforts of a diocese to offer Catholic education. The bishops saw themselves as having a special role to nurture Catholic schools and to serve the interests of the whole community and the opting-out procedure would damage that. This particularly exercised Cardinal Hume, who at the time gave frequent speeches critiquing the Conservative government's approach to education which he perceived as essentially utilitarian and was failing in its stated aim of promoting spiritual as well as material values. He told the North of England Education Conference in 1990 that: 'Training for a job or a profession and education are not co-extensive. Education will often include training for a job, but education is broader and greater and does not always have to serve a utilitarian purpose.'[40]

Not all Catholics agreed. The teachers and parents of the Cardinal Vaughan School, a heavily oversubscribed Catholic school in London's prosperous Holland Park, had run-ins with the cardinal and Westminster's Diocesan Education Service over proposals to set up a centralized Catholic sixth-form college. They believed the loss of the sixth form would damage the Vaughan and to them, an opt-out was a godsend, removing the school from diocesan control. Hume's efforts to block the plan came to nothing. The Vaughan and another of Westminster diocese's most successful West London schools, the London Oratory, opted out.

Meanwhile, meetings between the Cardinal Archbishop of Westminster and the education secretary, Kenneth Baker, took place on three occasions at Archbishop's House, events which clearly made a deep impression on the minister. Baker later recalled:

I was conscious that I was not dealing merely with a local education authority, or merely a trade union, or even the British Cabinet, but rather with one of the great and enduring institutions of Western civilisation. The tall, stooping figure of its representative, Basil Hume, is well known.

He conveys a sense of holiness, kindness and courtesy and it is not easy to argue with such a saintly man. But within that scarlet and purple apparition was the sinewy force of a prelate concerned with temporal as well as spiritual power.[41]

Yet despite this Catholic show of strength, on that occasion negotiations broke down and the government refused to exempt church schools from the right of 'opting out' allowed to schools in the Education Bill. Quite how big a blow this was to the Catholic Church in England and Wales is hard for outsiders to understand. Church schools have been integral to the development of Catholicism and its influence since its growth in Britain, post-Catholic emancipation, in the nineteenth century. They come under the authority of the bishops, and in that sense, lead directly back to Rome. So important were they from the beginning of modern Catholicism that Cardinal Manning held up the building of Westminster Cathedral to spend money on schools.

Ten years after Baker won his battle, Vincent Nichols, then an auxiliary bishop in London, became chairman of the Catholic Education Service (CES), a body that promotes the Catholic faith through education and is responsible for the English and Welsh bishops' national policy on education. Nichols had been close to Hume, and education has always been one of his specialist interests. Perhaps it was an awareness of the blow that Hume suffered, and a reluctance to endure the same, that meant Nichols was ready for a fight. In autumn 2006 the Labour government's education secretary, Alan Johnson, announced that he intended to make faith schools take 25 per cent of their pupils from non-faith backgrounds. The Church's lobbying of Labour MPs – including those who were still dependent on Catholic voters for their seats, as several IPSOS-Mori polls for *The Tablet* have shown – was key in defeating the matter fast. Nichols, by then ensconced in Birmingham as its archbishop, and also chairman of the Catholic bishops' education committee, insisted in a letter to Johnson that governors should remain the admission authorities of 2,000 Catholic schools, without political interference. 'Schools with a religious character are part of the solution for society, not part of the problem', he wrote, adding that it would be unfair if non-Catholic pupils in future were 'there by a new entitlement, and possibly even hostile to the religious aspects of the school'.[42]

But above all it was the support of ordinary Catholics for the schools and their involvement in the cause through a letter-writing campaign to MPs that caused Johnson to be outflanked. His schools minister, Lord Adonis, admitted in an interview with *The Tablet* that a meeting between the education secretary and forty concerned Labour MPs had been 'lively'.[43] Rather than make the 25 per cent quota of non-faith pupils mandatory, Johnson agreed that it would be voluntary for new faith schools.

A change of government did not make the relationship between the Catholic Church and politicians any easier over education. During David

Cameron's premiership – first at the helm of the coalition government and then the Tory administration elected in 2015 – the Church objected to the mandatory policy of restricting the number of faith-based admission to new schools to 50 per cent in over-subscribed areas, a policy first introduced as part of the Conservative–Liberal Democrat coalition agreement but without any public consultation or debate. The CES, answerable to Catholic bishops, lobbied for six years to require a change, arguing that it meant Catholic children would be turned away from Catholic schools. They saw this as a manifest injustice, particularly in West London where one in three Catholic children could not secure a place in a Catholic school. Malcolm McMahon, the Archbishop of Liverpool and the chairman of the CES, raised the matter with Michael Gove, education secretary of the time, but to no avail. The result: very few Catholic schools were built over a period of six years. Then, within weeks of Theresa May's appointment as prime minister, the cap was withdrawn and faith schools were allowed to select their pupils as they wished. As the announcement was made, it became clear that Number 10 had a hand in the U-turn, with a source telling the BBC that the cap had failed because it had not made faith schools more diverse and it had prevented new Catholic schools from opening, 'which are more successful, more popular and more ethnically diverse than other types of state school'.[44]

This was the message that the Catholic Church had been trying to convey for years but under Cameron it had fallen on deaf ears. But Mrs May, daughter of a high-church Anglican vicar, had long seemed more receptive to the concerns of the major Christian churches. She had also developed a relationship of mutual regard with Cardinal Vincent Nichols in her previous capacity as home secretary. The pair had worked together on human trafficking issues which had taken them to Rome to meet Pope Francis (discussed later in this chapter) and she was a guest at Hampton Court Palace alongside notable Catholic public figures, including Bank of England governor Mark Carney, when the cardinal celebrated Catholic vespers there in February 2016 – the first such Catholic service in 450 years. The cardinal had never developed such a relationship with David Cameron and is believed never to have visited Downing Street during his premiership. But he was through the door to see Mrs May soon after she took over in the wake of the EU referendum and had written her a fulsome letter of congratulation:

> I am personally delighted at your appointment. I know from the work we have done together that you have so many qualities to bring to the service of our countries at this time. I appreciate the maturity of judgement, the steely resolve, the sense of justice and the personal integrity and warmth you have always shown.[45]

It seems highly unlikely that when the cardinal visited Mrs May, he did not take the opportunity to discuss education, which had long been a passion of his and one of the most important concerns of the Catholic Church since restoration of the hierarchy in the nineteenth century. Others around Mrs May were also convinced of the importance of lifting the cap. One of her joint chiefs of staff, Fiona Hill, was a Catholic who at one time worked for PR man Mike Craven, chairman of governors at Cardinal Vaughan, while the other, Nick Timothy, had written on the influential website ConservativeHome, that the cap should be removed. Indeed his blog was couched in the same terms as the Number 10 source quoted by the BBC when explaining May's thinking, but he was writing eight months earlier:

> Given that there is growing demand for Roman Catholic schools, which are more likely to be ethnically diverse than other schools, more likely to be in poor areas, more likely to be rated Good or Outstanding by Ofsted, and more likely to provide what parents want, the rule should be replaced by a legal duty on faith schools to ensure that their pupils mix – perhaps through sport, performing arts, or school visits – with children of other backgrounds.[46]

As director of the New Schools Network, Timothy had also realized that if the Archdiocese of Westminster converted its schools to academies, it would become the largest academy group in the country. Indeed, the Catholic Church is one of the biggest players in faith education, responsible for two-thirds of all faith-based secondary schools. It has more than 2,000 schools educating 800,000 students. If May's decision is indeed enacted, it is likely to mean that the Catholic Church will become responsible for the education of even more children and that they have government confidence to do so. It also suggests a more constructive dialogue between Church and state over education but it is not without political risks. For years faith schools have been criticized by secular voices, including organizations such as the British Humanist Society and the National Secular Society, which frequently argue that the schools are divisive, privilege certain pupils, and unfairly turn away non-faith children. And with fears growing that other faith schools might not teach British values, the political mood for many years was to limit this type of schooling. The Catholic Church's take continued to be that it wanted to make its own decisions about education, that it was willing to educate non-Catholics – as indeed do many of its schools – but that if a school were to preserve the very ethos that made it attractive, it must have a majority intake of around seventy-five per cent of Catholic pupils.

Among the critics of Mrs May's decision to lift the cap on faith school admissions was sociology professor Linda Woodhead, who wrote on the London School of Economics' Religion and the Public Square website that the move was evidence of the government siding with 'religious hardliners', and that the new prime minister had been persuaded that the cap had to go because it contravened Catholic canon law – a suggestion which linked what was happening directly to Rome.[47] In fact, canon law does not say non-Catholics should not be educated in Catholic schools. It says that a

Catholic school must be based on Catholic doctrine, that the local bishop should approve those who teach religion and watch over Catholic schools in his diocese. It also stresses that 'the formation given in them is, in its academic standards, at least as outstanding as that in other schools in the area'.[48]

It is this focus on formation, ethos and high academic standards that has made Catholic schooling so popular with Catholic parents, even when they are not the strictest of adherents to Church teaching in other areas such as weekly Sunday Mass-going or birth control, and why they have supported their bishops so often when Catholic schools have come under attack.

There was not the same backing from the ordinary Catholic in the pew for the other major political rows of recent parliaments. The Church took on first Labour over gay adoption and the coalition government over same-sex marriage. Opposition to greater rights for gay people was not unique to the Catholic Church in Britain. The Vatican spoke out on the matter on several occasions, as did other bishops' conferences.

The first clash between the Catholic Church and the government over gay people came with the enactment of the Equality Act in 2007, which made discrimination in the provision of goods, facilities and services on the grounds of sexual orientation against the law. This meant that adoption agencies could no longer reject homosexual and lesbian couples as suitable parents.

The Catholic Church ran adoption agencies via its dioceses and, in line with its teaching, believed that children should be placed with a mother and a father (although they did sometimes place children with single parents). The Church asked for an exception to be made to the law, allowing Catholic agencies, which made up just 4 per cent of the sector, to continue their work, while gay people could still use the mainstream agencies. Cardinal Cormac Murphy-O'Connor went so far as to telephone Tony Blair to ask him personally for help, but he recalls that 'I didn't feel he could afford to squander political capital on the defence of Catholic adoption agencies against the intimidating forces of political correctness'.[49] In fact, the issue did cause divisions in the Cabinet. Lord Falconer, the Lord Chancellor, argued that no faith groups should be given exemptions while the Communities Minister, Ruth Kelly, who is herself a Catholic, asked the Cabinet to help the Catholic agencies. While Cardinal Murphy-O'Connor wrote perjoratively of political correctness, the Labour Government saw gay adoption as an issue of rights – something which had helped it find common ground with the Catholic Church in the area of international development.[50] Harriet Harman explained the government's rejection of exemption for the Church by saying: 'You can either be against discrimination or you can allow for it. You can't be a little against discrimination.'[51]

The Catholic Church in England and Wales – and in Scotland – similarly objected to same-sex marriage when legislation was first mooted by the coalition government in 2012. Vincent Nichols, who took over as Archbishop of Westminster from Cormac Murphy-O'Connor in 2009, was particularly forceful in attacking the proposal during a Christmas interview with the BBC when he said that the government had failed to announce its plans in advance and that 'from a democratic point of view, it's a shambles; George Orwell would be proud of that manoeuvre'.[52]

In objecting to same-sex marriage, Archbishop Nichols was following both traditional Catholic teaching and the lead of Benedict XVI, who had spoken in a pre-Christmas address of it destroying human nature. But it surprised Catholics who had previously noted Nichols showing a more compassionate approach when in 2010 he had angered conservative Catholics, critical of the so-called Soho 'Gay Masses', organized and held for homosexual Catholics, by suggesting that 'Anybody from the outside who is trying to cast a judgement on the people who come forward for Communion really ought to learn to hold their tongue'.[53]

Nichols's remark about judgement was in some ways prescient; it was made three years before Pope Francis's famous 'who am I to judge?' remark about homosexuals, a few months after his election. Nichols, elevated to the rank of cardinal in the first year of the Franciscan pontificate, quickly learned the new era's language of mercy and compassion, and spoke effectively during the Synods on marriage and the family, held in Rome during 2014 and 2015, about the need for the Church to understand problems more. But neither Nichols nor Pope Francis would go anywhere near gay marriage. As Vincent Nichols said in his 2012 pastoral letter on marriage at the time of the government's consultation period on changing the legal definition of marriage: 'The reasons given by our government for wanting to change the definition of marriage are those of equality and discrimination. But our present law does not discriminate unjustly when it requires both a man and a woman for marriage. It simply recognises and protects the distinctive nature of marriage.'[54]

Marriage was a natural institution and a sacrament, according to Catholic theology, ordained by God between a man and a woman, ordered for the good of the spouses and for procreation. The gap between the Church and the British government was not to be bridged.

There was greater success for the Catholic Church in its interventions over assisted dying. A series of private bills have been put before Parliament in recent years, attempting to make it legal for doctors to assist a dying patient to end their life. Four attempts were made by Lord Joffe between 2003 and 2006 to introduce bills in the House of Lords to legalize the assistance of suicide and were all defeated. Lord Falconer then introduced a similar bill in 2014 but it ran out of time before the general election, but was quickly followed by another effort, this time by Commons backbencher Rob Marris – and indeed the first opportunity that MPs had had to vote on the issue for twenty years – but was overwhelmingly defeated. Although polls suggested that the public was largely in favour of assisted suicide, the Church had played a role that may well have contributed to the decision of sizeable numbers of MPs to reject it. While the bishops were not noticeably engaged or outspoken themselves, they continually urged Catholics to engage in lobbying of MPs, providing briefing material online, developing contacts with Catholic healthcare workers and engaging with parishes.[55]

While their views on assisted dying were expressed sotto voce, the bishops do not always adopt this tactic. And when they do speak out over controversial issues in the public arena, an issue for them is the extent to which they connect between the pastoral and the prophetic. This is where the bishops can get it right and where they can get it wrong, as shown in their stance on abortion and on poverty.

The Catholic Church has been constant in its opposition to abortion in Britain since the Abortion Act of 1967, based on Church teaching that insists that every human being has a right to life from the moment of conception. The bishops have reflected this teaching, maintaining that abortion is an abhorrent sin, although in recent years their views have been more muted, suggesting it is a trauma for women, many of whom opt for abortion believing they have no alternative. But the bishops are not really heard; instead the Church's implacability is still most people's perception. When it comes to poverty, however, their pastoral voice is matched by the prophetic, and they are listened to in a way that suggests they capture both the imagination and the respect of the public.

While the Catholic Church is well known for its stance on abortion, it has an equally long history of concern about poverty in Britain, particularly since its work with Irish migrants in the nineteenth century. It has sought to provide institutions for the Catholic poor from hospitals to schools to orphanages, while in more recent years it has turned its attention to all the poor, regardless of creed. And its bishops have retained a vociferousness on these issues that regularly grabs the headlines.

This happened, of course, in the 1980s when both Catholic and Anglican bishops spoke out but it has happened again more recently. Archbishop Vincent Nichols condemned welfare cuts in an interview on the eve of his installation as a cardinal in February 2014. He described them as 'frankly a disgrace', saying that: 'The fact of people left for weeks on end without any support and therefore having to have recourse for food banks in a country as affluent as ours is a disgrace.'[56] Here the power of the Church in connecting with both the bottom and top of the pyramid of society can be seen.

Vincent Nichols's words had credibility because he cited evidence of people's suffering given to him from parish priests in his diocese. They also mirrored the moral integrity of Pope Francis, who also speaks for the poor and the marginalized. Nichols's comments on the impact of David Cameron's welfare policies had greater force because of their timing. He had spotted the PR opportunity of speaking out just before he was installed as a cardinal by the pope, enabling him to reinforce Francis's message about the poor to the British public. Indeed, Nichols's commentaries on the poor have noticeably increased since Pope Francis's election in March 2013. His homily at the ecumenical service for the martyred Salvadorean Archbishop

Oscar Romero, two months before Romero's beatification, evoked a passionate commitment to the poor – 'God loves his people, bestowing on them an innate dignity, especially on those who are denied almost everything else. Today, in the name of this martyr, we resolve again to be upholders of this God-given dignity of every person' – and a sense that Romero's example of solidarity with the poor in Latin America resonated in the UK.[57]

Concerns about people in poverty were also reflected in the Catholic Church's support for the Living Wage movement, another example of its commitment to Catholic Social Teaching outlined in papal encyclicals inspiring its interventions in public life. Its backing for the Living Wage caused union leader Dave Prentis, general secretary of Unison, to describe the Catholic Church as 'the force behind this movement'. Its bishops, he said, 'are showing real leadership'.[58] Again, this was a case of the Catholic Church stepping into public life with integrity, because its actions were derived from knowledge of people's lives coming from the grassroots, as well as authority coming from church teaching, with that authority rooted in Gospel values.

In sharp contrast, the message from the Catholic Church about abortion and its desire to see the law changed in Britain nearly always comes from the top down. Even when the bishops produce more nuanced, sympathetic statements, the public does not hear them talking of women they have spoken to, saying they are forced by poverty to seek abortion or what a struggle it has been to keep their baby. Instead they offer doctrine which alienates many people who stop listening. Perhaps the one churchman who did manage that strength from witness was Scotland's Cardinal Winning, who organized highly practical help for women so that they might choose to keep their children rather than opt for abortion.[59]

Even though both the Church of England and the Catholic Church have remained firmly in the public eye, sometimes clashing dramatically with the government in the process, Eliza Filby has suggested that they no longer play the same part as they once did in the nation's political conversation. After the departure of Margaret Thatcher from office, she argues, they too retreated from the public stage. According to Filby's book *God and Mrs Thatcher*, the upheavals of the 1980s changed Britain, and undermined its Christian culture. 'In her crusade to raise Albion from the ashes', Filby argued, 'Thatcher ended up destroying all that was familiar. The future was not to be conservative but consumerist, not English but cosmopolitan, not Christian but secular.'[60]

While the Churches have undoubtedly waned in influence, if that influence is measured by regular churchgoing, they do appear, despite Filby's arguments, to still punch above their weight in terms of their influence. There is still access to ministers and there are still headlines in the press. In recent years there has also been evidence of new partnerships between the churches and government. They may find their contribution in running schools is not as appreciated by politicians as it once was, but in a secular society where the price of things matters as much if not more than their value, there is enthusiasm for bringing the churches on board to run services. Governments think this is a useful way to save money by sub-contracting.

With the election of Pope Francis and the appointment of Justin Welby as Archbishop of Canterbury within days of one another in 2013, the Churches' commitment to speak up for the most vulnerable was powerfully reinforced. Spurred on by Pope Francis's call to help the victims of human trafficking, Cardinal Vincent Nichols worked with the then Home Secretary Theresa May on improving services in Britain for those caught up in the trade, and was instrumental in her speaking at a conference organized in Rome by the Vatican on human trafficking in April 2014. It was a clear endorsement by the British government of the pope's engagement. 'His Holiness Pope Francis has described modern slavery as "a crime against humanity",' said May. 'There can be few descriptions that so aptly match the appalling nature of this crime. The men, women and children who are forced, tricked and coerced into servitude and abuse, are often the world's most vulnerable.'[61]

For the Catholic Church, human trafficking is seen as much as an affront to human dignity as other life issues – abortion, contraception and euthanasia among them. Although its approach can lead to partnership with the British government it can also lead to direct confrontation, as the experience of Andrew Mitchell, the former secretary of state for international development discovered when he tried to take on Rome over birth control.

Mitchell, appointed to the post in the first coalition government administration of 2010, is in many ways warmly disposed towards the Catholic Church, praising its commitment to the developing world, having seen its work at firsthand. But he found its intransigence on the issue of contraception baffling. 'My main interest was as to whether we could persuade the Vatican to take a different view of contraception,' he told me.

Mitchell, in his Cabinet role, met Cardinal Peter Turkson, a Ghanaian viewed by many as one of the more progressive voices in the Church, who often speaks about issues of poverty in his capacity as president of the Pontifical Council of Justice and Peace. 'When I met him it was deeply depressing. He said we don't need contraception because women can tell when they are fertile. In fact what he said was women know when it is their fertile time because "they are sticky down there".'

Mitchell attempted to work with Rome over matters such as vaccination: 'In June 2011 we had the Gavi replenishment conference in London with Bill Gates, and the papal nuncio made a moving speech to people from 40 different countries. The speech was useful but he still only gave us 5,000 euros.'

But the principal hurdle remained contraception:

We had a family planning summit in 2012 which we ran with the Gates Foundation. My chief task was to keep people on the fairway. The problem is that the left sees family planning as an issue of human rights with abortion. I went to see Vincent Nichols and he was very helpful. He said stick to it [family planning] being about women choosing when to have children. But when I went to the Vatican I got lectured by a cardinal about bombing Libya – not very helpful. I thought that you really have to try because of the Catholic Church's influence on contraception. And I did respect what the Church did. I had seen through visits abroad with Cafod what the Catholic Church can achieve. I approached it with great respect and love but on contraception it was completely wrong.[62]

For all the intransigence and difficulty at finding common ground, and Rome's frequent presentation of itself as consistently principled, Mitchell's experience reveals that the Vatican is as engaged in realpolitik as any political fixers. And given its global reach, politicians realize it is worth working with the Catholic Church.

'The Church's role in the developing world is massive, it's hugely important through education and health care,' said Mitchell. 'Its quality is down to its values, its engagement with civic society, everything that it brings. If there are problems in the country then you have to go through international organizations and they can help. With contraception we both know where we stand, as a government we support Marie Stopes and they don't. We fund contraception in Africa. The reality is that we are sophisticated players and so we look for where there are common interests.

Those common interests shared with the Vatican are tackling conflict, bringing prosperity. They are obviously interested in the saving of souls but that is clearly not the only interest as their work shows.'[63]

Mario Conti, the retired Archbishop of Glasgow, addressed the issue of Church–government relations at the Colloquium held in Rome in 2010 to celebrate British–Holy See diplomatic ties, identifying a partnership between Britain and Rome that is in part fruitful, and in part testing.

'It is clear that the Church and the state have huge areas of shared concern and recognise the necessary engagement together. We are concerned about poverty, at home and abroad; we are concerned about the importance of education globally; and the work of establishing sure foundations for peace among peoples . . . So we respect one another even if we claim we are not listening enough to one another.[64]

Just as surely as the Church sees itself as serving our country's common good,' Conti went on, 'we are experiencing a sense that the country is aware of the Church's part.'

Five hundred years on from the break with Rome, there is clear evidence of a newfound alliance between the United Kingdom and the Catholic Church, yet tensions too. Rome has noted the United Kingdom's development as a secular nation and on occasion it is alarmed by it. It found the UK's legalizing of same-sex marriage deeply disturbing; it has never come to terms with the UK's record on abortion, and is similarly prepared to oppose assisted dying. 'Our anxiety is that the mood in Britain is changing on this matter,' a senior source in the Holy See said, despite the overwhelming rejection of the Assisted Dying Bill in 2015.[65]

And yet, there is pragmatism on the part of the Holy See as well. There might be clashes between the Church's values and those of the British government but there are also ways in which the two can do business, typified by the way the two institutions have come together to work on trafficking.

These partnerships, as well as the numbers of Catholics in the UK, and the country's international role, all mean that Britain is an important nation for the Holy See. But there is another intriguing reason why the UK is perceived as important to Rome: its very secular nature makes it matter. Rome has noted how the Catholic Church has found a role in the UK. 'It has gained a great deal of experience of existing in an increasingly secularised society,' said a senior Holy See official.[66]

Now that once devoutly Catholic nations are also becoming more secular – France, Italy and Spain are all undergoing this change too – the Church in these countries will also have to adapt. Cardinal Vincent Nichols, like his predecessors Basil Hume and Cormac Murphy-O'Connor, has recognized that influence sometimes requires persuasion rather than outright confrontation. This, he argues, is the way that the Catholic Church has done business in Britain for 150 years on issues such as education, with what he calls 'constant shuffling as a way of finding shared ambitions'. He cites as an example the way the Church has dealt with Catholic education, something which the Church has always treated as its absolute priority in Britain. 'There were definite overlaps of thinking in the postwar era about education, and now we are seeing it again with the issue of human trafficking.'[67]

The veteran parliamentarian Baroness (Shirley) Williams of Crosby, who is herself a Catholic, similarly recalls that the Church was prepared to do business with the government on education, when, as Labour secretary of state for education, she was heavily involved in introducing comprehensive schools in England and Wales.

> There was always strong support for comprehensive education from Catholic schools. I never had any problem as secretary of state for education with the idea of comprehensive schools from the bishops.
>
> There were a lot of Catholic children in places like Liverpool who were bright and missing out. The Church's position was that it was protective of Catholic schools but this didn't cause it to oppose what we were doing. This approach has helped education to continue to be one of the Church's greatest contributions to society.[68]

Lay Catholics, particularly those of a more progressive outlook, often consider the Church of England to be a 'laboratory' for the testing of new developments that might eventually be adopted by the universal Church, an idea first mooted by the Vaticanologist Peter Hebblethwaite.[69] Some of those developments – married clergy, women priests – have still not been accepted by Rome. But ironically, this idea of the 'lab' now seems to have been adopted by Rome with regards to England itself. The Catholic Church in this country has prepared the way for other national churches in other European countries as it has sought an accommodation with a secularised society.

Cardinal Nichols believes that the work that the English and Welsh bishops have done in recent years has come to be appreciated more by Rome. 'What was probably less understood in Rome were the particular nuances and the pastoral instincts you have here in England and Wales, how you guide yourself, the navigational system in terms of a being a long historical minority. I think that is changing; our strengths are now more understood and more appreciated.'[70]

Not all Catholics in England and Wales appreciate a nuanced approach and expect the cardinal to be much more overtly critical of the government and changes in society. This was evident when a vocal minority criticized him for allowing the gay community to hold special Masses. Nichols's response was to tell them to 'hold their tongue'. One of his critics wrote on the *Catholic Herald* website: 'It is very hard now, after years of form . . . not to come to the conclusion that Vincent Nichols is in fact a fifth columnist on a mission to undermine and if it were possible, even destroy Catholicism as we know it.'[71]

Nichols's approach is more subtle. 'My message has to be shaped by circumstances. You have to present Catholicism through finding a place of entry in the culture.'[72]

The experience in the UK suggests that there will always be difficulties for the Church but there is also room for manoeuvre. The adept diplomats at the heart of Rome's relations with other states recognize that the Church sometimes loses its battles. 'We live with it. Bishops have to recognise that these things happen and you move on. You need to maintain integrity but you don't make it an issue of lingering division,' said one Holy See diplomat regarding same-sex marriage laws.[73]

The Catholic Church is said to think in centuries. But when it comes to dealing with a fast-changing country like Britain, it has succeeded when it has acted as an institution of compromise rather than high-handed obduracy. Its strengths include its grassroots connections, giving its commentary on the issues dealt with by parliament a valuable veracity. This combined with its leadership built on centuries of tradition and on theology also gives its continued authority. So both its structure and its beliefs shape its capacity for influence. For Catholics, the Church represents the truth. But time and time again the modern papacy, when it comes to Britain, represents realpolitik.

However much the Second Vatican Council sought to tilt the balance towards greater collegiality, Rome remains at the centre of the Catholic Church, emphasized through the media's encouragement of a cult of personality, increasing the presence of the pope in public and in individuals' lives.

Even when it comes to relationships between nations and global institutions, personality matters as much as theology or political ideology, and that includes understanding the interests and concerns of a particular pope. This has clearly been the case in the relationship with Britain during the pontificates of John Paul II, Benedict XVI and Francis, chronicled in this book.

The individual character of a pope also heavily influences relations with Britain through its dealings with the Church of England. Layers of history matter too, for they influence perceptions, even if historical conflicts between Anglicans and Rome have waned in significance. Some issues remain unresolved including the authority of the pope as it is understood or not by the Church of England and the extent to which the Catholic Church assumes – and wishes – the Archbishop of Canterbury has more authority than he really has. Discussions involving officials might be key to ecumenical progress but friendship between leaders matters.

This is also true of politics and diplomacy. Negotiation and relationships have helped the relationship between the UK and the papacy to flourish. The two papal visits in 1982 and in 2010 were key to improving understanding, as was the accord that led to full diplomatic relations.

Like its relationship with the Church of England, the Catholic Church is developing areas with the UK government where they have common ground, be it combating human trafficking or sexual violence in war zones. The Church has a role in the public sphere where it can be a voice of moral authority. It has taken time for the UK to understand this and even today it seems to not quite 'get' the papacy and its potential for influence. In May 2016, during a visit to Rome to meet religious orders working at the grassroots to combat sexual violence in conflict, Foreign Office minister Baroness Anelay said: 'The Catholic Church may be small in numbers but it is tremendous in its reach and tremendous in the respect that it has around the world. Regardless of one's faith, one respects the work of the Church.' The minister had understood its reach but not its force; a Church with more than a billion members cannot be called 'small in numbers'.[74] This was surely an assessment derived from a British, rather than a global, perspective.

Yet there has been progress in relations between the papacy and the British, with greater warmth on both sides and less suspicion. The United Kingdom has appreciated the papacy's usefulness when it suits its purposes. Both can be high handed: the British in foreign affairs, Rome in its treatment of the Church of England.

Much of the progress in the relationship is down to pragmatism. Rome appreciates Britain's clout on the world stage, given it is the fifth largest economy globally and that it plays a significant role through Nato, its part in G7, its Commonwealth and the Anglican Communion. Hints, though, of a UK that is turning in on itself, being more suspicious of the part it plays in

Europe and in dealing with global problems such as the refugee crisis, worry Rome. Another growing mood in Britain, that of nationalism, does not: the papacy has long regarded both Northern Ireland and Scotland, in ecclesiological terms, as separate from England. Northern Ireland also shows that the Church can walk a tightrope – attempting to both support the people and show solidarity with them while denouncing violence even when the community may sympathise with the ultimate aims of men of violence.

While the key players, from the pope to the queen to the prime minister, have all profoundly influenced the relationship between the British and the papacy in the past thirty-five years, others have too. The role in Rome of British clerics, theologians and bishops at the heart of the Church has grown and is an often unappreciated way in which the United Kingdom plays an influential role in the Catholic Church. Then there are ordinary British Catholics who have played their part too. Once outsiders, they moved to the middle of things but were shut out, as the late Duke of Norfolk's personal librarian so memorably put it.[75] Now they are not only in the middle of things but even at the helm in many parts of British life. They have played their part in normalizing Catholicism and the papacy, helping to bring together the two institutions they hold most dear: their country and their Church.

Notes

1   Davie, Grace (1994), *Religion in Britain since 1945: Believing Without Belonging*, Oxford: Blackwell.

2   Office for National Statistics, Religion Data from the 2011 Census. http://webarchive.nationalarchives.gov.uk/20160105160709/http://www.ons.gov.uk/ons/rel/census/2011-census/key-statistics-for-local-authorities-in-england-and-wales/sty-what-is-your-religion.html

3   Figures on religion extrapolated from the British Attitudes Survey, by Bullivant, Stephen (2016), *Contemporary Catholicism in England and Wales*, Catholic Research Forum, Benedict XVI Centre for Religion and Society, St Mary's University, Twickenham.

4   Woodhead, Linda (2015), 'Why no religion is the new religion', British Academy lecture.

5   Bullivant, ibid.

6   Medhurst, Kenneth N. and George H. Moyser (1988), *Church and Politics in a Secular Age*, Oxford: Oxford University Press.

7   Bellah, Robert N. (1968), 'Civil Religion in America' in McLoughlin, William G. and Robert N. Bellah (eds), *Religion in America*, Boston, MA: Houghton Mifflin Company.

8   Marwick, Arthur (2003), *British Society since 1945*, London: Penguin, 4th ed., ix–xi.

9   Filby, Eliza (2015), *God and Mrs Thatcher*, London: Biteback.

10 Margaret Thatcher to Woodrow Wyatt, quoted by Campbell, John (2007), *The Iron Lady*, London: Vintage, 248.

11 For a detailed account of the diplomacy surrounding the papal visit, see Chapter 2.

12 Speeches quoted in Carpenter, Humphrey (1996), *Robert Runcie: The Reluctant Archbishop*, London: Hodder and Stoughton.

13 Quoted by McSmith, Andy (2010), *No Such Thing As Society: A History of Britain in the 1980s*, London: Hachette UK.

14 *Faith in the City: A Call for Action by Church and Nation* (1985), The Report of the Archbishop of Canterbury's Commission on Urban Priority Areas, Church House, London, 21.

15 Quoted by Raban, Jonathan (1989) in *God, Man and Mrs Thatcher*, London: Chatto and Windus.

16 Preston, Ronald H. (1983), *Church and Society in the Late Twentieth Century: The Economic and Political Task* (The Scott Holland Lectures), Canterbury: SCM-Canterbury Press, 1983.

17 Preston, ibid.

18 For a comprehensive account of Catholic Social Teaching, see *Compendium of the Social Doctrine of the Church* (2005), Pontifical Council for Justice and Peace, Vatican City: Libreria Editrice Vaticana http://www.vatican.va/roman_curia/pontifical_councils/justpeace/documents/rc_pc_justpeace_doc_20060526_compendio-dott-soc_en.html

19 Letter from Robert Runcie, 26 October 1983, quoted by Eliza Filby, ibid, 167.

20 Interview of Peter Hennessy (PH) by Catherine Pepinster (CP), October 2014.

21 See Chapter 9 for details of the Guildford Four.

22 Howard, Anthony (2005), *Basil Hume: The Monk Cardinal*, London: Hodder and Stoughton, 278.

23 Interview of Charles Wookey (CW) by Catherine Pepinster (CP), October 2015.

24 Interview of CW by CP, ibid.

25 Howard, ibid, 153–5.

26 Interview of CW by CP, ibid.

27 The report was leaked and damned in these terms by an anonymous minister to the *Sunday Times*, 1 December 1985.

28 Interview of CW by CP, ibid.

29 Interview of Cardinal Cormac Murphy-O'Connor (CMO'C) by Catherine Pepinster (CP), February 2015 and also referred to in Murphy O'Connor, Cormac (2015), *An English Spring*, Bloomsbury, London, 180–1.

30 Murphy-O'Connor, ibid, 181.

31 Howard, ibid, 288–91 and also see Chapter 8.

32 Interview of CMO'C by CP, ibid.

33 Cited by Filby, Eliza (2015), *God and Mrs Thatcher*, London: Biteback, 163.

34 Metropolitan Cathedral Archive, Worlock Papers, Series 13, Box X, A Toxteth riots; letter to Frank Judd, 11 July 1981.

35 Longley, Clifford (2000), *The Worlock Archive*, Clifford Longley, London: Geoffrey Chapman, 344.

36 Worlock Archive, letter from Michael Heseltine, 19 August 1981.

37 *Faith in the City*, ibid, 208.

38 Filby, ibid, 197.

39 'End of the ethos' (2014), *The Tablet*, 15 May, 2.

40 Quoted in Stanford, Peter (1993), *Cardinal Hume and the Changing Face of English Catholicism*, London: Geoffrey Chapman, 133.

41 Baker, Kenneth (1993), *The Turbulent Years: My Life in Politics*, London: Faber, 218.

42 Bates, Stephen and Tania Branagan, 'Catholics and Jews attack controls on faith school intakes as veil row grows', *The Guardian*, 17 October 2006. http://www.theguardian.com/politics/2006/oct/17/religion.faithschools

43 Macintyre, James (2006), '"We'd have done it differently"', *The Tablet*, 6 November, 6.

44 'Theresa May to relax faith schools admission rules' (2016), BBC News, 9 September. http://www.bbc.co.uk/news/uk-politics-37314149

45 'Cardinal Vincent offers support and prayers for Theresa May' (2016), Diocese of Westminster, 13 July. http://rcdow.org.uk/cardinal/news/cardinal-vincent-offers-support-and-prayers-for-theresa-may/

46 Timothy, Nick (2016), 'The wit and wisdom of Nick Timothy', ConservativeHome first published 26 January, reprinted July 14. http://www.conservativehome.com/parliament/2016/07/the-wit-and-wisdom-of-nick-timothy-11-the-laws-that-govern-faith-schools-discriminate-against-catholics.html

47 Woodhead, Linda (2016) 'The government changes to faith schools side with hardline religion', London School of Economics and Political Sphere, Religion and the Public Sphere, 30 September. http://blogs.lse.ac.uk/religion publicsphere/2016/09/the-governments-changes-to-faith-schools-sides-with-hardline-religion/

48 Catholic canon law, part three, Catholic education, 796–806. http://www.ourcatholicfaith.org/canonlaw/CANON793-821.html

49 Murphy-O'Connor, ibid, 189.

50 For this co-operation between Labour and the Holy See, see Chapter 3.

51 Bright, Martin and John Kampfner (2007), Interview: Harriet Harman, *New Statesman*, 29 January. http://www.newstatesman.com/uk-politics/2007/01/harman-labour-minister

52 'Archbishop of Westminster attacks gay marriage plan' (2012), BBC News 25 December. http://www.bbc.co.uk/news/uk-20840531

53 Jones, Sam (2014), 'Vincent Nichols: enigmatic archbishop stepping into pope's inner circle', *The Guardian*, 18 February. http://www.theguardian.com/world/2014/feb/18/vincent-nichols-archbishop-cardinal-profile

54 Nichols, Archbishop Vincent (2012), Pastoral letter on marriage, 10–11 March. http://rcdow.org.uk/cardinal/news/pastoral-letter-on-marriage/

55 Catholic Bishops' Conference of England and Wales, Christian Responsibility and Citizenship, http://www.cbcew.org.uk/CBCEW-Home/Departments/Christian-Responsibility-and-Citizenship

56 'People being left in destitution is a disgrace, says Archbishop' (2014), *Daily Telegraph*, 18 February. http://www.telegraph.co.uk/news/religion/10647064/People-being-left-in-destitution-is-a-disgrace-says-Archbishop.html

57 Cardinal Vincent Nichols, (2015), homily at the ecumenical service for Oscar Romero, St Martin in the Fields, London, 21 March.

58 Gamble, Rose (2015), 'Church "is force behind Living Wage campaign"', *The Tablet*, 7 November, 33.

59 See Chapter 10 for further details of Winning's effort.

60 Filby, ibid, 349.

61 May, Theresa (2014), 'A model that works: A government's role in combating human trafficking', at the Combating Human Trafficking – Church and Law Enforcement in Partnership summit, Vatican City State, 9 April. http://www.catholic-ew.org.uk/Home/Special-Events/Combating-Human-Trafficking-Rome-Conference/Speeches/Rt-Hon-Theresa-May
        See also Chapter 5.

62 Interview of Andrew Mitchell (AM) by Catherine Pepinster (CP), February 2015.

63 Interview of AM by CP, ibid.

64 Conti, Mario (2013), 1982, before and since: the relationship of Church and State, from Britain and the Holy See, in *Britain and the Holy See: A Celebration of 1982 and the Wider Relationship*, proceedings of the Rome Colloquium, Rome: British Embassy to the Holy See, 17.

65 Interview with a Holy See source.

66 Ibid.

67 Interview of Cardinal Vincent Nichols (VN) by Catherine Pepinster (CP), March 2015.

68 Interview of Baroness Shirley Williams by Catherine Pepinster, July 2015.

69 Hebblethwaite, Peter (1991), 'Despite Vatican, women on world agenda', *National Catholic Reporter*, 7 June. http://natcath.org/NCR_Online/archives2/1991b/060791/060791j.htm

70 Interview of VN by CP, ibid.

71 Quoted in Jones (2014), ibid.

72 Interview of VN by CP, ibid.

73 Interview with a Holy See unnamed source.

74 Gamble, Rose (2016), 'British minister praises work of Catholic congregations in conflict zones', *The Tablet* Online, 24 May. http://www.thetablet.co.uk/news/5599/0/british-minister-praises-work-of-catholic-congregations-in-conflict-zones

75 See Chapter 8, footnote 9.

SELECT BIBLIOGRAPHY

Baker, Kenneth, *The Turbulent Years: My Life in Politics*, London: Faber and Faber, 1993.

Bates, Stephen, *Royalty Inc: Britain's Best-Known Brand*, London: Aurum Press, 2015.

Bradley, Ian, *God Save The Queen: The Spiritual Heart of the Monarch*, London: Continuum, 2012.

Brewer, John D., with Gareth I. Higgins and Francis Teeney, *Religion, Civil Society and Peace in Northern Ireland*, Oxford: Oxford University Press, 2011.

Britain and the Holy See – proceedings of the 2012 Rome Colloquium, Rome: British Embassy to the Holy See, 2012.

Buckley, James J., Frederick Christian Bauerschmidt and Trent Pomplun (eds), *The Blackwell Companion to Catholicism*, Chichester: Wiley-Blackwell, 2011.

Burns, Jimmy, *Francis: Pope of Good Promise*, London: Constable, 2015.

Burns, Jimmy, *The Land That Lost Its Heroes: How Argentina Lost The Falklands War*, London: Bloomsbury, 2012.

Campbell, John, *The Iron Lady*, London: Vintage, 2007.

Carpenter, Humphrey, *Robert Runcie: The Reluctant Archbishop*, London: Hodder and Stoughton, 1996.

Chadwick, Owen, *Britain and the Vatican during the Second World War*, Cambridge: Cambridge University Press, 1987.

Conti, Mario, *It's Late! Final Pages of a Bishop's Journal*, Glasgow: Burns Publications, 2015.

Cornwell, John, *A Thief in the Night: The Mysterious Death of John Paul I*, New York: Simon & Schuster, 1989.

Cornwell, John, *Newman's Unquiet Grave: The Reluctant Saint*, London: Bloomsbury Continuum, 2010.

Davie, Grace, *Religion in Britain since 1945: Believing without Belonging*, Oxford: Blackwell, 1994.

Devine, Tom, *The Scottish Nation: A Modern History*, London: Penguin, 2012.

Duffy, Eamon, *Saints and Sinners: A History of the Popes*, New Haven, CT: Yale University Press, 2006.

Faith in the City: A Call for Action by Church and Nation, The Report of the Archbishop of Canterbury's Commission on Urban Priority Areas, London: Church House, 1985.

Filby, Eliza, *God and Mrs Thatcher*, London: Biteback, 2015.

Fischer, Tim, *Holy See, Unholy Me: 1,000 Days in Rome – Tales from My Times as Australian Ambassador to the Vatican*, Sydney: Harper Collins Australia, 2013.

FitzGerald, Garret, *All in a Life: Garret FitzGerald – an Autobiography*, Dublin: Gill and MacMillan, 1991.

Fox, Jonathan, *An Introduction to Religion and Politics: Theory and Practice*, Abingdon: Routledge, 2013.

Hebblethwaite, Peter, *In The Vatican*, Oxford: Oxford University Press, 1986.

Hook, Sidney, *The Hero in History*, Boston, MA: Beacon Press, 1960.

Hornsby-Smith, Michael P. (ed.), *Catholics in England 1950–2000: Historical and Sociological Perspectives*, London: Cassell, 1999.

Hornsby-Smith, Michael P., *Roman Catholics in England*, Cambridge: Cambridge University Press, 2008.

Howard, Anthony, *Basil Hume: The Monk Cardinal*, London: Headline, 2005.

Ivereigh, Austen, *The Great Reformer: Francis and the Making of a Radical Pope*, London: Allen & Unwin, 2015.

Longley, Clifford, *The Worlock Archive*, London: Geoffrey Chapman, 2000.

Martin, Christopher, *A Glimpse of Heaven: Catholic Churches in England and Wales*, Swindon: English Heritage, 2006.

Marwick, Arthur, *British Society since 1945*, London: Penguin, 2003.

McGinty, Stephen, *This Turbulent Priest: The Life of Cardinal Winning*, Harper Collins, 2003.

McLoughlin, William G. and Robert N. Bellah (eds), *Religion in America*, Boston, MA: Houghton Mifflin Company, 1968.

McSmith, Andy (2010), *No Such Thing as Society: A History of Britain in the 1980s*, London: Hachette UK.

Medhurst, Kenneth N. and George H. Moyser (1988), *Church and Politics in a Secular Age*, Oxford: Oxford University Press.

Moore, Charles, *Margaret Thatcher: The Authorized Biography, Volume One*, London: Allen Lane, 2013.

Moore, Charles, *Margaret Thatcher: The Authorised Biography, Volume Two – Everything She Wants*, London: Allen Lane, 2015.

Murphy-O'Connor, Cormac, *An English Spring*, London: Continuum, 2015.

Newman, John Henry, *Apologia Pro Vita Sua*, London: Penguin, 1994.

Nichols, Peter, *The Pope's Divisions*, London: Penguin, 1982.

Nuzzi, Gianluigi, *Merchants in the Temple: Inside Pope Francis' Secret Battle Against Corruption in the Vatican*, New York: Henry Holt and Co, 2015.

Nye, Joseph S. Jr, *The Powers to Lead*, Oxford: Oxford University Press, 2008.

Pimlott, Ben, *The Queen*, London: Harper Collins, 1996.

Preston, Ronald, *Church and Society in the Late Twentieth Century: The Economic and Political Task*, Canterbury: SCM-Canterbury Press, 1983.

Proctor, Robert, *Building the Modern Church*, Farnham: Ashgate, 2014.

Reese SJ, Thomas J., *Inside The Vatican: The Politics and Organization of the Catholic Church*, Cambridge, MA: Harvard University Press, 1997.

Roberts, Keith Daniel, *The Rise and Fall of Liverpool Sectarianism*, PhD thesis, University of Liverpool Repository, 2015. Available online: http://repository.liv.ac.uk/2010280/3/RobertsKei_April2015_2010280.pdf

Robertson, Geoffrey, *The Case of the Pope: Vatican Accountability for Human Rights Abuse*, London: Penguin, 2010.

Rooney, Francis, *The Global Vatican*, Lanham, MD: Rowman and Littlefield, 2013.

Scott, George, *The RCs: A Report on Roman Catholics Today*, London: Hutchinson, 1967.

Sewell, Dennis, *Catholics: Britain's Largest Minority*, London: Penguin Viking, 2001.

Stanford, Peter, *Cardinal Hume and the Changing Face of English Catholicism*, London: Geoffrey Chapman, 1993.

Stourton, Edward, *Absolute Truth: The Catholic Church in the World Today*, London: Viking, 1998.

Vallely, Paul, *Pope Francis: Untying the Knots – The Struggle for the Soul of Catholicism*, London: Bloomsbury, 2015.

Vatican Compendium of the Social Doctrine of the Church, Pontifical Council for Justice and Peace, Vatican City: Libreria Editrice Vaticana, 2005.

Walsh, Michael J., *The Westminster Cardinals*, London: Continuum, 2008.

Weber, Max and Sam Whimster, *The Essential Weber: A Reader*, Abingdon: Routledge Taylor & Francis, 2004.

Willner, Ann Ruth, *Charismatic Political Leadership: A Theory*, Princeton: Princeton University Press, 1968.

Wooldridge, Adrian and Micklethwait, John, *God Is Back: How the Global Rise of Faith Is Changing the World*, London: Penguin, 2009.

Vatican documents

Mit brennender Sorge – encyclical of Pius XI on the Church and the German Reich, 1937. http://w2.vatican.va/content/pius-xi/en/encyclicals/documents/hf_p-xi_enc_14031937_mit-brennender-sorge.html

Lumen Gentium – the dogmatic constitution of the Church, promulgated by Paul VI, 1964. http://www.vatican.va/archive/hist_councils/ii_vatican_council/documents/vat-ii_const_19641121_lumen-gentium_en.html

Gaudium et Spes – the pastoral constitution on the Church in the modern world, promulgated by Paul VI, 1965.

Humanae Vitae – encyclical of Paul VI on the regulation of birth, 1968. https://www.google.co.uk/#q=Humanae+Vitae&gws_rd=cr

Caritas in Veritate – encyclical of Benedict XVI on integral human development in charity and truth, 2009. http://w2.vatican.va/content/benedict-xvi/en/encyclicals/documents/hf_ben-xvi_enc_20090629_caritas-in-veritate.html

Anglicanorum Coetibus – apostolic constitution of Benedict XVI providing for personal ordinariates for Anglicans entering into full communion with the Catholic Church, 2009.

Evangelii Gaudium – apostolic constitution of Francis on the proclamation of the gospel in today's world, 2013. http://w2.vatican.va/content/francesco/en/apost_exhortations/documents/papa-francesco_esortazione-ap_20131124_evangelii-gaudium.html

Laudato Si' – encyclical of Francis on the care of our common home, 2015. http://w2.vatican.va/content/francesco/en/encyclicals/documents/papa-francesco_20150524_enciclica-laudato-si.html

Amoris Laetitia – post-synodal apostolic exhortation of Francis on love in the family, 2016. https://w2.vatican.va/content/francesco/en/apost_exhortations/documents/papa-francesco_esortazione-ap_20160319_amoris-laetitia.html

INDEX